D1514719

King Arthur

King Arthur

The Man Who Conquered Europe

CALEB HOWELLS

AMBERLEY

First published 2019

Amberley Publishing
The Hill, Stroud
Gloucestershire, GL5 4EP

www.amberley-books.com

British Library Cataloguing in Publication Data.
A catalogue record for this book is available from the British Library.

ISBN 978 1 4456 9083 4 (hardback)
ISBN 978 1 4456 9084 1 (ebook)

Typesetting and Origination by Amberley Publishing.
Printed in the UK.

Contents

Introduction

There is something very intriguing about Dark Age Britain. The very name bespeaks its mystery. The period sometimes referred to as the Arthurian Era, from roughly 400 to 600 CE, has been the subject of countless books, academic and mainstream, factual and speculative. One could write reams about virtually any aspect of the era because it is so poorly documented. However, the one individual who is honoured with being the subject of most of the speculation is King Arthur, the Once and Future King of Britain.

As the title bestowed upon him suggests, King Arthur is very much a figure of legend. Many tales about him include dragons, wizards, and magical swords. However, he is firmly rooted in a historical context. He is said to have been the mighty king of Britain who held off the invading Saxons for decades in the sixth century, and some accounts even credit him with the conquest of France and waging a war against the Romans. The immediate question that arises is, did King Arthur exist? Was he a real king, or even just a military leader, who simply had many embellished and fanciful tales written about him for one reason or another? Or, rather, was he always a figure of myth and folklore who was written into later historical records?

There is no universal agreement on the issue, nor does there even seem to be any real agreement as to what the general consensus is. Even those who conclude that there may well have been some truth to the legends simply pass King Arthur off as some mysterious, isolated, lone Roman war leader who helped the natives hold back the tide of the Saxons. Very rarely is any major portion of the legends taken seriously. It is often said that even if Arthur himself was a real person, he was certainly not a king, and there was absolutely no Lancelot, Merlin, Guinevere, Round Table or Code of Chivalry. Evidence for these elements of the legends, it is claimed, is totally lacking.

However, it seems that with many legendary figures, the mystery can be removed by identifying them with a well-known, well-documented historical character. This relies on the principle that the source for the legendary figure was, in fact, describing a real person but the description was too confused, inaccurate or masked for later readers to easily make the correct connection. However, if this identity is revealed, then there is no longer any mystery and instead of claiming that there are no authentic records of the person's existence, doubt can be removed once the legendary figure has been accurately identified. Although the legendary character is not necessarily completely accurate, the stories basically concern the same person.

To use a non-personal example, consider the tale of Atlantis. Supposedly invented by Plato in the fifth century BCE, Atlantis was a legendary island civilisation in the Atlantic whose people were defeated by the Greeks and which was subsequently destroyed by the gods by being submerged in the ocean. This seems to be complete fiction. Following the *exact* information about it, as given by Plato, there is no archaeological or oceanographic evidence for its existence, nor is it mentioned by any writer earlier than Plato. There seems to be no reason to doubt that the story was merely Plato's invention. However, extraordinary as the story seems to be, could it actually have been based on a real civilisation? Obviously, it cannot be *completely* accurate, but what if Plato's story of Atlantis was taken from somewhat inaccurate accounts of a real island civilisation that was attacked by the Greeks and that its eventual destruction was caused by dramatic but natural forces? If that civilisation could be identified, then that would naturally be the 'real' Atlantis.

A well-known idea, particularly developed in the mid-twentieth century, is that the Minoan civilisation was what the story of Atlantis actually referred to – in particular, the Minoan settlement on Thera. This was a volcanic island that erupted in the sixteenth or seventeenth century BCE. Its structure comprised one central island surrounded by a concentric ring of land, with one passageway from the sea to the central island. A fresco found on the island seems to confirm that this was the case. This is identical to Plato's description of Atlantis having concentric rings with a single channel from the sea to the island in the middle, the only difference being the number of rings (on Thera there was only one, whereas on Atlantis there were said to have been two).

The Minoans were one of the richest and most advanced nations of the ancient world. As such, they are immediately worthy candidates to have been the Atlanteans. But the similarities are more numerous and substantial than just that. The Minoans enjoyed bullfighting games, after which it seems they sacrificed the bulls, and this is described in Plato's account of the Atlanteans. The Minoans also made use of the resources on the island of Thera, mining and using red, black and white rocks for their buildings, exactly as Plato's Atlanteans did. (Thera had an abundance of stone in these colours due to it being a volcanic island.)

This identification of the Minoans with the Atlanteans seems to be confirmed by the fact that Plato gives the names of four Athenian kings who were involved in the successful war against Atlantis: Cecrops, Erechtheus, Erichthonius, and Erysichthon. All four of these individuals are known from standard Greek legend, and the time in which they were believed to have lived is the same as the period in which it is known that in real life the Minoans were being overthrown by the Greeks.

As for the actual destruction of Atlantis, this would have originated with accounts of the eruption on the island – one of the most cataclysmic events in recorded human history. During this volcanic eruption, the magma chamber underneath the island was emptied, causing a substantial amount of the island to literally collapse into the sea. This did not destroy the Minoan civilisation but it most certainly destroyed the Minoans' settlement on that island, and their civilisation as a whole collapsed just a few generations later.

So, if the story of Atlantis is simply an inaccurate account of the history of the Minoans on Thera, then suddenly 'Atlantis' becomes well-established reality. The idea that there is no record of it before Plato's time no longer applies because it described a very well-documented nation.

Whether one accepts this theory or not, it demonstrates the point being made. Something may seem to have been completely fabricated, whereas instead it could be a case of the author's sources not being accurate enough to immediately connect the story with known reality.

To move on to the main subject of this book: what if there really was a historical figure whose life corresponded to the stories of Arthur? What if, for whatever reason, the connection had simply not been made (or, more correctly, had been lost), causing the claim to be made that there are no records of Arthur before a certain point in history? This is not a case of attempting to find new evidence of an otherwise unattested historical figure; rather, it is a case of showing how the information about King Arthur, his kingdom, and his family, point to an already well-known and firmly established historical dynasty in Britain. His mighty European conquest is not fictional; it will be shown that it is nothing more than a slightly inaccurate account of a real event.

1

Establishing the Identity of King Arthur

When Did Arthur Live?

The first step to finding Arthur is to determine the period in which he was supposedly active. There appears to be an easy way to do this. A tenth-century chronicle called the *Welsh Annals* contains a record of important events in British history, starting from the mid-fifth century and ending when the chronicle was compiled. We will delve into the details of this record later on, but, in short, the *Welsh Annals* is accepted as placing Arthur's final victory against the Saxons in 516, and his last battle in 537. In the absence of other evidence, we would have to simply accept these dates. However, entries in the *Annals* must be, and are in practice, rejected if there is a sufficient amount of evidence to the contrary. For example, the death of a famous individual named Dubricius is recorded as being in 612, yet there is sufficient information provided by other sources that make it clear that this date is completely wrong. Now, most modern reference works hold that Dubricius was a late fifth-, early sixth-century individual. Similarly, there is an abundance of other information about Arthur and his activities that will allow us to position him in the stream of time, without needing to rely on the testimony of one chronicle.

The most clearly historical event with which Arthur is connected is the Battle of Badon. This battle was referred to by a writer of that time called Gildas, who claims to have been born in the year it took place, so its historicity is accepted by virtually all scholars. According to Gildas, the numerous battles between the native

Britons and the invading Saxons culminated in a battle fought at a place called Badon, resulting in a lengthy period of peace continuing up to the time of writing. According to the much later ninth-century *Historia Brittonum*, attributed to a writer named Nennius,[1] this event comes at the end of a list of twelve battles fought by Arthur. The Battle of Badon appears as Arthur's victory in the *Welsh Annals* for the year 516.

Though Gildas wrote about the battle much earlier than either of these two sources, he does not give any explicit dates. However, the fact that he was writing, by his own admission, forty-three years after the battle occurred means that we can work out the year, or at least the general period, if we can ascertain when he was writing. Fortunately, he addresses some comments to five kings who were ruling over different parts of Britain at the same time. There is no contemporary information about these kings other than the words of Gildas himself, who provides no dates, so we are forced to use the later medieval material to attempt to determine the reigns of these kings.

While the evidence is not completely clear for all five of the kings, most of the evidence indicates that these five kings were reigning – and therefore Gildas was writing – towards the end of the sixth century. This is not widely recognised, though it is nonetheless what the greater part of the evidence indicates. For a discussion of how such a conclusion was reached, see Appendix 1, 'The Dating of Gildas'.

If the Battle of Badon took place forty-three years before the end of the sixth century, it should have occurred at some point around the middle of that century. This conclusion is supported by Nennius, who gives much clearer historical information. Immediately after listing the twelve battles, which culminate in the Battle of Badon, he informs us:

In all these engagements the Britons were successful. For no strength can avail against the will of the Almighty. The more the Saxons were vanquished, the more they sought for new supplies of Saxons from Germany; so that kings, commanders, and military bands were invited over from almost every province. And this practice they continued till the reign of Ida.[2]

From the context of the passage, it is evident that the clause 'the more the Saxons were vanquished' refers to their defeats during the immediately aforementioned twelve battles. Since the text tells us that the more the Saxons were vanquished, the more they brought over fellow Germans to the island, the statement that this continued until the reign of Ida strongly implies that that was when the last battle was fought – the last battle being the one fought at Badon. According to the *Anglo-Saxon Chronicle* (*ASC*), written in the ninth century, Ida began ruling in 547 and ruled for twelve years. If 'until the reign of Ida' means until the *start* of his reign, then this source places the Battle of Badon in the year 547 (taking the *ASC* to be precisely accurate). Alternatively, if 'until the reign of Ida' simply means that it finished *at some point during* his reign, then this source places the battle sometime between 547 and 559. In either case, this information agrees with the evidence of Gildas.

Does this agree with later sources regarding the battle? Well, Geoffrey of Monmouth is the next writer to provide an account of Arthur's battles – this one being far more detailed than Nennius's. In Geoffrey's account, Arthur is appointed king and begins fighting against the Saxons after the death of his father, Uther. Uther is said to have perished at around the same time as Octa, with Octa having been killed in Uther's last battle. After Octa, three new Saxon leaders arose. One was named Colgrin, another was Badulph, and the third was Cheldric. All three are killed at, or immediately following, the Battle of Badon.

As we have already considered, Nennius's account indicates that the final battle took place either at the beginning of, or some time during, Ida's reign. However, the beginning of the Arthurian section refers to Octa receiving the kingdom of Kent and then says that it was 'then' that Arthur began fighting the Saxons. Unfortunately, there is no real information – reliable or otherwise – that allows us to pinpoint exactly when Octa became the king of Kent. However, the point to be noted is that Arthur's war against the Saxons is placed between the reigns of Octa and Ida.

The famous *Historia Regum Britanniae* (*HRB*), written in *c.* 1137 by Geoffrey of Monmouth, is similar in that it places Arthur's war in the time of the concurrent successors of Octa. Granted, this conflicts in that Nennius says that Arthur started fighting upon Octa becoming king, and the records show that Octa ruled for quite some time after that. Therefore, Geoffrey is presumably mistaken either in having Arthur only become king and begin fighting *after* the death of Octa (and Uther), or Octa did not really die during his battle against Uther, but died much later – this latter option would allow for the possibility that he had only recently become king when he fought Uther, who was then quickly succeeded by Arthur. In any case, both Geoffrey and Nennius are in agreement in that *at least some* of Arthur's Saxon war took place during the reign of a Saxon leader subsequent to Octa.

The significance of this is that the prominent leader of the Saxons before the start of the reign of Ida, according to the *Anglo-Saxon Chronicle*, was a certain Cerdic of Wessex. The correspondence between this Cerdic and Geoffrey's Cheldric has long been noted. Taking the *ASC* as it is, Cerdic died in 534. However, scholars have noted that there seem to be duplications in the records of the men of Wessex, and these duplications are separated by gaps of exactly nineteen years. There is a widely accepted theory that the duplications arose due to the chroniclers accidentally back-dating the events by dating them in relation to the wrong astronomical cycle. The astronomical cycle repeats every nineteen years. It is possible that as well as backdating events and keeping both the originals and the newly created duplicates in the record, the 'originals' have been backdated too, leaving the *true* original dates out of the record completely. Scholar David Dumville analysed the regnal years of the kings of Wessex and determined that Cerdic actually took the kingship in 538, rather than 519 as is claimed in the *ASC*.[3] Note the nineteen-year difference. His death, too, should be nineteen years later than the date of 534 that is present in the *ASC*; he would therefore have died in 553, though 554 is the more commonly suggested year by proponents of this theory.[4]

Of course, wherever the dates for these events were in relation to this astronomical cycle immediately prior to the *Anglo-Saxon Chronicle* being compiled, there is no guarantee that the dates had been kept accurately preserved for the roughly 400-year interval between the events occurring and the *ASC* being compiled; in other words, there is no guarantee that they are accurate to the very year. A few years either way for the actual death of Cerdic would be acceptable. In any case, we can see that this date ties in very closely with the date for the Battle of Badon that is indicated by Nennius. And as Geoffrey's Cheldric was supposed to have died immediately after that battle, this is a notable correspondence.

So the evidence, thus far, is consistent with a mid-sixth-century date for Badon. Another source for the dating of the battle is found in *The Red Book of Hergest*. This document is from *c.* 1400. Among numerous other things, it contains a chronicle known as *The Chronicle from Vortigern to King John*. Given that the chronicle ends in the very early 1200s, it is likely that this is the date of composition. The first entry informs us that there were 128 years from 'the age of Vortigern' to Arthur's victorious Battle of Badon. Assuming that this is a reference to the beginning of Vortigern's reign, which was, according to the *Historia Brittonum*, in 425, this would point to the Battle of Badon as having been fought in 553. Again, while allowing for an error of several years either side, it is clear that this source places the battle in the mid-sixth century.

From this consideration of the evidence, we can see that the climax of Arthur's victories against the Saxons took place around the middle of the sixth century. He is also recorded as having had a battle some twenty years later at a location called Camlann. This, by the earliest source that specifies it, was not fought primarily against the Saxons but was a civil war between Arthur and a relative named Mordred. This, if it really happened, would have taken place some time between the Battle of Badon and the time of Gildas' writing. Thus, it is placed well into the second half of the sixth century. This date is supported independently of the battle's temporal relation to Badon inasmuch as Mordred is claimed, in the earliest source which specifies it, to be a nephew of Urien Rheged. This Urien was a prominent king of the north of Britain who fought against the Angles of Northumbria. The *Historia Brittonum* provides us with the following dating information:

Ida reigned for twelve years; Adda his son reigned for eight years; Ethelric his son reigned four years; Theodoric son of Ida then reigned seven years; Freothwulf reigned six years; finally, Hussa reigned seven years.

As we have already noted, the *ASC* gives 547 as the start of Ida's reign. Therefore, Theodoric must have ruled from 571 to 578, while Hussa ruled from 584 to 591. These are the two Anglian kings whom Urien is recorded as fighting against.

From this and other evidence, it is universally agreed that Urien was active in the latter half of the sixth century. Assuming he was not more than seventy years old when fighting in *c.* 590, we can see that Urien was probably born no earlier than 520. Any nephew of his, therefore, cannot realistically have been active before the mid-sixth century at the earliest. Most likely, Mordred would not even have been born until around the middle of the century.

We find support for this conclusion by directly considering his father. He is named 'Lot' by Geoffrey of Monmouth, which is exchanged for 'Llew' in the Welsh accounts. The reason for these variable forms is most likely because they are both attempts to abbreviate the name 'Leudonus', which is the name of the king of Lot's territory in certain other records, such as the *Life of St Kentigern* and several genealogical records. Lot is called 'Lot of Lodonesia' by Geoffrey of Monmouth. Similarly, the aforementioned *Life* refers to 'Leudonus, from which the province over which he ruled obtained the name Leudonia'. There is every reason to conclude that this Leudonus was the person Geoffrey calls Lot, and he would therefore be the 'Llew ap (son of) Cynfarch' of the Welsh records.

There is much useful information that we can gather from this. Firstly, Kentigern was the grandson of Leudonus, whose daughter, Kentigern's mother, was raped by Owain, the son of Urien. If Urien was not born earlier than 520, then Owain's birth is likely to have been in the 540s. Assuming he did not rape a woman very much older than himself, this daughter of Leudonus was likewise most likely born in the 540s. Her son, then, was probably born *c.* 560 or a little later. That this is the correct general time frame is shown by the fact that his death is recorded in the *Welsh Annals* as being in 612.

Scholar Peter Bartrum estimates, based on more extensive information available concerning at least five children, that another daughter of Leudonus was born in 545.[5] This agrees with our estimate for her sister, the mother of Kentigern. Now, what can we conclude from this? Well, if Mordred was at least twenty years old when he tried to usurp the throne, then for the Battle of Camlann to have taken place in 537, as claimed by the *Welsh Annals*, he would have had to have been born no later than 517. In turn, his father Lot, or Leudonus, must have been born around 497 or earlier. This would make Leudonus around fifty years old when he fathered the two daughters in the 540s. Such a conclusion is unlikely.

Such a conclusion is also weakened by the records that state that he, Urien and Arawn were triplets. If Urien and Lot were born at the same time, then Urien would have been around 100 years old when fighting Hussa – unless, of course, we reject the date of 537 for Camlann.

If we use our revised estimate of *c.* 570 for the Battle of Camlann, then we can comfortably allow Mordred to have been twenty-five years old when it took place. This is more realistic than twenty, as he would have needed to have been able to raise sufficient support for his cause. This would put his birth in *c.* 545. Then we can allow a twenty-two-year generation gap back to Lot (Leudonus), putting his birth in *c.* 523, and then finally back to his father, Cynfarch, in *c.* 501. The year of 523 works well with the information concerning Urien, Lot's brother. So too does 545 fit well with the information concerning Owain, Mordred's first cousin.[6]

So, the evidence is clearly in favour of the later date of *c.* 570 for Camlann, which in turn conforms to a date of *c.* 550 for Badon.

However, we must now ask if the evidence is consistent in this regard. Does most of the other information in the Arthurian sources – such as dates (when they are given) and people who feature as contemporaries of Arthur – agree with the *c.* 550 and *c.* 570 dates for the battles of Badon and Camlann?

Consider the extensive information provided by Geoffrey of Monmouth. In his *Historia Regum Britanniae* there is a whole host of individuals mentioned as being present at Arthur's coronation some time after defeating the Saxons at Badon. Arthurian researcher Mike Ashley noted the following interesting fact: 'Almost all of the names are of princes and nobles alive in the mid-to-late sixth century.'[7]

Examples include the aforementioned Urien, as well as Dynod, the son of Pabo, a contemporary of Urien. In fact, the narrative in this account provides additional dating evidence in that it describes certain events that occurred at the same time as Arthur's coronation. Some of these events appear in independent sources, which therefore allows us to place them in time. One such event is the following: 'But St. Dubricius, from a pious desire of leading a hermit's life, made a voluntary resignation of his archiepiscopal dignity; and in his room was consecrated David.'[8] David's succession from Dubricius took place at an event known as the Synod of Brefi, which is dated to around 560 or 550 by modern reference works.[9] Another event in this passage is, 'In place of St. Samson, archbishop of Dole, was appointed, with the consent of Hoel, king of the Armorican Britons, Chelianus, a priest of Llandaff.'[10]

The 'Chelianus' in this account is actually Teilo, and this event is described in the *Life of St Teilo*.[11] It is placed before the death of the aforementioned David, who died in *c.* 584. Yet, it is placed while Teilo is in Armorica after having fled Britain to escape a great plague, known as the Yellow Plague. We shall see in Chapter Six that this plague most likely broke out in 563, and it is said to have ended after around seven years. Therefore, if Teilo became the Archbishop of Dol during this period, then we can see that this is more or less the same time at which the Synod of Brefi is supposed to have taken place.

How does this tie in with the information we have already considered? Geoffrey of Monmouth places this special coronation of Arthur's around twenty years after his victory over the Saxons at Badon. However, evidence will be presented in Chapter Six that there were really only a little more than twelve years between Arthur's victory at Badon and his special coronation. The information we have already considered points to that battle having been fought somewhere around the year 550. Therefore, if the Synod of Brefi took place around twenty years after that, then we arrive at *c.* 570 – not too far from the time in which the Synod is generally placed. And with the twenty years reduced to twelve years, this would place the Synod in *c.* 562, which is even closer to the commonly given year. The appointment of Teilo as the Archbishop of Dol similarly ties in with this.

So far, we have considered the information from Gildas, Nennius, and Geoffrey of Monmouth. However, there are other sources that should be considered. One such source is *Preiddeu Annwn*, a Welsh poem written some time between the writings of Nennius and Geoffrey of Monmouth. This speaks of a voyage made by Arthur, in which the composer of the poem participated – the author being a famous bard named Taliesin. Indeed, in another of Geoffrey of Monmouth's works, the *Life of Merlin*, Arthur is explicitly made a contemporary of Taliesin and another bard named Myrddin (spelt Merlinus by Geoffrey). Both these bards are held to have lived in the latter part of the sixth century.

While it is true that Geoffrey of Monmouth writes that Arthur abdicated his throne after the Battle of Camlann in 'the 542nd year of our Lord's incarnation', there are many instances in which a year that is expressed as being given relative to the Incarnation (that is, the birth) of Jesus, was meant to be relative to the Passion (that is, the death of Jesus). For evidence that a confusion between the Incarnation and the Passion did occur at times, see Appendix 2, 'The Thirty-three-year Error'. If this error took place here, and the starting point was actually meant to be the Passion, then the 542nd year after that – that is, 541 years after 33 CE – would bring us to the year 574 CE. It should be noted that the previously considered information from Geoffrey of Monmouth's *Historia Regum Britanniae* is totally inconsistent with Arthur dying in the 540s. A year of abdication in 574, on the other hand, would be completely in agreement with all the details about Arthur's special coronation, which point to this event as occurring in the 560s.

Another source that explicitly shows Arthur to have still been alive in the 560s or later is the *Life of St Gildas*. In fact, there are two *Lives*, written some time apart, one by an anonymous monk in the ninth century in Rhuys, Brittany, and the other in Glamorgan in the twelfth century. It is only the later one that mentions Arthur. In this version, the titular character is described as having left Britain to temporarily live in Ireland and preach there and, during this time, Arthur kills a rebellious brother of Gildas named Hueil. Gildas then returns to Britain to make peace with Arthur. In the earlier *Life*, while there is no mention of Gildas's brother being killed, the account tells us that Gildas was called to Ireland to preach by King Ainmericus, or Ainmuire mac (son of) Sétnai, as he is known in the Irish sources. This king reigned in the late 560s.[12]

That it is meant to be the same preaching trip is made clear by the fact that in both accounts Gildas travels to Rome immediately afterwards.

This is clear narrative evidence that Arthur was still alive and well in the 560s, if not the 570s. This is fully in agreement with the evidence for a *c.* 550 date for the Battle of Badon, a *c.* 560 date for Arthur's coronation, and a 574 date for his abdication. If Arthur was not more than eighty years old when he abdicated, then we can conclude that he was born no earlier than 494. What is the evidence regarding his birth?

There is a version of the *Book of Llandaff*, an important twelfth-century document concerning grants of land in south-east Wales, which includes a record of Arthur being crowned king as a teenager. In fact, he is specifically said to have been in the fifteenth year of his life, meaning he was fourteen years old. The record says that this was 506 years after the Incarnation of the Lord. If this should actually be understood to mean 506 years after the death of Jesus – that is, 506 years after 33 CE – then this would mean Arthur was fourteen years old in 539 – hence, his year of birth would have been 525. Alternatively, if the use of 'Incarnation' in this passage is correct, then this would simply mean that Arthur was crowned in 506 CE. This would make his year of birth 492. Such a year is a little too early by our above assumptions, but only just. It would mean that he was eighty-two years old when he abdicated, which is quite old but still acceptable.

However, there is another version of the Llandaff record which gives a different year for Arthur's crowning at the age of fourteen. This version gives the year as '517 years after the Incarnation of our Lord', which would put Arthur's birth in either 536 or 503, depending on the issue just discussed. Obviously, 536 is much too late, as it would mean that Arthur would have only been around fourteen at the time of the Battle of Badon. A birth year of 503, on the other hand, fits well with the dating of Badon and would make him seventy-one at the time of his abdication.

The Chronicles of England, produced by William Caxton in the fifteenth century, provides the date of '546 years after the Incarnation of our Lord' for Arthur's death. With the required thirty-three-year adjustment utilised in this case, this becomes

579 CE. If Arthur was born in 503, then this would mean that he would have been seventy-six when he died. On the other hand, if he was born in 492, then he would have been eighty-seven at his death. The younger age is preferable simply due to the inherent unlikelihood of a person living for longer than eighty years, especially at this time, but there is no way to definitively determine which birth year is correct.

However, we must ask whether or not a birth year of 503 fits the narrative information, such as the information provided in saints' lives. We have already seen how Arthur's age ties in with the *Life of St Gildas*, but that was about an event in the 560s or later, which evidently took place very late in Arthur's life. We will now see if there is any information which requires Arthur to have been born earlier than 503.

One significant *Life* in which he appears is the *Life of St Cadoc*. This was written in the eleventh century, and is therefore a relatively early source for Arthur. In this, the circumstances that led up to the birth of the titular character are described. A daughter of a chieftain named Brychan is eyed by Arthur, who is with Cai (Sir Kay) and Bedwyr (Sir Bedivere) in the land of Glamorgan. However, Arthur is informed that this woman is the lover of Gwynllyw, who is being pursued by Brychan, her father. Arthur intervenes and protects Gwynllyw. Subsequently, Gwynllyw and the woman have a child, and this child is Cadoc. Arthur may have been as young as fourteen at the time of this event, if that is how old he was when he was crowned king. Though a very young age, as a king, he would have wielded the necessary authority to protect a citizen, and he would still have been old enough to have engaged in the described activities. Therefore, we shall consider fourteen years old to be the youngest possible age for Arthur to have been when Cadoc was born.

There is no clear information regarding the year in which Cadoc was born. The only reasonably firmly dated event in his life is the Synod of Brefi. As we saw earlier, this is dated by most sources to have been in either *c. 550* or *c. 560*. By the time this event happened, Cadoc had been active for a while; however, there is, unfortunately, no way to be more specific than this. Therefore, a birth year of *c. 520* for this man is reasonable, and this would mean

Arthur would have been seventeen years old at the time of Cadoc's birth if Arthur was born in 503. Such an age is acceptable.

What about other *Lives*? The third one in which the king appears is the *Life of St Illtud*. Illtud was said to have been one of Arthur's cousins and one of the first things he does when he arrives in Britain, after being born and raised in Brittany, is to visit Arthur's court. Illtud probably lived until *c.* 580.[13] Assuming he lived for roughly eighty years, this would make him an exact contemporary of Arthur according to our estimated dates. Given that they were meant to have been cousins, this is logical. It would certainly be very unlikely for Arthur to have died at his last battle in 537 while his cousin continued living for another forty years.

These estimates of 503 for Arthur's birth and 579 for his death are much later than the dates given by the vast majority of modern sources. In fact, he is often referred to as a 'late fifth-, early sixth-century king'. Nonetheless, we have seen that the quoted sources point unmistakably to a *mid*-sixth-century reign for the king. It will be seen in the following section that this conclusion is further supported by Arthur's contemporaries as provided by a detailed early Welsh tale, *Culhwch ac Olwen*.

The early chronology given to Arthur is based almost entirely on the *Welsh Annals*. This record does not give any absolute dates, but simply presents a list of years, some of which have a brief description of an event next to them. Thus, the entries are only dated relative to each other. Therefore, finding a suitable date on which to anchor the annals is vital. Certain events can be cross-checked with external sources when such sources exist. For example, the second event listed is 'Easter altered on the Lord's Day by Pope Leo, Bishop of Rome'.

This event is known from external sources to have occurred in 457. The chronicle places the death of St Patrick four years later, in 461. The issue with this is that it is most commonly argued today that his death was actually in 493.[14] This later date is also found in some of the annals, such as the *Annals of Ulster* and the *Annals of the Four Masters*; however, it is strange that these sources *also* record Patrick's death around the year 460, so there was clearly some confusion. It has been suggested that there were two Patricks, the earlier also known as Palladius, this earlier Patrick being the one who died in *c*. 460, which would perhaps explain the confusion in the records.

Despite this apparently simple explanation, the next entry in the *Welsh Annals* does not conform to it. It gives the birth of David as being in the thirtieth year after Patrick left Menevia – that is, after he left for Ireland from Menevia, which is on the south-western tip of Wales. There is no evidence that Palladius, who was a native of Gaul, travelled to Menevia before reaching Ireland. On the other hand, the *Life of David* specifically mentions Patrick passing through south-west Wales before crossing over to Ireland. The *Life* then describes the birth of David, specifically noting that it took place thirty years after Patrick left for Ireland. Thus, it is certainly the later Patrick, not Palladius, who features in this entry in the *Welsh Annals*.

In line with the later date of Patrick's death, the date of his departure for Ireland has also been moved by modern scholars. One scholar suggested 456 as the date for this event.[15] If this is correct, then the birth of David, thirty years later, should have actually occurred in 486. If we assume that this is the year intended by the entry in the *Annals*, then when we count from this date, we come to 544 for the Battle of Badon. On the other hand, if we count from the secure year of 457 for the 'Easter' entry, then we come to 521 for the battle. But using the generally accepted anchoring of the *Annals*, which is based on more than just the 'Easter' entry, Badon took place in 516. Clearly, the *Annals* are not anywhere near perfectly reliable.

It must be admitted that many of the subsequent events are more or less accurately dated when working from the generally accepted anchoring – it is only by using secure dates that it was anchored in the first place. Examples include the 457 'Easter' date, the birth of Columba, the death of Bishop Benignus, and the conversion of the English by Augustine. All of these are more or less in their correct temporal positions if we assume that the generally accepted anchoring is correct. However, the example of the birth of David – and, possibly, the example of the death of Patrick – shows that it is possible for the entries to be wildly backdated at times.

The lists of years in the manuscripts are not one to a page, but generally make up several columns – often three – on each page.

It has been pointed out that the scribes copying a chronicle such as this may have, on occasion, put events in the wrong column, thus misdating them. Another possibility is that while transferring information regarding a particular event from one chronicle into their own chronicle, they may have misunderstood which column of years that event was supposed to belong to, whether it was the column on the left of the event or the column on the right. Such a mistake could produce a difference of as many as thirty years or so. It is possible that this is what happened with the battles of Badon and Camlann.

Alternatively, it may be that various events were dated relative to different anchor points, some of which were in error. It is not necessarily the case that the events were originally dated relative to whatever preceding event is now present in the chronicle. For example, in the *Chronicle from Vortigern to King John*, there is the statement that the Battle of Badon took place 128 years after the age of Vortigern. A scribe may have used a statement such as that to place the battle in his chronicle, while using other statements from different sources, using different anchor points, to place different events. If the anchor point used for Badon was wrong, then this would, as with the previous explanation, allow its date to be in error while the dates for most of the other entries are correct.

One simple anchor point that could have caused this error is 'the Incarnation of the Lord'. As with Arthur's abdication in *Historia Regum Britanniae*, perhaps Badon, the most renowned of Arthur's battles, was also an event which was known as having occurred X number of years after the Incarnation, or, alternatively, the Passion. If 'Passion' was used, and then this was mistakenly replaced for the more common 'Incarnation', then this would explain why it is dated in these annals as being around thirty-three years earlier than all the other evidence requires. This would mean that Badon should really be placed in the year 549. It is possible that this same explanation accounts for the Battle of Camlann, though it seems more likely that Camlann was actually dated relative to Badon, given that the two events are Arthur's greatest victory and his final defeat. In fact, this explanation may account for the roughly thirty-three-year error in the entry regarding David and, possibly, the entry regarding Patrick.

Whatever the cause of the error, it is clear that almost every other piece of evidence for Arthur shows that he must have lived long past the middle of the sixth century, and every other piece of evidence for Badon specifically indicates that it took place around the year 550. Similarly, the evidence regarding Mordred prevents him from having been alive as early as 537, let alone fighting in a battle. A date closer to 570 for Camlann must be true, in view of all the other evidence regarding his family.

With this information in mind, we have a clear period in which to look for Arthur and we will be able to see if there is a suitable historical figure who fits this time period.

Where Did Arthur Live?

The next step to finding Arthur is to work out the area in which he lived and was active. The first possible reference to him occurs in *Y Gododdin*, which is a sixth- or seventh-century poem describing a British defeat at a place called Catraeth, supposedly written by the late sixth-century poet Aneirin. The poem is set in the North, with the Gododdin being a tribe who lived around southern Scotland and northern England. The poem also mentions several northern locations, and Catraeth itself is commonly held to be Catterick, North Yorkshire. One of the warriors who fought in the battle is allegorically stated to have killed many men, 'though he was no Arthur'. The famous king is here being used as a comparative device to place superlative praise on the warrior, which is, in itself, testimony to the immense reputation of King Arthur.

This reference does not necessarily mean that he was active in the north of Britain, but it does mean that he was famous in that area, so it would be logical to conclude that his sphere of influence at least included that area. Should we, therefore, look for Arthur's dynasty there? We should certainly look for someone who had some degree of influence in the North, but it is not necessarily the case that Arthur lived there.

There was definitely an Arthur who lived in that area in the sixth century – Artuir mac Aedan. However, neither the information about the King Arthur of legend, nor the implied information about the Arthur mentioned in *Y Gododdin*, is compatible with the information about Artuir mac Aedan. The main issue is that he lived too late to be the King Arthur of legend. His father, Aedan mac Gabrain, became king of Dal Riata in 574 after the death of his uncle Conall mac Comgaill, according to *The Annals of Ulster*. *The Annals of Tigernach* records the death of 'Aodhan son of Gabran' in 604 in the seventy-fourth year of his age, which would place his birth in 531. This would put the birth of his son Artuir somewhere in the early 550s, if not later. This is decades from the estimated dates given for Arthur's life in the previous section. Artuir cannot have been the Arthur who fought at Badon around 550. Artuir could also not have had any hand in the events that led to the birth of Cadoc, whose birth was in the early sixth century. Nor could he have been the King Arthur who interacted with Padarn, another individual who lived in the first half of the sixth century. This is just some of the information which shows that Artuir mac Aedan lived too late to be King Arthur. There are many other reasons for the connection to be unsupported, such as the lack of correspondence between Arthur's family and Artuir's family, but the incompatibility of the dates of their lives is sufficient to prove the point.[16]

Regarding the Arthur of *Y Gododdin*, it is highly unlikely that Artuir mac Aedan is the Arthur in question. There is no issue with the chronology of the matter, as the events of the poem are believed to have occurred around 600. Artuir was already dead by then, having been killed in battle either in 594 or 596.[17] The issue is in the purpose of the text. It has been pointed out that all the numerous soldiers referred to in the poem are praised to an extreme degree, and there is certainly no criticism of them. Therefore, the line 'He fed black ravens on the wall of the fortress, although he was not Arthur' must be understood in this light. Such a statement would certainly imply that Arthur was known for being an incredible soldier – the subject of the stanza was said to have killed at least 300 others in the battle – but it can be seen that the actual meaning gives him a reputation of far greater magnitude. The only consistent interpretation of the line is that Arthur is being used as a figure of virtually incomparable stature. In other words, the correct understanding of the line should be that the soldier is being praised for the fact that he accomplished all that he did *even though* he wasn't Arthur.

Remarkably, this has been used as an argument against the famous king's historicity, using the logic that the Arthur in question was understood to be a legendary, or perhaps even mythical, figure in the early 600s when this poem was composed. However, a consideration of the context of the line and the position of Arthur and his family eliminates the necessity for such a conclusion.

Arthur is indeed being used as a figure of virtually incomparable stature, but incomparable to what? The individual to whom the stanza is referring is Gwawrddur. This person is almost entirely unknown from other records, which is testimony to his insignificance. He is merely a soldier, albeit a very good one. King Arthur, on the other hand, is frequently referred to as 'Emperor' in Welsh literature, with its earliest known use being in the tenth-century poem *Geraint son of Erbin*. In the eleventh-century *Life of St Cadoc* he is referred to as 'the most illustrious king of Britannia'. In the ninth-century *Historia Britonnum* he is said to have been the leader of an alliance of British kings and military leaders. Clearly, King Arthur was not just any warrior. If a mighty king – such as Maelgwn Gwynedd, the incredibly powerful king of north Wales in Arthur's time – had been the subject of the stanza, *then* it might be logical to conclude that the Arthur of the stanza must be a superhuman figure. As it is, there is no reason why the mighty King Arthur, if he really was nearly as powerful as the sources claim, could not have been used as a figure of unapproachable reputation for this obscure Gwawrddur to be compared with. It would be akin to comparing a soldier who took part in a particular battle in twelfth-century Asia with the mighty Genghis Khan himself. There is no issue with such a concept.

There is, however, an issue in supposing that Artuir mac Aedan could have had such an astonishing reputation. That is not to say that his dynasty was a minor one, but there is simply no basis for supposing that anyone of that family could have achieved such unparalleled prestige. This is particularly evident regarding Artuir himself, for in the entry for 'the slaying of the sons of Aedan' in the Irish annals, *The Annals of Tigernach*, lists them as Bran, Domangort, Eochaid Fionn and Artuir. In *The Annals of Ulster*, Artuir (with Eochaid Fionn) is not even listed. How could this possibly be, if Artuir was a mighty man of such stunning reputation? Is that the sort of person whom the annalists would leave out of their records? Or, if they did include him, would they list him last? Such observations make it virtually certain that Artuir mac Aedan could not have been the Arthur of *Y Gododdin*. On the same grounds – the matter of reputation – it is exceedingly unlikely that the Arthur of *Y Gododdin* could be anyone other than 'the most illustrious king of Britannia', the King Arthur of legend.

Another early poem which mentions Arthur is *Pa Gur*. It lists several battles fought by him and his warrior Cai (Sir Kay). There is a reference to Arthur fighting in Mynyd Eiddyn, which is Edinburgh. The other battles have no certain location, but this mention of Edinburgh shows that – according to this early source – Arthur was active in that area. Aneirin, the author of *Y Gododdin*, was the court poet of the northern kings Urien and Owain. Therefore, the fact that Arthur was mentioned in that poem shows he was well known in the northern area. And not just well known, but he possessed an exceedingly great reputation in that area. This agrees with the mention in *Pa Gur* of him fighting in Edinburgh.

Historia Brittonum

We can compare this information with the earliest definite reference to King Arthur, which is in the *Historia Brittonum*. It records twelve battles Arthur fought against the Saxons during their invasion of Britain. Not all the locations are known with certainty, but several are, and these can help us to identify Arthur's area of activity.

The seventh battle is said to have taken place in 'the wood Celidon, which the Britons call Cat Coit Celidon'. This can confidently be identified as the Caledonian Forest in southern Scotland. The eleventh battle was said to have been on Mount Agned, which Geoffrey of Monmouth, writing in the twelfth century, identified as Edinburgh. This would fit with the mention of Arthur fighting at Edinburgh in *Pa Gur*.

These two battles again point towards a northern area of activity for Arthur. This fully supports the evidence from *Y Gododdin*, that Arthur was active in the north of Britain. But, as asked before, does this mean that he was a northern king, or warrior? Before we can make any such conclusion, we must take into consideration *all* the evidence. Nennius provides us with more details about Arthur.

At the end of some manuscripts of *Historia Brittonum* there are a series of 'wonders' of Britain, in a section called *De Mirabilibus Britanniae*. The twelfth and thirteenth wonders concern Arthur. The first of these is to do with a paw print on top of a mound of stones, allegedly the paw print of Arthur's hunting dog Cabal, or Cavall. This was said to have been formed 'when hunting the porker Troynt', which is a reference to an event described at length in the slightly later tale *Culhwch ac Olwen*. In the Nennius document, it is said to have been in the region of Buelt, which is the medieval cantref of Buellt in Mid Wales. It further says that the mound of stones on which the paw print is located is called Carn Cabal, which is virtually certain to be the modern Carn Gafallt in Powys, in the former area of Buellt. Therefore, this information shows that Arthur was also active in Wales. More specifically, Buellt was a cantref in the southern half of Wales, just below the border between the north and the south.

The second reference to Arthur in the Wonders of Britain is regarding his son, Amr. Apparently, Arthur himself killed Amr and he lies buried in a tumulus in the region of 'Ercing', which is the medieval kingdom of Ergyng. This kingdom encompassed much of modern Herefordshire and Gloucestershire, bordering the kingdom of Gwent (or Monmouthshire) in Wales. In medieval times, this area was part of Wales. Again, this information places Arthur's area of activity in the south, this time around the border of south-east Wales and England.

So far, the information is suggesting a warrior active both in southern Scotland and southern Wales. This is quite a peculiar separation of localities. Still, let us continue examining the sources and see where they lead us.

Culhwch ac Olwen

The tenth-century tale *Culhwch ac Olwen*, part of the famous Mabinogi collection, contains a story of King Arthur and his men embarking on a series of almost impossible missions. The most dramatic of these is a boar hunt: the attack of 'Twrch Trwyth' on Ireland and Wales. Though this particular telling of the story seems, on linguistic grounds, to have been constructed in the tenth century, the fact that the tale was referenced in passing in the ninth century

Historia Brittonum shows that the story had existed since at least before that time. And although the boar is not specifically said to have gone through Buellt in *HB*, the general area is the same, with the hunt taking place predominantly through the southern half of Wales. This story contains a wealth of information regarding where Arthur was active and where his main contacts were.

Many of the individuals in Arthur's court list are based in Wales; this is known from a comparison with other sources. However, it seems especially beneficial to discuss the characters who are – or probably are – historical figures of the sixth century. If we can establish that they are historical, then the information about them is more likely to be useful than the information about someone about whom there is no independent corroboration.

The *Harleian MS 3859* contains a series of king lists, which are known as the Harleian genealogies. One of the names on the king lists appears in Arthur's court list in *Culhwch ac Olwen*. This name is Rhun ap Neithon (spelt Nwython in the Welsh tale). He is listed as a seventh-generation descendant of Magnus Maximus (d. 388), which places him in precisely the right era for the Arthurian story. He is included in the king list of Ynys Manaw, which is the Isle of Man. This island is situated slightly further north than York. It was part of the territory of the northern kingdom of Rheged for a while in the sixth century, so this character reiterates the connection between King Arthur and the North.

Gwythyr ap Greidawl is another character who seems to have been a real figure. In later sources, particularly the Welsh Triads, he is said to have been the father of Gwenhwyfar, Arthur's wife. In the later medieval romance tales, the father of Gwenhywfar – that is, Guinevere – is said to be Leodegrance. This individual was supposedly the king of Carohaise, which is probably Carhaix in Brittany. Therefore, the father of Guinevere was supposed to have ruled in Brittany, but evidently had relations with Arthur's area of activity.

The Welsh Triads actually list three Guineveres, but none of their fathers are called Leodegrance. Therefore, it is impossible to say which of the fathers is represented by Leodegrance. With the possibility that it was Gwythyr being the case, it is significant to note that in the *Life of St Paul Aurelian*, a certain Count Withur appears as ruling in Brittany. There is no reason for him to have been invented; certainly not for purposes of linking the events of the *Life* to the popular Arthurian tales, for he is not said to have been the father of Guinevere or a relative of Arthur. He is simply there, in the account. It is, therefore, likely that this Count Withur was a real person, and he would have been an exact contemporary of Gwythyr. Additionally, he is said in the *Life* to have come from Gwent, which borders Ergyng, thus putting him right into the area of Arthur's activity.

Strongly associated with Gwythyr is a man called Gwyn ap Nudd, who is regularly connected to the North. This could well be a son of the historical Nudd Hael of Selcovia (southern Scotland) in the mid-sixth century. Alternatively, he may have been the son of Nudd ap Ceidio, another individual from the north of Britain. In either case, this character reinforces Arthur's connection with the North.

Another character in Arthur's court list is Iona, king of France. This is clearly Ionas, a king of Brittany who was killed by the infamous Count Conomor in Arthur's time. Again, here is a historical ruler from Brittany, supposedly serving Arthur in South Wales. This alliance with Brittany is reaffirmed in *Culhwch ac Olwen* when Arthur summons men from Armorica and Normandy.

Odgar, son of Aedd, king of Ireland, is another character mentioned in the story. Though Odgar himself is not known from other sources, it is known that one of the kings of Ireland in Arthur's time was Aed mac Ainmuirech. Another Irish king at the same time was Aed Dub mac Suibni. Either of these kings could be the Aedd of the tale. A character from the Welsh tale named Maelwys, the son of Baeddan, likewise, appears to be a historical prince of Ireland. He is known from the Irish annals as Mael Umai mac Baidan.

Samson Finsych may well be the famous Samson of Dol. His father was Amon Ddu, the son of Budic of Brittany, and his mother was Anna of Gwent. He spent much of his life in both locations. Provided this is the Samson of the *Culhwch* tale, it again shows Arthur's connection with either Brittany or south-east Wales.

Taliesin is another character who is probably historical. This man was supposedly the chief of the bards, and is perhaps best known for his service to Urien, the powerful king of Rheged, the kingdom of southern Scotland and northern England. However, as well as being associated with the northern area, Taliesin was said to have been the son of a certain Henwg. This latter individual appears in the *Life of St Samson* as a cousin of Samson of Dol, making Taliesin and Samson first cousins once removed. Their family relationship may be the reason for them being listed next to each other in Arthur's court list. The church of Llanhennock in Monmouthshire, south-east Wales, is apparently named after Taliesin's father.

Morvudd, the daughter of Urien of Rheged, is also listed in the story. While she herself is not positively historical, her father Urien is widely accepted as a real historical figure. This yet again illustrates Arthur's alliance with the North.

Finally, Gildas is one of the last main figures in the court list whose historicity is without doubt. He was a member of a large royal family who were originally from southern Scotland, though he was said to have travelled to the south of Britain to be taught by Illtud in his famous school, Llanilltud Fawr (or Llantwit Major, as it is known in English), in Glamorgan, South Wales. He was also said to have gone to Somerset (just across the Bristol Channel from Glamorgan), to Ireland, Brittany and even to Rome.

The result of this brief analysis of the historical figures in Arthur's court list is that we now have a very good idea of the areas over which Arthur had influence and alliances. But even better than that, the story provides information about Arthur's position. None of the other sources that we have looked at have clarified anything more than Arthur's role as a military leader. But in *Culhwch ac Olwen*, there is frequent mention of 'Arthur's Palace'. When Culhwch finally gets to meet his cousin, Arthur, he greets him by referring to him as 'Sovereign Ruler of this Island.' Clearly, Arthur was far more than a military leader; he was a royal ruler. And more than just *a* royal ruler; he was *the* ruler of the island, Britain. This is consistent with the roughly contemporary (if not older) poem *Geraint son of Erbin*, in which Arthur is called Emperor.

So according to this information, Arthur was a king of the highest rank. He had allies in Brittany, being able to call men to his aid from that country. He also had associates in Ireland, as well as allies from the northern kingdom of Rheged – and the associated Isle of Man – and possibly from the bordering Scottish kingdom of Selcovia. Yet Arthur himself was active in the southern half of Wales.

Even if the specific details provided in the tale are not all correct, there cannot be very many sixth-century figures who fit even the general picture that is developing.

The Location of Gelliwig and Kernyw

A more controversial location that the tale connects with Arthur is Kernyw. In this region named Kernyw, Arthur is said to have had a court called Gelliwig, and this place also appears in the Triad, *The Three Tribal Thrones of the Island of Britain*, as one of Arthur's courts. 'Kernyw' is the Welsh word for Cornwall, but there are also other places in Britain by that name. The uncertainty is unfortunate, since the references in *Culhwch ac Olwen* strongly imply that it is Arthur's main camp. Hence, this is the earliest piece of information regarding Arthur's own area of rulership, rather than just the areas in which he was active.

The Kernyw of this story is commonly taken to be Cornwall, and the town of Callington in Cornwall is known in Cornish as Kelliwik. However, 'Kernyw' was also the name of a place in South Wales. It is unclear where the exact area was that it originally covered. In modern-day Newport, south-west Gwent, there is 'Coedkernew', which means 'Cernyw wood'. In the *Book of Llandaff*, there is a location by the name of 'Llan Cerniu', or 'the holy estate of Cernyw'. A place by this name no longer survives, but it was said to have been by the River Dore, which is just to the north of Gwent and runs along much of the eastern side of Herefordshire. Thus, with one surviving location bearing the name in the south-west of Gwent, and one location bearing the name in the north of Gwent, it seems 'Cernyw' more or less covered the same area as Gwent. Perhaps it was another name for Gwent, or was just a large region within it. It is therefore very significant to note that modern-day Gelli Farm, Llanvetherine, Gwent, was historically known as 'Gelliwig'. The most significant issue to be addressed for the purpose of locating King Arthur is to answer the question of whether the 'Kernyw' of the tale is Cornwall, or the region of Cernyw in South Wales.

Towards the end of the tale, it is said that Arthur 'summoned all of Kernyw and Dyfneint' to him. Earlier, there is a man called Gwynnhyvar, the mayor of Kernyw and Dyfneint. These names are usually translated as Cornwall and Devon. However, Dyfneint was the name for the kingdom of Dumnonia, which encompassed all of modern Cornwall and Devon.[18] It is difficult to see how a man could have had power over Dumnonia *and* Cornwall, when the latter is an area inside the former. On the other hand, if the intended meaning was that Gwynnhyvar was the mayor of Dumnonia and Cernyw (that is, Gwent, or a major component thereof), then the statement makes sense.

After gathering all the men of Dyfneint and Kernyw to him, Arthur says, 'Twrch Trwyth has slain many of my men, but, by the valour of warriors, while I live he shall not go into Kernyw.'

It is important to note that, by this point in the story, the boar has not entered the territory of Gwent. After a great deal of fighting in west Wales, the boar is said to have gone to Llwch Ewin, which would seem to be Llyn Llech Owain. This is near Ammanford, to the west of Glamorgan, which is, itself, to the west of Gwent. The next location is Llwch Tawy, which would correspond to the origin of the River Tawe (now known as Llyn y Fan Fawr, but referred to as Llyn Llwch Towe in the sixteenth century). This lake is at the foot of Fan Brycheiniog, and is in the region above Glamorgan.

Next, 'Twrch Trwyth went from there to between Tawy and Euyas.' Euyas would be the region of Ewyas, no longer extant but memorialised by Ewyas Harold and the Vale of Ewyas. This area, as indicated by those existing place names, was to the north-east of Glamorgan. Therefore, 'between the River Tawe and the region of Ewyas' would be somewhere a little way above Glamorgan.

It is at this point that Arthur gathers all of Dyfneint and Kernyw to him – that is, most probably, Dumnonia and Gwent. Then, he 'resolved that he would send a body of knights, with the dogs of the Island, as far as Euyas, who should return thence to the Severn, and that tried warriors should traverse the Island, and force him [Twrch Trwyth] into the Severn'. This passage is very puzzling to understand if Cornwall is intended by Kernyw. Arthur has just said that he would not allow the great boar to enter Kernyw, and now he is ordering his men to try and force the enemy – currently in

Wales – into the Severn. The next battle is said to have taken place between Llyn Lliwan and Aber Gwy. Aber Gwy is the mouth of the River Wye, on the Severn, and Llyn Lliwan is one of the wonders mentioned by Nennius. He wrote that 'the mouth of that river flows into the Severn', which would thus mean that both locations, Aber Gwy and Llyn Lliwan, are on the Severn. Hence, between the two locations would also be somewhere on the banks of the Severn. Unfortunately, since we do not know where Llyn Lliwan was, this is not particularly helpful.

Nonetheless, the mouth of the River Wye is some way into Gwent, so the location of this battle on the Severn depends on whether Llyn Lliwan was to the east or the west of the Wye. But considering Arthur's men were approaching from the west, and Llyn Lliwan is listed before the mouth of the Wye, it seems likely that Llyn Lliwan was to the west (making it the nearer of the two locations from the point of view of Arthur's men). Thus, the battle appears to be set near, though not necessarily within, the western border of Gwent. So, this means that Arthur has got his men to pursue Twrch Trwyth and push him from, presumably, where he was last said to have been, which was somewhere above Glamorgan, all the way down to the Severn somewhere around the eastern border of that kingdom. This is the very opposite of what one would expect if Arthur did not want him to reach Cornwall. The boar was 40 km or so from the coast of the Severn, well away from Cornwall and not even heading in the right direction. Forcing the boar up into north Wales, east into England or back into west Wales would have achieved his purpose. Forcing the enemy south-east to the banks of the Severn is one of the few possible actions that would run counter to Arthur's intention. By forcing them into the Severn, Arthur was forcing Twrch Trwyth closer to the south-west peninsular of Britain.

On the other hand, Arthur's actions are sensible if the region of Cernyw in Gwent was intended by Kernyw. Though it involved skirting near the western side of the region, by forcing Twrch Trwyth onto the other side of the Severn (the side on which Cornwall is located) he was leaving a great boundary between the boar and Kernyw. In fact, immediately after saying that he would not allow Twrch Trwyth to enter Kernyw, Arthur said, 'And I will not follow him any longer, but I will oppose him life to life.'

Such a statement makes sense if Arthur was currently *in* the vicinity of Kernyw and was determined to drive Twrch Trwyth out of Wales by means of the Severn just to the west of the kingdom. On the other hand, the line does not make sense if Kernyw was intended to mean Cornwall, because Arthur does continue following the boar all the way to 'Cornwall' after the battle on the Severn. Arthur's statement becomes meaningless. It could be argued that it was simply a case of Arthur having no choice but to continue following Twrch Trwyth because he was heading towards Cornwall, which was the very place Arthur did not want him to go, meaning that he simply had to contradict his earlier declaration. However, it would still be a puzzle as to why that line was included in the tale. If the region of Cernyw in Gwent was meant by Kernyw, then when the boar did finally reach it and Arthur pursued him, they were still in the same vicinity as they had been before, and Arthur's statement is not contradicted.

When the boar does reach Kernyw and attack it, it might be argued that the text implies that the boar was on the other side of the Severn at this point, meaning that it must have been Cornwall to which he charged. However, such a conclusion goes beyond what was written. This is the description of the battle on the Severn:

And Arthur fell upon him together with the champions of Britain. And Osla Kyllellvawr drew near, and Manawyddan the son of Llyr, and Kacmwri the servant of Arthur, and Gwyngelli, and they seized hold of him, catching him first by his feet, and plunged him in the Severn, so that it overwhelmed him. On the one side, Mabon the son of Modron spurred his steed and snatched his razor from him, and Kyledyr Wyllt came up with him on the other side, upon another steed, in the Severn, and took from him the scissors. But before they could obtain the comb, he had regained the ground with his feet, and from the moment that he reached the shore, neither dog, nor man, nor horse could overtake him until he came to Kernyw.

As can be seen from that description, nowhere is it said that Twrch Trwyth was forced onto the other side of the river. He was plunged *into* the river, but then a little later he 'regained the ground with his feet'. When it then says he 'reached the shore', there is no reason to conclude that this meant anything but the shore he had been forced away from. From the likely location on the banks of the Severn, it is only a short distance to the western side of Gwent, and thus Cernyw. This is a far more logical scenario than supposing that this enemy charged all the way from the mouth of the River Severn to Cornwall, some 150 km away.

In view of the weight of evidence, it must be acknowledged that the Kernyw that Arthur was concerned about, and therefore where his important base 'Gelliwig' would have been located, was Gwent, or in Gwent.

Before moving on with this conclusion, let us first see if it is consistent with the other information about Arthur and his area of control. Another early Welsh story is Geraint and Enid, also part of the Mabinogi collection of tales, and this places Arthur's court at Caerleon-upon-Usk; this is a locality in Newport, Gwent. Geoffrey of Monmouth, likewise, placed Arthur's court there. He also claimed that Dubricius, a famous bishop of Glamorgan, was the person who crowned Arthur both as a teenager and an adult. King Arthur also appears in the *Lives* of *Cadoc*, *Gildas*, and *Illtud* – all of whom lived in Glamorgan. He also appears in several other saints' lives, sometimes appearing in Brittany or even Cornwall, both of which locations are consistent with the information that has been gleaned from *Culhwch ac Olwen*. Most sources describe him as the king of all Britain, but one of the few sources which places him as the king of a specific area is *The Chronicles of England*, published in the late fifteenth century by William Caxton. This states plainly that Arthur was to be crowned king of Glamorgan. Therefore, it is indeed consistent with the later evidence to place Arthur's centre of activity in the area of Glamorgan and Gwent.

The entire story of *Culhwch ac Olwen* is invaluable in assessing Arthur's area of activity and, most importantly of all, the location of his base. As we have seen, this prose tale provides us with the information that Arthur was not just a war leader but actually a royal ruler. It also reveals that this was a person who had associates in Ireland, the North, and could also call on men from

Brittany. And, finally, we have a location for Arthur's own base of operations, which is placed in Gwent in south Wales.

A considerable amount of progress can be made with this information alone. We are looking for a king of one of the dynasties who had power over the area of Gwent, or at least had connections with that area and would have a base there. For any candidate to be viable in light of the evidence of reputation from *Y Gododdin* and the title of 'Sovereign Ruler' bestowed on Arthur in *Culhwch ac Olwen*, there must be evidence that he was extremely powerful and well respected. To secure the candidate, there must be good evidence for connections with Ireland, Brittany and the North. If such an individual had family members who correspond well with family members described in the legends, then the identification can be taken to be as good as confirmed.

From the constant allusions to an 'Arthurian mystery', it is easy to assume that such an individual does not exist – or at least, that they have so far been elusive to modern researchers. It should be easy enough to test this claim, for there are innumerable surviving king lists of the various kingdoms of Wales. Though it is possible that Arthur was simply a member of a dynasty allied to Gwent, the more obvious conclusion is that he was part of the actual Gwentian dynasty. Hence, that is where we will look first.

The Gwentian Dynasty

The *Harleian MS 3859* provides a list of kings of Gwent and of the neighbouring kingdom of Glywysing, modern-day Glamorgan. It seems that Gwent was originally under the control of Glywysing in the immediate post-Roman era, and only split into a separate kingdom after several generations of kings. Therefore, the list for Glywysing goes back further in time than the list for Gwent. Even so, the list does not go back far enough to establish a definite date (for example, by starting with a firmly dated Roman emperor such as Magnus Maximus, as some of the lists do), but the dates of the individuals can be checked elsewhere. For the kingdom of Glywysing, the first king named is Teudubric. The second is Atroys. Then it is Morcant, and then Iudhail. These latter two are also the first two names in the list of the kings of Gwent. Iudhail's son on the Glywysing side is listed as Fernmail. This individual is known from the *Welsh Annals* as Ffernfael son of Iudhail, or Ithael. The *Welsh Annals* records his death as being in 775. Assuming an age of death of around seventy and approximately twenty-two years between each generation, his ancestor Teudubric's birth should have been in *c.* 617.

There is an issue with this calculation, though. Virtually every other source attests to there being an extra individual – Meurig – between Atroys and Teudubric. This would indicate that Teudubric's birth was closer to *c.* 595. It is evident that the Harleian genealogies are not always strictly father-to-son relationships, but are sometimes lists of succession. This is particularly noticeable by looking at the Brycheiniog list, in which many of the Roman emperors are listed as if they were father and son even when there was no family connection. For example, the Roman Emperor Galerius, who succeeded Emperor Diocletian, is listed as 'Galerii map Diocletiani' even though they were not even related. Probably, then, Atroys is listed immediately after Teudubric because he became king very soon after the death of Teudubric, without much time for the independent rule of Meurig – or perhaps Atroys became king while Teudubric was still alive, leaving no independent rule at all for Meurig.

If the suggested dates for the birth of Teudubric (more commonly spelt 'Tewdrig') are correct, this would mean that the Harleian king list for Glywysing does not cover the period in which King Arthur would have lived. These dates, or ones close to them, are generally accepted as being correct. If the current view *is* correct, then the Harleian genealogies are useless for our current purpose, which is to see who the ruler of this part of the country was during Arthur's time.

However, basing the dates of an entire dynasty on one reference in the *Welsh Annals* is more than a little unwise. The members of this Glamorgan dynasty feature frequently in numerous early sources, so it is possible to check how well these suggested dates tie in with the abundance of other information we have at our disposal.

The members of the dynasty appear in several saints' lives, as well as the Llandaff charters and the Llancarfan charters (attached to the *Life of St Cadoc*). At the end of the twelfth-century *Life of*

St Teilo, there is a brief summary that describes how the Church of Llandaff continued to grow in churches and territories, which were given to it by Teilo's contemporary kings. A list of those kings then follows, with the first one listed being Tewdrig son of Teithfallt. From many other records, such as the twelfth-century *Book of Llandaff*, we know that the Tewdrig of the Glamorgan dynasty was indeed 'ap Teithfallt'. So according to this *Life*, Teudubric, or Tewdrig, was a contemporary of Teilo. The latter individual is generally held to have been born around the year 500, being a 'younger contemporary of Dewi [David]'.[19] The sources, such as the *Life of St Teilo* and the *Life of St Oudoceus*, explicitly tell us that he outlived the great plague, which most likely ended in *c.* 570 (see Chapter Six). Yet he cannot have lived for very much longer. His death was likely in *c.* 580. This is much too early for Tewdrig to have given land grants in Teilo's lifetime if the former was born *c.* 595, as suggested by the sources that include Meurig between Atroys and Tewdrig. He must reasonably have been born *at least* fifteen years before Teilo's death, likely more, which would make the year of his birth no later than 565.

Meurig also appears in the *Life of St Oudoceus* as the king who was present, with his sons Athrwys (the 'Atroys' of the *Harleian MS 3859*) and Idnerth, at Oudoceus's elevation to the bishopric of Llandaff. In the *Life*, Oudoceus succeeded Teilo as bishop, and as Teilo died in *c.* 580, this would have had to have happened that year or earlier. It is implied that it happened more or less as soon as Teilo and Oudoceus returned to Britain after the end of the great plague, which ended *c.* 570. But even if we take the later date of 580 as the latest possible year for Oudoceus's appointment, Meurig must have been born around 565 at the very latest for him to have been present as a king.

However, the fact that his sons Athrwys and Idnerth are also recorded as being among those by whom Oudoceus was chosen shows that they are clearly not infants at this time. It seems safe to assume that they must have been upwards of around fifteen years of age when this appointment took place, which was in *c.* 580 at the latest. Thus, these two sons of Meurig should have been born no later than *c.* 565. Assuming, as previously, an average of twenty-two years per generation, this would place Meurig's birth in 543 at the latest. Tewdrig, in turn, would have been born around 521.

This is supported by the Llancarfan charters. There is a record of a certain Euan Buurr, who was said to have killed two sons of his sister – Atgan and Aidnerth. It seems reasonable to conclude that Aidnerth and Idnerth are one and the same, especially since the charter says: 'Euan being compelled came, and kings with him, to the presence of Cadoc and Illtud, and confessed to them his crimes.' Clearly, the murder of these two individuals was a very significant incident, even causing kings to get involved in the settling of the matter. Undoubtedly if the two individuals were royal, it would make a great deal of sense for Aidnerth to be Idnerth, the son of King Meurig. No other individual with a similar name from this general time period and location is known.

With this being the case, it is necessary to note that the witnesses for the resultant charter include Cadfan and Finnian the Irishman. This latter individual is either Finnian of Clonard or Finnian of Moville. Of these two, the first died long before the end of the great plague, but the second died in 579, which fits.[20] Likewise, Cadfan died in 590. In addition to these witnesses, the quote above regarding Euan also reveals that Illtud and Cadoc were present; however, Illtud, as we reasoned earlier, was most likely dead by *c.* 580. Cadoc, too, is believed to have died around the same time.[21] Therefore, if they were still active to address the aftermath of Idnerth's death, then Idnerth must have been killed sometime before *c.* 580. This corroborates the conclusion that the appointment of Oudoceus as bishop, which occurred while Idnerth was still alive, took place before 580.

So, based on this information, Tewdrig should have been born around 521 at the latest. His father Teithfallt would then have been born around 499, making him more or less exactly contemporary with Arthur. One of the other characters in Arthur's court list in *Culhwch ac Olwen* is a certain 'Teithi Hen'. Perhaps this is Teithfallt. However, there is far more information about the Glamorgan dynasty that needs to be considered before arriving at such a conclusion.

The conclusion that Teithfallt was more or less the exact contemporary of Arthur is somewhat supported by Meurig and

Athrwys being contemporaries of Oudoceus, who – according to his *Life* – was the son of Budic ap Cybydan of Brittany. This Budic was born around 500, and would thus have probably begun having sons around 520 or later.[22] The *Life of St Oudoceus* states that Budic had at least two sons before Oudoceus, so he may have been born relatively late in his life – though just how late, we cannot know. He was likely no more than forty years old at the time of Oudoceus's birth, which would mean Oudoceus was probably born before 540. This would put most of his *floruit* in the sixth century. Yet he is shown, in the *Book of Llandaff*, as being a contemporary of Ithael ap Morgan ap Athrwys. In one charter, even two sons of Ithael (Meurig and Ffernfael) are witnesses. Consider what this requires.

Let us assume that Oudoceus did not live beyond ninety and that he served as bishop until the day he died. Let us also assume that the two sons of Ithael who appear as witnesses were as young as fifteen years old when this land grant was made. If we make 540 the latest year Oudoceus was likely to have been born, then 630 is the latest that that any land grant featuring him as a witness could have occurred. Thus, if we allow the two sons of Ithael to have been as young as fifteen years old when the land grant to which they appear as witnesses was made, then they would have been born in 615. If we again use twenty-two years as the standard male generation, then we can estimate that their father Ithael would have been born *c.* 593, with Morgan being born *c.* 571. Another twenty-two-year generation gap would bring us to *c.* 549 for the birth of Athrwys, and then *c.* 527 for Meurig, *c.* 505 for Tewdrig, and finally, *c.* 483 for Teithfallt. Even if we reduce the generation gap to twenty years, this would still only produce an estimate of *c.* 495 for Teithfallt's birth.

This conclusion, however, would conflict with information found in the same source – the *Book of Llandaff*. This source records that Meurig married Onbrawst, the daughter of Gwrgan Fawr, the king of Ergyng (to the north-east of Gwent). Gwrgan's father is recorded in this source as Cynfyn; his father, in turn, is recorded as Pebiau (also spelt 'Peibio' and 'Peibo' in other sources). This Pebiau gives several grants of land to Dubricius, as does his father Erb on one occasion. However, the *Life of St Dubricius*, contained in the *Book of Llandaff*, informs us that Dubricius was actually the illegitimate son of Pebiau's daughter Eurddil. This would make Dubricius's mother the sister of Cynfyn, Gwrgan's father. Thus, Dubricius and Gwrgan were first cousins. Dubricius's dates are not totally certain, but virtually all authorities agree that his life extended from some time in the late fifth century to the early sixth.[23] Peter Bartrum, for instance, estimates his birth to have been in 465.[24] Without evidence to the contrary, we can assume that his first cousin Gwrgan would have been born at roughly the same time.

Using *c.* 465 for Gwrgan's birth, his daughter Onbrawst would likely have been born *c.* 487. Her son Athrwys, then, should have been born around twenty years later, in 507; it was possibly as little as eighteen years later, due to the shorter expected female generation, making the birth year 505. This makes Athrwys, rather than his great-grandfather Teithfallt, a contemporary of Arthur.

This chronological scenario is further supported by the information regarding a well-known individual mentioned earlier – Samson of Dol. From the earliest information about him, found in his *Life*, he is known to have been the son of Anna of Gwent, and this Anna is stated by several sources to have been the daughter of Meurig.[25] His *Life* tells us that he was trained at Illtud's school at the age of five. Considering Illtud was unlikely to have been older than eighty when he died in *c.* 580, we can estimate that he was born in *c.* 500. As he was said to have been a cousin of Arthur, this seems like a good estimate. Using this as his birth year, we can further assume that his school was not founded before *c.* 520, or possibly somewhat later. If Samson was sent to the school at the age of five, then Samson should have been born somewhere in the region of 520 at the earliest. And he cannot have been born much later than this, for he is recorded as having attended one of the councils of Paris in 553.[26] If, once again, we use the estimate of twenty-two years per generation, then we come to *c.* 476 for the birth of his grandfather Meurig (though this may be a little too early, as the female generation was likely shorter than the twenty-two years of the male generation). This corroborates the conclusion that Athrwys, the son of Meurig, was born around the beginning of the 500s.

There are records of another daughter of Meurig – Gwenonwy – marrying Gwyndaf, the son of 'Emyr Llydaw', that is, Budic of

Brittany.[27] Their son was Hywyn, who is said to have accompanied Cadfan when he came to Britain from Armorica.[28] As we saw earlier, Cadfan died in 590 and was therefore a mid-sixth-century individual. As Hywyn was his contemporary, the expected birth date of his mother Gwenonwy is consistent with the previously considered information that points to an early sixth-century birth for the children of Meurig.

Additional support for the dynasty being positioned here continues to be found in the charters of the *Book of Llandaff*. Athrwys is recorded as the king of Gwent after his father's death, and witnesses to the land grant are disciples, and therefore contemporaries, of Dubricius. The father of this Athrwys is specifically identified as Meurig, so it is definitely the pertinent Athrwys. Peter Bartrum, who subscribes to the commonly accepted later dates for this dynasty, acknowledges the issue and writes: 'A king of Gwent of this name is not known ... to have lived at that time.'[29] But it is, nonetheless, what this source tells us. And as we have just seen, it is in perfect agreement with the information regarding Gwrgan and his familial relationship to Dubricius; Oudoceus and his familial relationship to Budic; Samson and his familial relationship to Athrwys, and so on.

Yet another familial relationship that supports this conclusion is found in the *Life of St Cadoc*, of the eleventh century. This document records the ancestry of the titular religious figure. His mother was said to have been the daughter of Brychan, son of Marchell, daughter of Tewdrig ap Teithfallt. This is not just any Tewdrig ap Teithfallt, for the record specifically states that this Tewdrig was martyred in Gwent, and it then connects said martyrdom with Merthyr Tewdrig (now Mathern, Gwent). This story of being martyred in Gwent and then being buried at Merthyr Tewdrig is told in the *Book of Llandaff* in an account concerning the death of Tewdrig, also called 'ap Teithfallt', the father of Meurig. Therefore, it is unambiguously the same Tewdrig who is meant in this record concerning the ancestry of Cadoc. As we discussed earlier in this chapter, Cadoc may have been born around the year 520. Even if we allow his mother to have been young at the time – perhaps as young as eighteen – we cannot escape the fact that Brychan, a grandson of Tewdrig ap Teithfallt, would likely have been born around 480. Again using eighteen for a female generation (that of Marchell to Brychan) and twenty-two for a male generation (that of Tewdrig to Marchell), Tewdrig would have been born around 440.

This issue will be discussed at greater length in Chapter Seven, but for now, it is sufficient to note that Meurig does not appear as a prince in the *Cognatio Brychan*, which is a document containing a record of Brychan's birth and children. It mentions Tewdrig ap Teithfallt as well as his daughter Marchell, the mother of Brychan. But it does not mention Meurig. In fact, Marchell is said to have been an only daughter. This statement appears shortly before the description of Marchell being sent over to Ireland, followed by her marriage to the Irish king Anlach and the subsequent birth of Brychan. Based on this information, it would appear that, while Tewdrig was born in *c.* 440, Meurig was not fathered until at least around the time of Brychan's birth in *c.* 480. Based on the information concerning Samson, we estimated that Meurig was probably born around 476. These dates must be somewhere near correct, as Meurig outlived the great plague and was therefore still alive after *c.* 570. This is much more likely if he was born around 476–480 than if he was born around 462, as Marchell probably was.

Conclusions

We can now start to see how the various pieces of information fit together. What follows is a suggested scenario that fits all of the information considered.

Near the beginning of this section, we saw that Tewdrig was shown to have been a contemporary of Teilo, the former having made land grants to the Church of Llandaff in the lifetime of the latter. Teilo lived from *c.* 500 to *c.* 580. Tewdrig is said to have been old when he died, so if he was born around 440, then he probably died *c.* 520. This fits comfortably in the lifetime of Teilo.

Meurig, the son of Tewdrig, outlived the great plague and was there for Oudoceus's appointment as bishop in *c.* 570. While being very old, this is possible if he was born around the year 480. His two grown sons, Athrwys and Idnerth, were present for this. Athrwys was evidently the eldest as he is always listed first and Idnerth is never recorded as a king. Twenty-two years after *c.* 480 brings us to *c.* 502 for the year of Athrwys's birth. Therefore, when Oudoceus was made bishop, Meurig was about ninety, Athrwys was about sixty-eight, and Idnerth was presumably somewhat younger.

At some point between this appointment – *c.* 570 – and 580, Idnerth and Atgan were killed by an uncle, one of Onbrawst's brothers. This brother must have been born quite late in Gwrgan's life, perhaps when he was as old as forty. This would mean that he would have been in his sixties when he killed Idnerth and Atgan. Similarly with the two victims, they may have been born quite late in Meurig's life; there is nothing to indicate that this could not have been the case. If they were born when Meurig was about forty, they would have been in their fifties when they were murdered.

Oudoceus was a contemporary of Teilo. He was probably born around the year 540. He became bishop in *c.* 570, serving as such until, possibly, *c.* 630. By this time, Ffernfael and Meurig, great-grandsons of Athrwys, were old enough to be counted as witnesses.

Gwrgan Fawr, a first cousin of Dubricius, was born *c.* 465. Onbrawst was born twenty to twenty-two years later in *c.* 485–487. She gave birth to Athrwys around eighteen years later in *c.* 503–505.

A sister of Athrwys named Anna married a man named Amon. Their child, Samson, was born *c.* 520 and attended the council held at Paris in 553. Another sister, Gwenonwy, gave birth to Hywyn, who became the companion of Cadfan, a mid-sixth-century individual.

Athrwys, now as the king of Gwent after his father's death in the early 570s, makes a land grant in the presence of several disciples of Dubricius, who was dead by the middle of the sixth century.

Meurig's sister was born in *c.* 462, quite some time before he was. She gave birth to Brychan in *c.* 480, who then fathered the mother of Cadoc. Cadoc, finally, was born in *c.* 520.

This understanding of the information is completely internally consistent. None of it is impossible or requires any gross anachronisms from any of the sources, which is the case for the popular dates given to this dynasty.

However, there is one last piece of information that we must address: the record in the *Welsh Annals* of Ffernfael ap Ithel dying in 775. Unless each generation from Athrwys to Ffernfael was separated by ninety years (which would be completely at odds with the information about Oudoceus's contemporary kings), this is simply impossible. So what is the explanation for this? Well, it is taken for granted that this is Ffernfael ap Ithel ap Morgan ap Athrwys, when, in fact, this need not be the case. In the Harleian genealogies, there is a record of a certain Ithel ap Athrwys ap Ffernfael ap Ithel ap Morgan ap Athrwys. It may well be the case that the Ffernfael who died in 775 was the son of this later Ithel. This is one of the main pieces of evidence used in an effort to prove that Athrwys cannot have been Arthur, due to having lived much too late, but given the weight of the entirety of the other evidence, which supports the earlier position, and the obvious option of a later Ithel, this is hardly valid.

We have now arrived at a historical scenario that has very interesting parallels to the Arthurian legends. The evidence points to King Arthur having a significant base in the area of Gwent. By analysing the information about the various members of the dynasty of Glamorgan and Gwent, the evidence points to Athrwys being born around the beginning of the 500s. In fact, our estimates – though they are admittedly only estimates – put his birth around the year 503 specifically. This makes him an exact contemporary of the legendary King Arthur. In fact, if his name was Arthur then there would be little reason to doubt that they were one and the same. As it is, his name is recorded as 'Atroys' in the earliest surviving record, which does not appear particularly similar to 'Arthur'.

One explanation is that it was Irish influence that led to 'Arthur' being spelt 'Athrwys'. Meurig's sister married an Irish prince and their son ruled Brycheiniog, which borders Glamorgan. As 'Artuir' is an Irish form of the name 'Arthur' (as in Artuir mac Aedan), it is not unreasonable to suppose that the intimate Irish connections of Meurig and his family led to their king lists recording Meurig's son as Artuir, rather than Arthur. This explanation would still allow for the populace at large to continue calling him by their British form 'Arthur'. But from the form 'Artuir' – which may have been rendered as 'Artoyr' in the Welsh from the *Harleian MS 3859* and 'Arthwyr' in the Welsh from the *Book of Llandaff* – a simple scribal mistake would change the 'r' into an 's'. This mistake was quite common.[30] This would then give 'Artoys', or 'Arthwys'.

This name is found in the individual of Arthwys ap Mar. From a consideration of Peter Bartrum's *A Welsh Classical Dictionary*, he is apparently the only person in recorded British history with a name of that exact spelling.[31] Therefore, it is very likely that his name is not a genuine British name, but it went through the processes just described, though the Irish influences would have come from the Irish of the north of Britain – perhaps from Dal Riata – rather than the Irish of Brycheiniog. Significantly, his name is spelt 'Athrwys' in later records, demonstrating a change from 'Arth' to 'Athr'. It is plausible, then, for an 'Artoys' or 'Arthwys' of the Glamorgan records to have been changed into 'Atroys' or 'Athrwys'.

In summary, one possible process that could have led to 'Arthur' becoming 'Atroys' over a 400–500-year period can be shown as follows: Arthur – Artuir – Artoyr – Artoys – Atroys. Of course, the change from 'Art' to 'Atr' may have happened at any point. This is merely one possible course of transmission.

Another possible explanation, suggested by Barber and Pykitt, is that 'Athrwys' is a corruption of 'Arturus' or 'Arthurus', which is how Arthur's name is spelt in many Latin records.[32] Consider the fact that, as already mentioned, Arthwys ap Mar is apparently the only person recorded as having a name with that exact spelling. There are some other individuals recorded as having a similar name, but their names are spelt 'Arthrwys'. And as mentioned before, Arthwys ap Mar even appears as 'Athrwys' in later records. It is often claimed that 'Athrwys' and 'Arthwys' are distinct, regular, genuine names, but this opinion is unsupported by the evidence. In reality, it seems far more likely that 'Arthwys' and 'Athrwys' are both simply variant spellings of 'Arthrwys'. Although, given the earliest spelling found for any of these forms, it should be more correct to speak of 'Arthwys' and 'Athrwys' as variant spellings of 'Artroys'. This can easily be dismissed as nothing more than a scribal or oral corruption of 'Artorius', the likely contemporary Latin form of Arthur's name.[33]

In any case, whether these are viewed as reasonable explanations of the difference between the name of Arthur and that of Athrwys ap Meurig or not, this is the man who was heir to the Glamorgan throne at the time of King Arthur's supposed life. If the members of his family can be seen to correspond to the characters in the Arthurian legend, then it will be safe to conclude that Athrwys ap Meurig was the legendary King Arthur, regardless of how his name came to be corrupted.

2

The Family of King Arthur

Uthyr Pendragon

We have already seen a connection between the families of Arthur and Athrwys in that both of them are recorded as having a sister named Anna. However, far more important is Arthur's father, Uthyr Pendragon, who plays a very large role in Geoffrey of Monmouth's *Historia Regum Britanniae*. If the Arthur of the legend really was Athrwys ap Meurig, then why is it that his father was referred to as 'Uthyr Pendragon'? Firstly, 'Pendragon' is a title, not a name. This is explicitly shown to be the case in Geoffrey's account, wherein Uthyr acquires the title after a dragon-shaped comet appears in the sky upon his older brother's death. Geoffrey gives the etymology as 'dragon's head', while the majority of modern scholars believe it means 'head dragon', in the sense of 'chief warrior'.

In this case, why was Arthur's father not recorded as 'Meurig Pendragon'? Why was his birth name said to have been Uthyr? There are several possible explanations for this.

The first, and perhaps simplest, is that the tradition of Arthur's father being named Uthyr is a misunderstanding of Nennius's words, which state that Arthur was 'map uter'. However, Nennius goes on to say that he was called this because from his birth he was terrible. Therefore, 'map uter' was intended to mean 'terrible son', not 'son of Uter'. But a misreading of this comment of Nennius's could easily have led to the mistaken idea that Arthur was the son of a certain 'Uthyr'. However, Uthyr Pendragon already appears in the ninth- or tenth-century poem *Pa Gur*, not very long after the ninth-century *Historia*, and the 'map uter' comment only appears in two manuscript versions, so it is unlikely to have been in the original. It seems more likely that, rather than the comment in Nennius producing the belief that Arthur's father was called Uthyr, the reverse is true.

Another suggested explanation is that there has been some confusion with Arthur's father and his father-in-law.[1] The Welsh Triads tell us that one of Arthur's fathers-in-law (for he was said to have had three wives, all of whom were called Gwenhwyfar) was a man by the name of Gwythyr. As discussed earlier, he was probably the same as the Withur mentioned in the *Life of St Paul Aurelian* as a ruler in Brittany. It should not be too difficult to conceive how 'Withur' could become construed into 'Uthyr'. This is a possible explanation, and it might have contributed to Arthur being persistently called the son of Uthyr, but there are good reasons for concluding it was not the main cause.

Significantly, Arthur was supposed to have begun ruling after the death of his father, when he was either fourteen or fifteen years old. As discussed previously, this was probably around the year 517, meaning Uthyr should have died then at the latest. However, Withur's appearances in Paul's *Life* require him to have been alive long after that year. So even if there was some confusion between Arthur's father and his father-in-law, the fact that neither Withur nor Meurig were dead early in the sixth century require an additional explanation for Arthur's legendary father – who was it that Arthur succeeded in 517?

But the issue is more extensive than just this. *Pa Gur* is based during Arthur's reign, after he has already fought many battles. Yet, it refers to one of the individuals with Arthur, a certain Mabon son of Modron, as 'the servant of Uthyr Pendragon'. It is difficult to see why the poem would have stated this had Uthyr been dead by this time. This suggests that Uthyr was still alive at this point in Arthur's life, though admittedly this may have just been some careless wording on the part of the poet.

However, bearing in mind the statement that one of Arthur's men was 'the servant of Uthyr Pendragon', it is worth considering the elegy of Uthyr Pendragon, entitled *Marwnat Vthyr Pen*. This is commonly, and understandably, assumed to be Arthur's father.

However, in lines thirteen and fourteen, the speaker, who is taken to be Uthyr, says: 'I shared my shelter, a ninth share in Arthur's valour.'

Other translations differ, but the essential meaning is usually the same. The lines tell us that Uthyr shared his 'shelter' – or refuge, as other translations put it – and then this is immediately followed by an apparent parallelism: 'a ninth share in Arthur's valour.' It very much seems to be the case that Uthyr is referring to himself in the third person as 'Arthur', and this is the conclusion of Arthurian researchers Wilson and Blackett.

If this is correct, then it would mean that 'Uthyr' was not a name at all, but a title for Arthur himself. This would explain why Arthur's companion Mabon ap Modron is called 'the servant of Uthyr Pendragon' in *Pa Gur*, despite the poem being based well into Arthur's reign. The Uthyr Pendragon in question, presumably, was Arthur himself. This is supported by the fact that, just a few lines after the statement concerning Mabon, Arthur refers to him and two others as 'my servants'.

So if the entirety of 'Uthyr Pendragon' is actually a title, then what does 'Uthyr' mean? According to a modern reference work, the word 'uthr' means 'awful' or 'awesome', originally meaning something high or lofty.[2] This makes perfect sense as part of a title. Hence, it seems that the full title of 'Uthyr Pendragon' meant something to the effect of 'Fearsome Chief Warrior'. And, as we have seen, it seems to have been used by King Arthur himself. Why, then, is it used as the name of Arthur's father in Geoffrey of Monmouth's *Historia Regum Britanniae*? In addition to Geoffrey's book, the Welsh poem *The Dialogue of Arthur and the Eagle* calls a certain Eliwlod the son of Madog ap Uthyr and the nephew of Arthur, implying that Uthyr was Arthur's father.

If Uthyr Pendragon was a title, and if there is conflicting evidence as to whether it was used by Arthur himself or by his father, then the logical conclusion would be that it was used by both. This is no different to the common practice among modern writers of referring to both Arthur and his father as 'Pendragons'. All this means is that 'Uthyr' was part of the title as well, so Arthur and Meurig were both 'Uthyr Pendragons'.

But is there actually any evidence that Meurig ap Tewdrig was known by the title 'Uthyr Pendragon'? Some evidence can be found from the information about the family of Myrddin Wyllt, one of the figures to have contributed to the legendary Merlin.

Myrddin is repeatedly said to have been the son of a certain Morfryn, such as in *The Dialogue Between Myrddin and His Sister Gwenddydd*. In Triad Series Three, No. 129, his father's name is given as Madog Morfryn. In the Iolo MSS, Madog Morfryn is said to have been the son of Morydd ap Mar ap Ceneu ap Coel Godebog.[3] But there is a problem with this ancestry. Myrddin was supposedly born around 544. Yet his supposed ancestor Coel Godebog, also known as Coel Hen, was the father-in-law of Cunedda, who was born before the start of the fifth century; some modern reference works place Cunedda's birth as early as 370.[4] If we follow the estimate that Cunedda's father-in-law Coel was born around 360, then to get to 544 in four generations would require each generation to be forty-six years apart.[5] This is very unlikely.

In a seventeenth-century record of Myrddin Wyllt, he is made the grandson of a certain Meurig, king of Dyfed. Considering the Iolo MSS are later than this, the seventeenth-century record is likely to be more accurate. Morydd, therefore, may well be a corruption of Meurig, and if Mar ap Ceneu really did have a son called Morydd, this would explain why Myrddin's lineage was placed onto the kings of the north of Britain, rather than the kings of south Wales, Dyfed being a kingdom of south-west Wales. That Myrddin really was from the dynasty of south Wales and not the dynasty of north Britain is supported by Geoffrey's *Life of Merlin*, which says that Merlin (Myrddin) was a king of the south Welsh. This being the case, it is far more logical that his father Morfryn would have been the son of this Meurig of Dyfed, in south Wales, than the son of a king of the north of Britain.

So who was Meurig of Dyfed? He also appears in *Brut Tysilio*, a Welsh version of *Historia Regum Britanniae*, as a contemporary of Arthur, but as Peter Bartrum points out, 'there is no independent evidence for a king of Dyfed named Meurig in the time of Arthur in history or legend'.[6] The king lists show that the king of Dyfed in Arthur's time would either have been Aircol Lawhir or his son Vortipor. So how can the reference to Meurig be explained, both as the grandfather of Myrddin and as one of the kings present in *Brut Tysilio*?

At the very beginning of the *Cognatio Brychan*, there is the statement that Brycheiniog was 'a part of Demetia, that is, South Wales'. Here, the document is apparently viewing the term 'Demetia' – the Latin form of 'Dyfed' – as synonymous with south Wales, even though the actual kingdom of Dyfed only covered the western half of south Wales. Whether this usage is technically correct or not, it shows how at least some old British documents used the term. This is supported by the fact that the *Historia Regum Britanniae* (*HRB*) refers to Gloucester as being situated on the border of Loegria, which is England, and Demetia. This only makes sense if Demetia is being used in the sense of south Wales in general, for the *kingdom* of Dyfed did not border England. Also of significance is the fact that, in the Brecon manuscripts, Brycheiniog was part of Tewdrig's territory, yet Tewdrig was the king of Glamorgan. So it seems that either the rulership of the kings of Glamorgan extended into at least part of the kingdom of Dyfed, or 'Demetia' could be used to mean the entirety of south Wales – the evidence from the *HRB* supports the latter conclusion. Either way, it would seem that 'Meurig of Dyfed' was actually Meurig ap Tewdrig, since he was the only king with that name at that time in that area. So if Myrddin was his grandson, and Myrddin's father was Morfryn, then this would mean that Morfryn was the son of Meurig.

To summarise so far, it seems that Myrddin Wyllt was the son of Morfryn ap Meurig ap Tewdrig. Notice again, however, that Morfryn is also called Madog Morfryn. As mentioned earlier, the Welsh poem *The Dialogue of Arthur and the Eagle* gives Arthur a brother, Madog ap Uthyr. Could it be that this Madog ap Uthyr is the same as Madog Morfryn ap Meurig? If so, then it would indicate that Meurig was the 'Uthyr' of this record.

Admittedly, this conclusion relies on some late sources, but it must be noted that, although it is the late and potentially unreliable Iolo MSS that provide Morfryn with the additional name 'Madog', it makes him the son of Morydd, not Meurig. Therefore, it cannot have been invented to make Meurig the same as Uthyr. So while this is by no means definitive evidence that Meurig was Uthyr, there is little reason to be overly suspicious of the sources used to come to this conclusion.

At this point, we have seen that the evidence indicates that Uthyr Pendragon was a title used by King Arthur, but that it was also a title for his father. If King Arthur was Athrwys ap Meurig, then Meurig should have been known by the title as well. As we have seen, there is some evidence that this was the case. What we have so far, then, is evidence that the title was passed from father to son. Recall that Uthyr Pendragon was supposed to have died when Arthur was young, yet Meurig was still alive after the great plague, which ended around 570 (see Chapter Six). Could it be that Meurig's father Tewdrig also used the title, and the legends of Uthyr came about as a result of Tewdrig the 'Uthyr Pendragon' being mistaken for Meurig the 'Uthyr Pendragon', the father of Arthur? An examination of the life and death of Tewdrig will reveal whether this is a plausible explanation.

One of the most detailed episodes of Tewdrig's life is contained in the *Book of Llandaff*. It describes the events surrounding his death in some detail, but it also provides some general information about his reign. One line of the relevant section begins: 'King Tewdrig when he was in his kingdom, enjoying peace and administering justice with his people…'

This is in accord with the following line found in Geoffrey of Monmouth's *Historia Regum Britanniae*: 'After this victory Uther repaired to the city of Alclud, where he settled the affairs of that province, and restored peace everywhere … At last, when he had established peace in the northern provinces…'[7]

So Uthyr and Tewdrig both enjoyed kingdoms of peace, though just as Tewdrig administered justice among the people, so there was the necessity for Uthyr to do the same. In fact, regarding the 'taming' of the Scots, *HRB* says that it was due to Uthyr's 'strict administration of justice'. The account goes further, explaining that wrongdoers *everywhere* were terrified of Uthyr, knowing that they would be punished. Additionally, the account in the *Book of Llandaff* tells us that while Tewdrig ruled the kingdom, he was never overcome, but was always victorious in battle. Clearly, all this information about Tewdrig's reign agrees with the information given in *HRB* about Uthyr's reign.

To move on to the more specific information about the circumstances surrounding his death, the account tells us that

Tewdrig abdicated in favour of his son Meurig. Similarly, Uthyr relinquished the throne and left the kingdom in the hands of his son-in-law, Lot of Lodonesia.[8] While Meurig was reigning, the Saxons invaded the country and caused a great deal of trouble for him. In fact, according to the *Book of Llandaff's* account, Meurig would have been 'altogether dispossessed' without the help of his father. Therefore, Tewdrig came to his assistance. Likewise, Uthyr was forced to come to Lot's assistance, due to the latter being unable to effectively lead the British armies against the Saxons.

The battle between Tewdrig and the Saxons famously occurred at the ford of Tintern. In contrast, the battle between Uthyr and the Saxons supposedly took place in Verulam, modern-day St Albans. It must be noted, though, that the geographical placement of events is notoriously unreliable in Geoffrey of Monmouth's *HRB*. This will be demonstrated clearly in the following two chapters. In both accounts, nevertheless, the battle is a victory for the Britons, ending with the Saxons 'turning their backs' and fleeing. Both Uthyr and Tewdrig are specifically described as having rejoiced at this victory.

During the battle Tewdrig was wounded by a lance, a wound that lead to his death three days later. Similarly, the account in *Historia Regum Britanniae* tells us that Uthyr's illness increased after the victory. Shortly afterwards, the Saxons allegedly poisoned a spring from which Uthyr used to drink. The very next time he drank from it, he died a sudden death. This parallels the account of Tewdrig's death, which is said to have occurred by a spring. Additionally, in both accounts, the aged king is carried in a cart, though Tewdrig is only said to have been carried in a cart after he was mortally wounded, whereas Uthyr was said to have been carried in the cart both before and after the battle.

The two accounts contain sufficient differences to demonstrate their independence, yet they are nonetheless strikingly similar. In both cases, the aged king has left the kingdom in the hands of his son, or son-in-law. This new leader is having trouble fighting the Saxons, requiring the former king to return from retirement and give his assistance. The Britons are victorious, but the king's condition deteriorates after the battle. Being carried in a cart, he later dies by a spring. The reader can decide whether the two accounts seem to have derived from the same event, which would logically equate Tewdrig with Uthyr Pendragon.

Next, let us take one step back in Uthyr's life. Perhaps the most famous event in his legendary life is the attack on Cornwall, in which he kills a ruler there known as Gorlois and then takes Gorlois's wife for himself, leading to the birth of Arthur and Anna. Obviously, if this was an event that involved Tewdrig rather than Meurig, then it cannot have led to the birth of Arthur and Anna. It may have been a case of 'Uthyr Pendragon's son' being assumed to be Arthur due to the confusion between Meurig and Tewdrig.[9] Alternatively, it may be that Meurig had already been born and the event with Tewdrig and Cornwall simply happened around the time of Arthur's birth, hence the association. So the question is, did something like the famous Cornwall incident happen to Tewdrig?

There are records of a certain Theodoricus, king of Cornwall, who attacked a large group of Irish missionaries upon their landing in the country. They were led by Gwinear, the son of an Irish king, who had been converted to Christianity by the famous Patrick of the fifth century. Gwinear was said to have first gone to Brittany and lived there for a while, before returning to Ireland. There, he gathered a large group of almost 800 people, before setting off for Brittany again. However, so the story goes, they were driven off course by the wind and landed in Cornwall. Within a short space of time, Theodoricus turned his attention to the party and massacred the group of missionaries, including Gwinear.

It is interesting to note that when Uthyr first goes to attack Gorlois, Geoffrey says that Gorlois decided not to engage Uthyr in battle until he could get assistance from Ireland. So the Irish connection is there in both stories. Additionally, though the Gwinear legend claims that it was just a landing party of missionaries, the fact that there were almost 800 of them certainly implies that it may well not have been that innocent. In fact, there is at least one surviving version of the legend that specifically states Gwinear's father warned Theodoricus that Gwinear was travelling to Cornwall to attack him.[10] Regardless, the legend of Gorlois would be from the perspective of those on Tewdrig's side, being a legend from south Wales. Both legends are from different parts of the country, both having their own propaganda twists and being recorded at different times, which would account for how different they are. But, as we have just noted, at least one version of the Gwinear legend does present it as an attack.

However, Gorlois is portrayed as the duke of Cornwall in Geoffrey's story. So how does this relate to Gwinear, the Irish prince? Well, while there is no record of him having gone to Cornwall before the event that led directly to his death, he was, as we have already noted, supposed to have settled in Armorica. One of the regions in Armorica was Cornugallia, as it is spelt in the *Life of St Oudoceus* – the modern region of Cornouaille. Its name shares an origin with the name of Cornwall, as is made clearer by the fact that the Cornish word for Cornwall is 'Kernow', while the Breton word for Cornouaille is 'Kernev'. Additionally, both regions were sometimes referred to by the Latin 'Cornubia'. Thus, it is very easy to see how the two locations may have been confused for one another at times. Gwinear, then, could have been a duke of Cornouaille during the time he spent in that area.

There was extensive contact between the inhabitants of Britain and the inhabitants of Brittany (Armorica). The Bretons on the Continent had an especially close relationship with the inhabitants of south-east Wales and Cornwall. For example, we saw in a previous section how Withur, a count of Leon in Brittany, came from Gwent. Furthermore, Tewdrig was supposedly the son of a princess of Brittany (see the following section discussing Ambrosius). Thus, there is nothing at all implausible about the idea that Gwinear, as the duke of Cornouaille, would have been at the court of Tewdrig in south-east Wales.

When Gorlois discovers Uthyr's unhealthy admiration for his wife Igerna, Gorlois and his wife leave Uthyr's court and return to 'Cornwall' (presumably Cornouaille, if Gorlois was Gwinear). The statement that Gorlois decided not to engage with Uthyr until he could get assistance from Ireland appears in the account at this point. Perhaps this is reflected in the Gwinear legend when Gwinear is described as sailing from Brittany to Ireland, and then leaving Ireland with his company of several hundred men with the intent of attacking Theodoricus.

In the *HRB*, Gorlois secures his wife in one part of Cornwall and secures himself in another town. Uthyr's men are described as besieging Gorlois's town, while Uthyr himself and several others make efforts to enter Igerna's town. This is possibly a reflection of the part of the Gwinear story in which Theodoricus caused Gwinear's arrival party to be separated into two. In the *HRB*, it is Igerna's town that is penetrated first, while Gorlois is killed during the events that unfolded after Uthyr had managed to enter the town. This corresponds to the Gwinear legend inasmuch as it is the half of the forces without Gwinear present that is defeated first, and then only after that is Gwinear's party defeated and their leader killed.[11]

In the accounts of Theodoricus, he is said to have made peace with Gwinear's surviving associates and kinsmen after Gwinear's death. While this does not correlate with anything in Geoffrey of Monmouth's account, there is a later version that does include such a claim. *Arthur a Kaledvwlch*, a fourteenth-century Welsh text, says that after this incident Uthyr prepared a feast for the whole island and 'made peace with the kinsmen of Gwrleis and his allies'.

While the two stories are not as clearly consistent with each other as are the stories of the deaths of Tewdrig and Uthyr, it can be seen that there are nonetheless a number of important similarities throughout the stories of Gorlois and Gwinear, which indicate that they may well be referring to the same original event. It is to be expected that the same event might be described in very different ways when both accounts come from opposing sides, and have gone through several hundred years of transmission.

It is commonly claimed that the king of this legend was Tewdwr Mawr, the son of Hoel of Brittany. However, Tewdwr only ruled in Cornwall from around 577, many decades after the arrival of Gwinear. Thus, the logical conclusion is that the 'Theodoricus' of this account is his exact contemporary, Tewdrig of Gwent and Glywysing. This record of him being the king of Cornwall corresponds with the concept of Tewdrig's grandson Athrwys, as King Arthur, having control of Dumnonia, as he does in *Culhwch ac Olwen*.

But is it really plausible that 'Gwinear' developed into 'Gorlois'? Well, bear in mind the fact that the name was actually spelt 'Gwrleis' in the Welsh texts, as can be seen from the quote from *Arthur a Kaledvwlch*. One step that could have led to 'Gwinear' becoming 'Gwrleis' is the common error of mistaking an 'r' for an 's'. This would have made 'Gwineas'. If, then, the 'n' was ever mistaken for an 'r' and 'l' next to each other, this would have produced 'Gwirleas'. With just these two scribal corruptions, one of which is known to have been common, we get a name very close to the legendary 'Gwrleis'. Whether this is actually what took place or not is impossible to say, but we do know that some of Geoffrey's character names are rather far from the original. For example, consider the fact that Urien's brother, whose name is spelt Arawn or even Aron in many British sources, is called Augusel by Geoffrey of Monmouth.[12] Granted, these extreme misspellings are rare in *HRB*, but we can see that converting Gwinear to Gorlois is, at least, not beyond the established limits for Geoffrey.

The most significant question to answer now is, when exactly did this event happen? According to Geoffrey of Monmouth, it was some time after Uthyr had succeeded his brother, Ambrosius, as king. Ambrosius's death was marked by the famous appearance of a star, 'darting forth a ray, at the end of which was a globe of fire in form of a dragon, out of whose mouth issued forth two rays'. This can only be the appearance of a comet, which often have two tails. According to the *Chronicle of Edessa*, which seems to have been compiled in the mid-sixth century and is therefore an early and very valuable source, there was a sign seen in heaven that resembled a spear. Again, this is almost certainly a comet. The year in which this spear-like heavenly sign was seen is 499. Meanwhile, in Bede's *Chronica Maiora*, Ambrosius's victory against the Saxons is dated to the reign of the Roman emperor Zeno, who was emperor from the 470s until 491. Therefore, the year of 499 for Ambrosius's death is perfectly plausible and seems to be the most likely conclusion. By extension, then, this would be the year of Uthyr's (Tewdrig's) accession.

This seems to clear up the question of whether the birth of 'Uthyr's' son Meurig was mistaken for the birth of 'Uthyr's' son Arthur. As previously discussed, it seems that Arthur was born in the year 503. The battle in Cornwall must have happened shortly before that time, which fits with a 499 date for Ambrosius's death and Uthyr's accession. Therefore, if Tewdrig was the 'Uthyr' of this account, then it can only be the case that the association with Arthur's birth was simply due to it having occurred around the same time, since Meurig was born in *c.* 480, long before this time. But if the battle between Tewdrig and Gwinear was the same as the battle between Uthyr and Gorlois, then the former should likewise have taken place around 499–503. So what does the evidence show?

The year in which this event took place is not known with complete certainty. The account says that Patrick, the religious teacher who is said to have preached in Ireland from 432 to 493, was the one who converted Gwinear. Therefore, the cutting short of Gwinear's life would probably have been some time in the late fifth, early sixth century. *The Lives of the British Saints* by Baring-Gould and Fisher contains a lengthy discussion of the related arrival of the Irish 'Saint Breaca' and concludes that the evidence gives 'the close of the fifth century, or the very beginning of the sixth, as the date of their arrival in Cornwall, approximately 500'.[13] Thus, the evidence supports the notion that Tewdrig's slaying of Gwinear occurred about the same time as, or a little before, Arthur's birth in 503.

But what about earlier in Uthyr's career? Very soon after Ambrosius died, and therefore presumably still in the year 499, Uthyr fought and defeated Pascentius, one of Vortigern's sons who had allied himself with the Irish, in Dyfed. Is there evidence that Tewdrig fought against the Irish in Dyfed at this time?

According to one modern reference work, 'The Irish names in the list of Demetian kings end abruptly about 500, and are replaced by men with Roman names and Roman titles... It is evident that a successful campaign... ousted the Irish dynasty, and replaced it with men who used names and titulature more Roman than in most of Wales.'[14] So the evidence is that the Irish were expelled from Dyfed around the time of Ambrosius's death, though admittedly this does not tell us who did it. The aforementioned source concludes that it was a campaign led by Tewdrig, on the basis that the Brecon manuscripts seem to show that he sent an army into Dyfed and across to Ireland at about the right time. In reality, this event did not occur at the correct time; it will be explained shortly that the Brecon manuscripts indicate that this event took place around 480 and is therefore unrelated to the expulsion of the Irish around 500.

However, it is interesting to note the description of Tewdrig in *The Genealogy of Iestyn son of Gwrgan*. It says that he 'drove the infidel Saxons and Irish out of the country'. So according to this source, which gives no indication of desiring to make Tewdrig seem like Uthyr Pendragon, Tewdrig drove the Irish out of the country. It does not specify where exactly these Irish had been living, but records such as the *Historia Brittonum* inform us that the Irish had already been driven out of north Wales long before Tewdrig's time. So the Irish that Tewdrig drove from the country cannot have been living in north Wales, yet the Irish were mainly concentrated in the western half of the country. So, with this pattern of concentration being the case – yet the north being excluded from the equation – it is likely that Dyfed, in the south-west, is the part of the country from which Tewdrig expelled the Irish. Therefore, while this does not *prove* that he was the one who expelled them out of Dyfed in *c.* 500, it certainly makes it the most probable scenario. In this way, the evidence of the events of Tewdrig's life continues to be consistent with the tale of Uthyr Pendragon.

However, not every significant moment in Uthyr's life occurred while he was king. While Ambrosius was ruling, the *Historia* reports that he sent his brother Uthyr on a mission to Ireland to retrieve the 'Giants' Dance'; this was to be raised as a monument over the graves of several hundred British leaders who had been massacred by the Saxons during a supposed peace conference. The story portrays the result of this to be Stonehenge. Obviously, this element of the legend must be fictional, as Stonehenge was constructed many centuries before Ambrosius's time. Perhaps Geoffrey's source simply included some local legend about the origin of Stonehenge, but it is also a distinct possibility that Uthyr really did lead a mission over to Ireland after he and his brother fought and crushed the Saxons after the massacre.

As mentioned earlier, Bede places the initial counter-campaign against the Saxons, with Ambrosius as the leader of this campaign, to within the years 474 and 491. And, as we have seen, he probably died in 499. According to Geoffrey of Monmouth, it was only after he defeated the Saxons and restored the churches of Britain that he went to where the British leaders had been slain and decided to erect a monument in their memory. Thus, a date of around

480 seems about right for the expedition to Ireland, if it has any historical basis.

The Brecon manuscripts, such as the *Cognatio Brychan* and the *De Situ Brecheiniog*, inform us that Tewdrig sent his daughter over to Ireland to be married to a king named Anlach, and they then had a child named Brychan. He and his family will be discussed in depth in Chapter Seven of this book, but briefly, a comparison of the above mentioned manuscripts with list four of the *Harleian MS 3859* reveals that he was a seventh-generation descendant of Magnus Maximus. As Maximus was born around 335, a seventh-generation descendant – assuming just over twenty years per generation – should be born somewhere around 480. Counting backwards from his descendants also produces a date of around 480 for Brychan's birth. Thus, though it is impossible to calculate the exact year for Tewdrig sending his daughter to Ireland or for Uthyr heading an expedition to Ireland, the estimated dates are very compatible.

Granted, the nature of the journeys to Ireland are not identical, as in one of them it results in a battle against an Irish king and is led by Uthyr himself, whereas in the other it is merely a daughter being sent to Ireland for the purposes of a marriage alliance. However, both sources (the *Historia* and the Brecon manuscripts) were written hundreds of years after the events to which they pertain, so this easily accounts for the differences. It is possible that they both preserve only parts of the original event. Tewdrig may, in fact, have accompanied his daughter to Ireland; in turn, the account in *HRB* may simply have left out the marriage alliance due to the purpose of the account being about the monument created in memory of the slain British chiefs. The battle fought between Uthyr and the Irish king may be completely fictional. We know that the story is at least partially fictional, for Stonehenge was not stolen from Ireland in the fifth century. The battle between Uthyr and the Irish king upon arrival may have been an additional invention, for the purpose of neatly linking it with the later battles against the Irish in Dyfed, which were supposedly led by the same Irish king in hopes of revenge.

One piece of evidence that points toward their similarity is the fact that, in the *Cognatio Brychan*, Tewdrig's daughter Marchell is sent over to Ireland to be married to Anlach not simply for the sake of the marriage alliance itself, but rather to get her away from a pestilence that was currently afflicting Britain. It is interesting, then, to note the reason given in *HRB* for the stones from the monument being taken from Ireland in particular. At first, Ambrosius objects to the idea of taking the Giants' Dance from Ireland to serve as the monument, saying that Britain is 'furnished with stones fit for the work'. However, Merlin then tells the king that the stones that make up the Giants' Dance have medicinal properties. In fact, he says that they would unfailingly cure a person of sickness. The account then says: 'When the Britons heard this, they resolved to send for the stones.'

So, in this account, it is really the desire to possess something that will cure sickness that motivates the king to organise this incursion into Ireland. Now, it must be reiterated that we know that Stonehenge was *not* brought over from Ireland by anyone in the fifth century. So this aspect of the legend simply must be in error. Thus, if an expedition to Ireland really was conducted in the late fifth century, it is most likely that it was really for the purpose of bringing relief from a pestilence in Britain, as stated by the *Cognatio Brychan* and implied by Geoffrey's *HRB*. It would then simply be the case that the false association between the expedition to Ireland and the monument erected for the slain British chiefs developed only within the line of transmission that reached Geoffrey, accounting for its absence in the Brecon manuscripts. These latter documents, for their part, simply excluded the information that Marchell was accompanied by her father, Tewdrig.

In any case, whatever the exact origin was, this demonstrates that both Tewdrig and Uthyr were connected with some journey to Ireland at about the same time, and both, apparently, to provide relief from sickness. We have also seen that the evidence points to both Tewdrig and Uthyr later driving out the Irish from Dyfed. At around the same time, *c.* 500, Tewdrig and Uthyr fought a battle in Cornwall against Gwinear, or Gorlois, a man associated with the Irish, and killed him, afterward making peace with his kinsmen and allies. Later, Tewdrig and Uthyr abdicate in favour of their son, or son-in-law. Due to this man struggling to defeat the Saxons, Tewdrig and Uthyr return as old men to give their assistance, leading to a victory for the Britons. Soon after this victory, their condition deteriorates and they are carried in a cart. Immediately after stopping by a spring, they die – this death occurring while Athrwys and Arthur were young. Athrwys and Arthur, who both have a sister named Anna and, probably, a brother named Madog, then rule in exactly the same area – Glamorgan and Gwent – during the sixth century.

However, one major difference is the lineages of Uthyr and Tewdrig. According to Geoffrey of Monmouth, Uthyr was the brother of Ambrosius, and they were the younger sons of Constantine, the king of Britain. In contrast, Tewdrig was the son of Teithfallt, and there is no record of Ambrosius being his brother. Can the family of Athrwys explain this aspect of the legend?

Ambrosius Aurelianus

The closest thing to a contemporary source that we have, and therefore the source that contains the most reliable information, is *De Excidio*, by Gildas (also known as *On The Ruin and Conquest of Britain*). Gildas was writing in *c.* 591 and was born forty-three years earlier, *c.* 548. This means that he could have known and spoken to contemporaries of Ambrosius himself. Therefore, what he tells us about Ambrosius is far more important than what any later writers said about him.

In light of the extensive legends about Ambrosius having a brother called Uthyr who fought alongside him, it is very interesting that Gildas says that the Britons 'took arms under the conduct of Ambrosius Aurelianus, a modest man, who of all the Roman nation was then alone in the confusion of this troubled period by chance left alive'. As can be seen by the fact that Ambrosius was 'alone', there is no room for Uthyr in the historical reality. Ambrosius did not have a warrior-brother who fought alongside him. The next line of Gildas's reveals that Ambrosius did, however, have children, and these children had surviving descendants. Could it be – considering Uthyr was said to have succeeded Ambrosius – that Ambrosius was not the elder brother of Uthyr, but his father? We have seen that the stories of Uthyr Pendragon came from the activities of Tewdrig (and misapplied to 'Uthyr Pendragon' the father of Arthur), so if Uthyr was really the son of Ambrosius, Ambrosius would have to be Tewdrig's father Teithfallt. What does the information reveal about Teithfallt?

Unfortunately, there is not nearly as much information about Tewdrig's father as there is for Tewdrig himself, but there is still some that we can use. Firstly, there is the time period in which he lived. According to Geoffrey of Monmouth, Ambrosius and Uthyr were still children at the time of Vortigern's murder of their older brother Constans and his subsequent accession to the throne of Britain. Of course, if Ambrosius was really the *father* of Uthyr, then we can exclude Uthyr (that is, Tewdrig) from the historical reality behind this legend. Therefore, Ambrosius alone would have been a child when Vortigern came to power.

Nennius tells us that this was in the year of the consulships of Valentinian and Theodosius, who can only be Valentinian III and Theodosius II, whose joint rule began when Valentinian rose to power in 425. He then refers to an event occurring in the fourth year of Vortigern's reign, placing this in the reigns of Taurus and Felix, who ruled together in 428. Therefore, Vortigern rose to power in 425.

Was Teithfallt a child at this time? Well, as explained earlier, Brychan was born in *c.* 480 and was a seventh-generation descendant of Magnus Maximus, born *c.* 335. This makes Teithfallt, his great-grandfather, a fourth-generation descendant. Using roughly twenty to twenty-two years per generation, this brings us to *c.* 420 for the year of Teithfallt's birth. This is also the year we get when we count backwards from Brychan's birth of *c.* 480. Therefore, we can very confidently place Teithfallt's birth in *c.* 420. He would thus have been about five years old when Vortigern became king. Hence, he is perfectly chronologically placed to be Ambrosius.

But what about the name 'Ambrosius Aurelianus'? We have explained 'Uthyr Pendragon' as being a title, but Ambrosius Aurelianus is clearly a proper Latin name – Aurelius Ambrosius being the name of a bishop in the fourth century. So perhaps this was a Latin name that Teithfallt used, being, as he supposedly was, the descendant of a Roman emperor. But is there any evidence that this was actually the case?

Consider the family of Cadoc. His *Life* informs us that he had an uncle named Paul. This Paul had nine brothers, including

Cadoc's father. Paul is said to have received the land of Penychen, which is an area in Glamorgan. This is set in the late fifth, early sixth century.

In the *Life of St Paul Aurelian*, the subject of the *Life* is said to have been the son of the count of Penychen, and is said to have had eight brothers. This, too, is set in the late fifth, early sixth century. It seems very probable that the two families are one and the same. Note that Paul Aurelian is said to have had eight brothers, while Paul the uncle of Cadoc is said to have had nine. In the account in the *Life of St Cadoc*, one of Paul's brothers did not receive any land, for he chose to pursue a religious life. All eight other brothers, however, did receive land. This would explain why the *Life of St Paul Aurelian* only records Paul as having eight brothers. The notion that these two contemporary families are the same one is made additionally likely by the fact that the *Life of St Paul Aurelian* claims that Paul sprang from a family most noble in the eyes of the world, which would be explained by the genealogical material supplied by the *Life of St Cadoc* and reiterated in the *Jesus College MS 20* to the effect that Cadoc (and therefore his uncle Paul) was descended from the Roman emperor Magnus Maximus. Additionally, Paul Aurelian's father is referred to in the text as 'Perphirius', which means 'clad in purple' – purple being the imperial colour.

So what is the significance of all this? Well, it would mean that Paul Aurelian was descended from Magnus Maximus. Teithfallt was also a descendant of Maximus, though through one of Maximus's other sons. If the name 'Aurelian(us)' was used by the descendants of Maximus through one of his sons, it is not at all improbable that it could have been used by the descendants of Maximus through one of his other sons. In fact, Barber and Pykitt claim that Afrella, the name of one of Meurig's daughters, is the Welsh version of the name Aurelia.[15]

What we have seen so far is that Teithfallt, the predecessor of the man whose life corresponds to Uthyr's, was a child at the time of Vortigern's usurpation, and it is plausible that he would have used the name Aurelianus. We have also seen that, considering Ambrosius was more probably the father than the brother of Uthyr, it would have been Ambrosius alone who was taken away to Brittany. But is there any evidence that Teithfallt was in Brittany?

Because of the lack of information about Teithfallt in comparison to his son Tewdrig, there is unfortunately no explicit information about where he was for most of his life. However, some of the information that is still available shows that he was at least connected with Brittany. In *Bonedd y Gwyr Gogledd*, Teithfallt is called Tudfwlch, and is quite rightly referred to as the prince of Kernyw. In this document, he is said to have been married to Dywanw, daughter of Amlawdd Wledig. And who was Amlawdd Wledig?

First of all, when did he live? The *Jesus College MS 20* tells us that he was married to Gwen, daughter of Cunedda Wledig. As Cunedda was probably born somewhere around 370, and his daughter was probably married to a man somewhat older than her, Amlawdd must have been born no later than the early fifth century. Additionally, to have been the father-in-law of Teithfallt, who was born *c.* 420, it is likely that he was born approximately fifteen to twenty-five years before Teithfallt's birth, though it could potentially have been even earlier than that. So he seems to have lived sometime in the early fifth century.

Next, *where* did he live? His pedigree records him as the son of Kynwal ap Ffrwdwr ap Gwrfawr ap Kadien ap Kynan ap Eudaf.[16] Kynan, usually spelt Cynan, was the founder of the kings of Brittany. In fact, a comparison of this with the pedigree of Geoffrey of Monmouth's 'Aldroenus' – presented as a king of Brittany – shows an interesting similarity. Under the Welsh version of the name, Aldwr, he is said to have been the son of Kynfawr ap Tudwal ap Gwrwawr ap Gadeon ap Cynan ap Eudaf. In these two lists, only Ffrwdwr and Tudwal are particularly different. Due to the similarity of their sons' names, Kynwal and Kynfawr (spelt 'Kynwawr' in the earliest version), 'Ffrwdwr' can probably just be regarded as an extreme corruption of 'Tudwal'. Given the lateness of the source in which 'Ffrwdwr' appears, this corruption should not be considered too unlikely.

Hence, it seems that Amlawdd was actually identical to his contemporary 'relative' Aldwr, the king of Brittany in the early fifth century; that is, they were the same person. This conclusion is strongly supported by the fact that a woman called Rieingulid is said to have been Amlawdd's daughter in the *Life of St Illtud*, while *The Lives of the British Saints* remarks that one account makes Rieingulid the daughter of Aldwr.[17] Evidently, the original name of this person was something like 'Amlawddwr' or even 'Anblawddwr', given the spelling of the name in the *Life of St Illtud*. This then became shortened to Amblawdd and then Amlawdd through one line of transmission, while becoming shortened to Alawddwr and then Aldwr through another line of transmission.

Evidence for this intermediate step of 'Alawddwr' can be seen in the poem *Cadair Teyrnon*, purportedly by Taliesin. The poem seems to be directed at Arthur, and refers to him as being of the race of 'Aladwr'.

This being the case, we can see now that the evidence points to Teithfallt marrying a daughter of the king of Brittany. In fact, we can even pin this marriage down to the period during which Ambrosius was supposed to have been in Brittany. In *Bonedd y Saint*, Tywanwedd daughter of Amlawdd Wledig is recorded as the wife of a certain 'Hawystl Gloff'. Tywanwedd appears to be the same as Dywanw, and is accepted as such by Peter Bartrum.[18] Therefore, this is either a previous or subsequent marriage to her marriage to Teithfallt, or alternatively, Hawystl Gloff is an epithet for Teithfallt. Considering one of the sons of Tywanwedd and Hawystl is named Tudur, which is a common version of the name Tewdrig in many records – yet Tewdrig's father was Teithfallt – it is most likely that Hawystl Gloff was, in fact, Teithfallt.[19]

This evidence brings us to two interesting points. First of all, and most significant to our current issue, is the fact that this means that Dywanw(edd) the daughter of Amlawdd Wledig was not just *a* wife of Teithfallt, but was specifically the mother of Tewdrig, or Tudur, as it is spelt in *Bonedd y Saint*. And as has been explained previously, Tewdrig must have been born *c.* 440. Ambrosius, meanwhile, was supposedly in Brittany from 425 – when Vortigern took over – until he returned and vanquished the Saxons, which Bede places between 474 and 491. So if Teithfallt married Dywanwedd, the daughter of the king of Brittany, and had Tewdrig *c.* 440, then either he was in Brittany during this time or Dywanwedd was in Britain. There is no way of knowing which option is correct. This information does not prove that Teithfallt was in Brittany when Ambrosius was said to have been there, but it does require that *either* he went there or his future wife came to Britain during the time in question.

The second interesting point we gain from this evidence is in the meaning of the name. Hawystl Gloff is a title that translates into 'Augustulus the Lame'. Why would Teithfallt have been known by this title? Nothing is known about Teithfallt's life that explains this title, but in Geoffrey of Monmouth's *HRB*, Ambrosius is said to have been confined to a sickbed at Winchester shortly before he died, for which reason Uthyr had to lead the army to Dyfed to fight the Irish-Saxon alliance.[20] The origin of this part of the legend of Ambrosius may well be linked to the reason for Teithfallt being termed 'the Lame'.

'Augustus' was used as a title for the emperors of Rome, and 'Augustulus' essentially means 'Little Augustus' – or, in other words, 'Little Emperor'. The reason this is so significant is because it confirms Teithfallt's extremely high position among the kings of Britain. Perhaps the 'Little' element of the title was an acknowledgement of the position of the Roman emperor on the Continent, but in any case it shows that Teithfallt was viewed as an emperor of sorts. This brings to mind Nennius's description of Ambrosius as 'the great king among the kings of Britain'.

In the information provided about Teithfallt in *The Genealogy of Iestyn the Son of Gwrgan*, we are told that he was a 'wise and heroic monarch' who 'fought powerfully with the Saxons, and vanquished them'. This is exactly the kind of description one would expect if Teithfallt was really the famous Ambrosius. However, there is a more specific point of similarity to be noted. In Geoffrey of Monmouth's book, Merlin tells Vortigern the following: 'Ambrosius shall be crowned. He shall bring peace to the nation; he shall restore the churches.'

This comment about restoring the churches is reiterated later on, such as when the account tells us that he 'gave orders for the restoration of the churches'. In *The Genealogy*, meanwhile, immediately after stating that Teithfallt fought and vanquished the Saxons, it says that he 'passed a law that made it imperative on all to contribute a portion of their wealth towards supporting religion, the clergy, learning, and the repairs of churches'. The very next sentence, apparently by way of explanation, tells us that many Saxons came to Wales in his time, slew a huge number of the natives, and burned churches and choirs. This exactly parallels the story from the *Historia Regum Britanniae*.

As for how Teithfallt and Tewdrig could have been mistaken for brothers, producing the accounts of Ambrosius and Uthyr as brothers, there are a number of possibilities. One possibility is that the title 'Uthyr Pendragon' may have been used by Teithfallt as well as by Tewdrig, Meurig and Athrwys. If so, this would mean that there would have been records of 'Uthyr' as a young child being taken away to Brittany, as well as records reporting the same for 'Ambrosius'. The reason given in the legend is that Vortigern wanted them dead, due to them being the rightful heirs to Britain. Thus, if we suppose that Teithfallt was known as 'Uthyr' as well as 'Ambrosius Aurelianus', then given that the 'Uthyr' of the records and the 'Ambrosius' of the records would have been described as children at the same moment in history (Vortigern's rise to power), the logical conclusion to explain how they could both be described as the heir would have been that they were brothers.

Alternatively, the explanation may lie in the fact that Teithfallt's wife was a daughter of Amlawdd. According to the Welsh sources, Igerna, the wife of Gorlois, was also a daughter of Amlawdd. She became Uthyr's wife after her first husband's death. Though there is no mention of Tewdrig marrying Gwinear's wife in the accounts concerning Gwinear's death, if we suppose that this did happen and that she really was a daughter of Amlawdd, this would mean that Teithfallt and Tewdrig were brothers-in-law. From this, we can see how they may, sometimes, have been referred to simply as brothers.

Similarly, due to the mistaken belief that the wife of Gorlois, or Gwinear, was Arthur's mother, Teithfallt would have been considered the uncle of Arthur, just like Ambrosius in the legends.

It may have been a combination of these factors that resulted in a chronicler becoming convinced that Teithfallt – or Ambrosius, as we are theorising – and Tewdrig, or Uthyr, were brothers, when in reality they were father and son.

But what about the idea that Ambrosius was the heir to the throne of Britain? Can this status really be attributed to Teithfallt?

As already mentioned, Teithfallt is recorded as being a descendant of the Roman emperor Magnus Maximus. It will be seen in Chapter Seven how the available evidence points to the conclusion that this Glamorgan dynasty was actually the senior line of descent from Maximus, being the descendants of his eldest son. Thus, from the evidence we have, we arrive at the conclusion that Teithfallt was indeed the heir to the throne of Britain, at least inasmuch as senior descent from Magnus Maximus could give someone that claim. This ties in perfectly with his title of 'Augustulus', which indicates that he was considered to have been a kind of emperor.

For a discussion of Ambrosius's supposed older brother Constans and their father Constantine see Appendix 3, 'Constans and the Family of Brittany'.

So, though there are not nearly as many sources for the events of Teithfallt's life as there are for Tewdrig's, we have seen from the information we do have that there is a remarkable match between Teithfallt and Ambrosius Aurelianus. We have seen that they were exact contemporaries, Ambrosius being a child in *c*. 425 and Teithfallt being born in *c*. 420. We have seen that there is reason to believe Teithfallt may have used the name 'Aurelianus', sharing Paul Aurelian's descent from Magnus Maximus. We have seen that there is a very real possibility that he was in Brittany during the time period in which Ambrosius was in Brittany, his son Tewdrig being born to the daughter of the king of Brittany in *c*. 440. We have seen that he was known by a title meaning 'Little Emperor', which accords with Ambrosius's position as high king. We have seen that he was a mighty warrior against the Saxons, as was Ambrosius, and we have seen that he organised the restoration of the churches that were destroyed during the Saxons' raids, as his contemporary Ambrosius was said to have done. Something evidently occurred after his victories against the Saxons that led to him later becoming known as 'lame', while Ambrosius is said to have been confined to a sickbed towards the end of his life. We have also seen that there are several plausible explanations for how Teithfallt and Tewdrig could have become mistaken for brothers, like Ambrosius and Uthyr are in the legends. Finally, we have seen that Teithfallt really was the heir to the throne of Britain, just as Ambrosius was supposed to have been.

Teithfallt was then succeeded by Tewdrig, the man whose life closely parallels the life of Uthyr Pendragon, the successor of Ambrosius Aurelianus. Tewdrig died early in the sixth century when Athrwys was young, just as Uthyr died early in the sixth century when Arthur was young. Both Athrwys and Arthur had a sister named Anna, and the evidence also indicates that they both had a brother named Madog. Through the greater part of the sixth century, as exact contemporaries, Athrwys and Arthur both ruled from Glamorgan and Gwent.

In view of all this information regarding the Glamorgan dynasty and its resemblance to the Arthurian dynasty of legend, there does not seem to be any reason to question Athrwys's identity as King Arthur.

How This Fits in with Other Information

There are also other identifications that could be made. One such example is in *Historia Regum Brittaniae*. Arthur's sister Anna is said to have married Lot of Lothian, and their children are Gawain and Mordred. However, the native Welsh sources consistently make the parents of these characters Gwyar and Lleu. While one can see how 'Lot' and 'Lleu' are related, the names 'Gwyar' and 'Anna' are hardly similar at all. It is therefore notable that *The Chronicles of England*, produced in the fifteenth century by William Caxton, tells us that Arthur's sister Anna married a certain Aloth son of Eleyn of Brittany – obviously a completely different man to Lleu ap Cynfarch of Lothian in the North.

Lothian was alternatively known as Leudonia or Lodonesia, while Brittany was known as Llydaw. What seems to have happened, then, is that Geoffrey's source mistook Aloth of Llydaw for Lleu of Leudonia due to the similarity of the names of their localities and thus combined the information about them, thus making Anna the husband of Lleu, when, in fact, that was Gywar (evidently another of Arthur's sisters). So who was Aloth, the actual husband of Anna?

There is no individual known to sixth-century history by that name. What we know from history is that Anna, the sister of Athrwys, married a man called Amon Ddu. He was the son of Emyr Llydaw, the ruler of Brittany in the sixth century. In Welsh, 'dd' is pronounced 'th', so what seems to have happened is that

'Amon Ddu' became corrupted, at least partly by oral transmission, into 'Aloth'. The name of his father, Eleyn, seems to be a scribal error for Amon's father Emyr. Interestingly, the 'm' has become an 'l' in both names, for whatever reason.

In *The Chronicles of England*, Eleyn is said to be the cousin of Hoel of Brittany. In reality, Hoel was Emyr Llydaw's son, so this could be viewed as an objection to the identification of Eleyn with Emyr. However, Hoel was also known by the name Riwal, which was indeed the name of one of Emyr's cousins, so this would explain the confusion of the sources. It could have been the case that 'Riwal' was used in the source for the name of the cousin of Eleyn, referring to Emyr's cousin Riwal, and then this name was substituted for 'Hoel' because the writer knew that 'Riwal' was a name used by Hoel, so he assumed that Hoel was the pertinent individual.

In the *Petit Bruit* of the early fourteenth century, Arthur is succeeded by three sons: Adeluf, Morgan, and Patrick. Athrwys, we know from history, was succeeded by his sons Ithel and Morgan. Ithel corresponds to Adeluf, and Morgan is obviously the same as Morgan, though admittedly there is no Patrick to be found. What is particularly interesting about this record is that the Morgan of the *Petit Bruit* is called Morgan the Black. In Welsh, that would be Morgan Du, or Ddu. In the *Historia Regum Britanniae*, Geoffrey writes of a king of the south Welsh called Margadud. He is shown to be an active king around the time of the Battle of Chester, which took place in *c.* 616. He subsequently appears as a king, though not necessarily active in battle, in the reign of Cadwallon, which was from *c.* 625 to *c.* 634. It is generally held that there is no independent evidence of his existence, and as such, he is considered fictitious. The king of Dyfed, in south-west Wales, at this time was probably either Vortipor's son Cincar or his grandson Petr. The king of the other half of south Wales was, according to the generally accepted chronology of the Glamorgan dynasty, Meurig ap Tewdrig. However, as we have established, the evidence actually indicates that Athrwys likely ended his rule in the 570s, some time during Oudoceus's tenure as bishop after the end of the Yellow Plague. He was then succeeded by his sons Morgan and Ithel.

There are several early tales of some of Arthur's sons, such as Amr, Gwydre, and Duran, dying during the king's lifetime. It is possible that this caused him to have an issue with regards to having an heir. This is supported by the fact that there are two different fates given to Arthur's wife in the legends, implying that the legends are actually describing two different people. According to Geoffrey of Monmouth, she joined Mordred when he usurped the kingdom while Arthur was away in Brittany. However, as the conflict between Mordred and Arthur is being described, she is said to have become a nun at Caerleon and lived out the rest of her life like that. On the other hand, there is a legend that Arthur, after the Battle of Camlann, pursued Guinevere up into Scotland and killed her for her unfaithfulness.[21] One explanation for this apparent discrepancy is the idea that, after his unfaithful wife was slain, Arthur remarried, and this final wife was the one who became a nun. But for Arthur to have remarried at such a late stage in his life, it is a reasonable speculation that he was still in need of an heir, supporting the idea that all his sons born before the Battle of Camlann had already died, such as Amr, Gwydre and Duran.

This being the case, it is quite likely that Morgan and Ithel were born *c.* 570. It is even possible that Athrwys's son Morgan is the Morgan who is recorded as dying in 665 in the *Welsh Annals*. In any case, Morgan was the king of the south Welsh during the time in which Geoffrey claims that 'Margadud' was the king of the south Welsh. Considering this, it is a virtual certainty that Geoffrey's 'Margadud' is a corruption of 'Morgan Du' – that is, Morgan the Black, the son of King Arthur according to the *Petit Bruit*. This is internally consistent with the idea that Arthur's succeeding children were born late enough to be active in the first half of the seventh century.

As was discussed in the previous chapter, Athrwys had a brother called Idnerth and a brother called Atgan. This Atgan could well be the origin of Edmund Spenser's Artegal, the half-brother of Arthur. Arthur and Artegal were said to be related through their mother, which is consistent with the fact that the record in the *Life of St Cadoc* specifically says that Idnerth and Atgan were the sons of the same woman.

Related to this, there is Euan Buurr, the son of Gwrgan Fawr (thus, the maternal uncle of Arthur, as his mother Onbrawst was a daughter of Gwrgan Fawr). In *Culhwch ac Olwen*, several sons of a man called 'Iaen' are listed, and they are said to be related to Arthur on his father's side. Another possible translation, however, is 'their father's side', rather than 'his father's side'.[22] If this alternative translation is valid, then perhaps this Iaen was actually Euan, the brother of Athrwys's mother. It must be noted that 'Iaen' was not a common name. From a consideration of Peter Bartrum's *A Welsh Classical Dictionary*, it seems that he is the only individual ever recorded as having that name. Also of note is the fact that there was a certain individual known as 'Ieuan Gwas Padrig ap Llywelyn'. Yet, in *Bonedd y Saint*, his first name is spelt 'Euan'. Evidently, then, 'Euan' Buurr is simply an alternative spelling of 'Ieuan' Buurr. From the full 'Ieuan', it is easier to see how this may be linked to 'Iaen'. Since 'Iaen' apparently appears nowhere else as the name of anyone, it does seem very probable that this is simply a corruption of 'Ieuan', which was a name borne by a number of persons in British history and legend.

Another relative who can be identified is Gwrfoddw Hen, one of Arthur's maternal uncles in *Culhwch ac Olwen*. As Athrwys's mother was Onbrawst, from the royal family of Ergyng, we should expect to find Gwrfoddw there. And, indeed, we do. In one of the charters in the *Book of Llandaff*, there is a king of Ergyng called Gwrfoddw who appears as a contemporary of Bishop Ufelwy. This bishop was also present for one of Meurig's land grants, showing that he was of the correct time period.[23] His parentage is not given, but the fact that he is explicitly described as a king of Ergyng points toward the very real possibility that he was a son of Gwrgan Fawr, the king of Ergyng around this same period, and was thus one of Athrwys's maternal uncles.

There is also evidence that Athrwys was a relative of Cador and his son Constantine, as Arthur was said to have been. In the *Life of St Winwaloe*, there is a 'Fracan' who appears, and he is said to have been the cousin of 'Catovius' the king of Dumnonia. This must be Cadwy, the king of Dumnonia in the genealogies. His name is also sometimes spelt 'Cador', and this Cador of Cornwall is, in Geoffrey of Monmouth's history, the father of Constantine the successor of Arthur. When Arthur hands over the throne to him, it is said that Constantine is his kinsman, though the exact relationship is not stated. Yet here in the *Life of St Winwaloe*, we have a clear statement that Cadwy was a cousin of Fracan. And who was Fracan? This is simply an alternate spelling of 'Brychan' – in fact, Brychan's name is spelt 'Vrachan' in the *Jesus College* genealogies. There is no other Brychan or Fracan known of in this era and location, so it is safe to assume that the Fracan of this *Life* is Brychan the cousin of Athrwys. This being the case, since Fracan is described as the cousin of Cadwy, Athrwys must have likewise been a relative of Cadwy. We do not know what the relationship was, but it apparently existed.

Near the outset of the previous chapter, Artuir mac Aedan was rejected as King Arthur partly on the basis of his lack of reputation and prestige. Can the same be said for Athrwys? There is not very much information about Athrwys himself that we can use to assess this, but we have already seen that his great-grandfather, Teithfallt, had an extremely high position as the 'Little Emperor'. The *Book of Llandaff* indicates that Tewdrig, his successor, was likewise very well regarded. He was said to have always been victorious in battle. In fact, when describing these past victories, the account contains the statement that 'when his face was seen in battle, the enemy immediately were turned to flight'. We have also seen evidence that he fought all across the entirety of south Wales, from Dyfed in the west to the River Wye in the east, and he was also regarded as the king of Cornwall, in which place he also fought. He therefore held sway over a very large area, and must have been a mighty king. The extent of his power and influence is further seen from a record which reports that Tewdrig had defeated a certain King Maxentius in Brittany and forced him to relinquish his lands.[24]

Also significant is the fact that Morgan Mwynfawr, Athrwys's son, is listed in the Welsh Triads as one of the 'Three Red Ravagers of the Isle of Britain', along with Arthur himself. That is how mighty a warrior the son of Athrwys was regarded. So although there is no direct evidence regarding Athrwys's fame and might, there is every reason to believe – from the evidence about the power of his family – that he was powerful enough to have been the King Arthur of legend. He is often described as a 'petty king' of one small corner of Wales. But this is an unsustainable opinion. His territory extended from Ergyng in the east to Gower in the west, forming a kingdom certainly as large as the famously powerful kingdom of Gwynedd, ruled by the mighty King Maelgwn.

An extremely significant point is the fact that, as mentioned previously, Teithfallt was the heir to the kingdom of Britain by virtue of his descent from the eldest son of Maximus (the evidence for this is covered in detail in Chapter Seven). The fact that he was evidently known by the title 'Augustulus' demonstrates that this was a fact which did indeed have a bearing on the power he exerted. Thus, Teithfallt's descendants through the senior male line would have likewise been considered the rightful emperors of Britain. This is a characteristic which no suggested Arthurian candidate possesses but Athrwys ap Meurig ap Tewdrig ap Teithfallt. Furthermore, Athrwys's mother Onbrawst was the daughter of Gwrgan Fawr. Gwrgan's power is indicated by his title, 'Fawr', meaning 'the Great'. Thus, not only was Athrwys the senior descendant of the Roman emperor Magnus Maximus, but the marriage which produced his birth actually united this imperial line with a powerful native dynasty. It can genuinely be said that, according to the available evidence, Athrwys was the heir to the throne of Britain. He was not an obscure figure. The Welsh sources refer to Arthur as 'Emperor', and the *Life of St Cadoc* calls him 'the most illustrious king of Britannia'. Athrwys truly does fulfil this criterion.

Earlier, we also said that the real King Arthur would have had to have had connections to Ireland, the north of Britain, and Brittany. It has already been explained that Tewdrig sent his daughter, Marchell, to Ireland and that she married King Anlach. So the Glamorgan dynasty had a marriage alliance in Ireland. The result of that marriage was Brychan, Athrwys's cousin. Several of Brychan's daughters married Northern kings and princes, such as Gwawr to Elidyr, the uncle of Urien Rheged. Additionally, Brychan's daughter Nyfain married Cynfarch, the father of Urien Rheged.[25] So the Glamorgan dynasty had marriage alliances to the North as well. In fact, this is particularly significant because the family of Cynfarch is exactly the family with which Arthur is connected in the legends.

Regarding Brittany, it has already been established that several of Meurig's daughters married several sons of Budic of Brittany, also known as Emyr Llydaw. So the Glamorgan dynasty also had marriage alliances in Brittany. Like the connections to the North, this is particularly interesting due to the fact that it is specifically the family of Budic which is connected to King Arthur in the legends. For example, Budic's son Hoel was said to have fought alongside Arthur in some of the famous twelve battles. And in addition to the marriage alliances, the example of Tewdrig overthrowing King Maxentius of Brittany shows that the Glamorgan dynasty did in fact extend at least a degree of power over Brittany.

So, in its familial connections and sphere of influence, in its power and prestige, and in the lives and names of its members, the Glamorgan dynasty is an astonishing parallel to the supposedly non-existent Arthurian dynasty of legend.

However, the primary purpose of this book is not to discuss this sixth-century King Arthur. While it is certainly a very interesting subject, and much more could be said about the evidence for his legendary activities and the true nature of the Knights of the Round Table and the Code of Chivalry and the stories of Lancelot and the Holy Grail, the purpose of this book is to analyse a much less discussed aspect of the Arthurian stories. Though it can and has been established that many of the facets of the legend are based on real people, things, and events, this says nothing of the great European conquest. The King Arthur who lived in the sixth century and fought the Saxons was unmistakably Athrwys. But Athrwys did not wage war against Rome. If so much of the tale of Arthur's family as recorded by Geoffrey of Monmouth seems to have come from true history, how is it that such a major portion of the story of Arthur's own life – about half, in fact – had no basis in reality? Is it really logical to think that Geoffrey of Monmouth invented an entire portion of Arthur's life from his own imagination?

Other researchers have likewise concluded that there simply must have been some historical basis to the story, and have either attempted to connect the story with an already known historical event, or attempted to devise a speculative scenario which limits the area of activity to somewhere other than Europe, avoiding the issue altogether. However, many of these proposed explanations of the first type fall short on the grounds of limited similarity between the real event and the Arthurian story. Explanations of the second type rely on speculatively constructed scenarios that, by nature, cannot be proven. If a genuinely historical pattern of events was found that corresponded to the pattern of events portrayed in the Arthurian story, then that would obviously be a much more preferable explanation.

This book will first examine what the boundaries of accuracy in Geoffrey of Monmouth's *Historia Regum Britanniae* are. This will allow an informed assessment to be made of certain theories regarding the origin of the European conquest.

3

The History of the Kings of Britain: Book Four

Geoffrey of Monmouth has been much derided over the years. The reason stems from the work of his that we have already discussed, written in *c.* 1137: *Historia Regum Britanniae*, or *The History of the Kings of Britain*. It purports to recount the history of the British nation from the time of the Trojan War, the Britons allegedly being descendants of the Trojans, to the time of Cadwaladr of the seventh century. He claimed that this was a translation of 'a very ancient book in the British tongue'. The majority of modern scholars do not consider this claim to be true. There have been numerous investigations into the book by a variety of people – many with the intention of proving that it was indeed based on an ancient Welsh book as Geoffrey claimed, rather than it being largely invented by Geoffrey himself.

One argument in favour of Geoffrey's truthfulness is the fact that there are numerous historical errors within the *HRB*. For example, there are many substantial differences between Caesar's contemporary account of his two invasions of Britain, in what is known as *De Bello Gallico*, and what Geoffrey of Monmouth describes. This is very unexpected if Geoffrey was creating the history from his own research, as is now claimed. He was a very learned man – an Oxford cleric for most of his life, in fact. If he really was creating his own account of history with the intention of passing it off as fact, one would think he would have been very careful about his research. In fact, the abundance of mistakes present in the book – to make no mention of the misspelt names of historical figures – seems remarkable for the work of such an educated man.

As well as mistakes, what is absent from the book is also significant. Once again using the example of Caesar's invasion of Britain, it is interesting to note how Geoffrey describes the first battle in his account of this invasion. In some parts he is very detailed; an exact choreography is given of the fight between Julius Caesar and the British warrior Nennius, for example. Yet absolutely nothing is mentioned of the tactics used by the Britons, nor the fact that they even had chariots and cavalry, nor the fact that the Romans were so out of their depth during this initial attack. Not a single comment is made about how the Romans 'could neither keep their ranks, nor get firm footing, nor follow their standards,' or how they were 'altogether untrained in this mode of battle,' or how the Britons 'surrounded them with their cavalry and chariots,' as Caesar described.[1] The Roman leader related in immense detail the Britons' method of fighting and, particularly, the way they used their chariots. Yet Geoffrey does not even mention that the Britons had chariots.

It is astonishing to consider that when describing the first battle with Caesar, Geoffrey makes absolutely nothing of the impressive and overwhelming tactics that the Britons used, while Caesar himself described them in great detail. If Geoffrey was working with Caesar's account of the battle, then it logically follows that he would have placed a huge emphasis on the amazing tactics employed by the Britons to defeat the Romans. The fact that it is *not* there, perhaps more than anything else, indicates that Geoffrey was not using Caesar's account.

But surely he would have had access to it, being a man of his position? There is every reason to think that this was the case, but the absence of major Briton-favouring details and the presence of significant 'errors' in the account (with no apparent benefit to Geoffrey) strongly indicates that he did not use Caesar's own work. This does not conform to the viewpoint that he was simply using all the sources available to him in an effort to construct his own historical account. Evidently he was not, otherwise he would have made use of Caesar's contemporary account.

It may be very significant that the initial attack on Caesar's forces when he arrived at the shore is not described in Geoffrey's work.

After Caesar's fleet arrives at the shore, Cassivellaunus, the leader on the British side, gathers several kings of Britain to a town called Dorobellum, where they discuss what to do. The kings, according to Geoffrey, 'gave their advice to march directly to Caesar's camp, and drive them out of the country before they could take any city or town'. Then, 'To this proposal they all agreed, and advanced towards the shore where Julius Caesar had pitched his camp. And now both armies drew out in order of battle...'[2]

So the battle now being described takes place *after* Caesar had already managed to pitch his camp on the shore. It is not the attack on Caesar's army as his fleet is attempting to land. That attack, where the Romans are viciously opposed by the Britons, is not described or even referenced in Geoffrey's book. Why would that be? According to Julius Caesar himself, the British ambassadors apologised for the attack on his fleet as it was arriving and claimed it had been done by the common people.

If this really was the case, then it would be understandable for the British histories to not contain any mention of it. An eighth-century historian named Bede – who, although being English, was willing to use the native British sources – does not mention it, nor does Gildas, nor Nennius, nor, as we have just seen, does Geoffrey. So it seems that the Britons never retained any memory or record of that incident. The fact that Geoffrey follows the other British records in not mentioning it strongly indicates that he was using a British source, not a Roman one; it was certainly not Caesar's own account.

However, the 'problem' with this conclusion is that Geoffrey includes many details that are not present in any of the surviving British records, yet are known to be true from Caesar's own words. For example, Nennius does not mention Mandubracius, the Trinovantian king who allied himself with Caesar. Bede mentions him, calling him Androgeus, but simply writes: 'In the meantime, the strong city of Trinovantum, with its commander Androgeus, surrendered to Caesar, giving him forty hostages.'[3]

It is only Geoffrey who provides the accurate detail that it was Mandubracius, whom he also calls Androgeus, who took the initiative to make contact with Caesar and appeal for his help. Nor does Bede mention the fact that Cassivellaunus was at war with the

Trinovantes, yet Geoffrey of Monmouth does. Nor does Bede say anything of the yearly tribute imposed upon the Britons. Nennius mentions that Caesar had received tribute from Britain, but that is all the detail he gives. It is only Geoffrey who supplies the additional, and accurate, detail that it was a yearly tribute that was agreed upon. There are many more details that are common only to Geoffrey and Caesar, but these examples should be sufficient to demonstrate the point.

The question is, how did Geoffrey get this information? If he had used Caesar's account of the invasion, then why did he not describe the marvellous actions of the Britons that are recorded there but not in native sources? If he did not use Caesar's account – and the aforementioned evidence favours the conclusion that he did not – then it logically follows that he had access to other, native, sources that contained the information. In other words, he had access to historically accurate sources that are not directly known to us today.

Then there are other pieces of evidence that demonstrate the point more definitively; accurate details Geoffrey includes that are not included in any native account *nor* Caesar's account. For example, due to our modern understanding, it is safe to conclude that Cassivellaunus's stronghold was a hill fort. Caesar himself says that the town was 'admirably fortified by nature and art'; presumably 'art' means man-made defences in this context. This statement implies that it had significant natural defences, which it would do if it were at the top of a hill. The hill fort at Wheathampstead is a commonly suggested site for the final battle, though this is by no means certain. Yet out of Gildas, Bede, Nennius and Geoffrey, it is only Geoffrey who contains the information that the final battle took place on a 'mountain', as he calls it. But it can hardly be supposed that Geoffrey read Caesar's passing remark and used that to form his detailed account of the mountain siege, when he completely ignores most of the much more noticeable details in *De Bello Gallico*. Such a concept is inconsistent in the extreme. Additionally, he makes no mention of the mountain having a town atop it as Caesar does, showing that he had an independent source of information.

However, some might still insist that, just because Geoffrey apparently had access to another source of information, this does not mean he was telling the truth about translating one particular book. The most common claim is that he used essentially all the British sources available to him. In terms of narrative sources, the three major ones are Gildas, Bede and Nennius. Gildas does not give any detail about Caesar's invasion whatsoever, so for this analysis there is only Bede and Nennius. But consider the following.

Both Nennius and Geoffrey exaggerate the time between the first two arrivals (three arrivals are present in both texts), but the exaggeration is greater in Nennius's *HB* than in Geoffrey's *HRB*. Nennius claims that Caesar returned three years later, while Geoffrey says it was two years. There is no reason for this to be so if Geoffrey had used and embellished Nennius's work. He also does not contain any of the numerical information provided by Nennius, yet plenty of numerical information is contained elsewhere in the book, so it is not a case of Geoffrey not wanting to include it for the sake of simplifying the narrative. Additionally, Nennius's brief account records that Caesar 'defeated them [the Britons] near a place called Trinovantum,' yet Geoffrey, who frequently mentions Trinovantum, instead places the final battle near Dorobernia. Bede does not say where it took place, so if Geoffrey was just using Gildas, Bede and Nennius as sources, it would logically follow that Geoffrey would use the only piece of information about the location of the battle available to him. But he did not.

Undoubtedly, Geoffrey had read the *Historia Brittonum*. But if the fact that the few details that are provided by Nennius – such as the number of ships in Caesar's fleet – are not present in *HRB* may be taken as evidence that Geoffrey did not even bother consulting Nennius for additional information, then the only apparent reason why this would be so is if he really was telling the truth when he claimed to simply be translating one particular book.

But this argument still might be dismissed in the eyes of some, on the basis that Geoffrey could conceivably have had access to other native sources that contained the accurate details (as well as the mistakes) not contained in the sources still available to us. However, if this is the case – if the ancient book did not exist, but Geoffrey of Monmouth was simply using a huge variety of purely British sources, many of which are now lost to us, and was attempting to pass off the final result of that collection as a translation of one particular ancient book given to him by Walter of Oxford – then one wonders why Geoffrey lamented at the lack of information written about the kings of Britain at the outset of his work. If there were plenty of other reliable sources of information, then Geoffrey's contemporaries should have been aware of them too, and would have picked up on the dishonesty at the very start of the book.

Of course, some might claim that the lost sources were oral tales known only to him, but at this point we would simply be contriving explanations to justify the commonly held view that he was lying about the existence of the ancient book.

If, on the other hand, we take the view that he was simply translating – or, accounting for the possibility of embellishments, working directly from – one particular ancient Welsh source, then all that improbability is removed. All the inconsistencies between his book and the British sources still available to us, as well as the Roman sources, are merely the natural result of an independent and genuine ancient British scribe writing what he knew.

The reason this is so significant is due to the nature of the study of history. If a writer claims to be copying or translating an earlier work, the truth of that claim is a vital factor in determining the evidence for the reality of an event. The writer himself is not contemporary with the event, so the existence of something closer to contemporary needs to be determined before making any judgements about what really happened. In Geoffrey's case, because his work contains descriptions of events that are, to the best of our knowledge, not recounted anywhere else in history, the existence of his ancient Welsh book, which would naturally have been closer in time to the supposed events than Geoffrey himself was, is of major importance to establishing the historicity of said events.

That it would still be the one and only source describing many of these events is not an issue in terms of historical studies. Scholars regularly accept the reality of events based on the testimony of only one writer. For example, much of what happened in first-century Judea is known purely through the writings of Flavius Josephus, yet they are accepted as factual; it is also worth noting that there are many more historical records from first-century Judea than there are from Dark Age Britain.

As just outlined, it is wholly reasonable to conclude that Geoffrey really was using an ancient source as opposed to his own imagination. If this is the case, then there is every reason to treat it largely like any other ancient historical work, such as the work of Bede in the eighth century – it should be considered just as valid a reflection of reality.[4] Of course, coming to us as a translated work, there may be a significant amount of geographical errors owing to inaccurate translations of the Celtic or even simply archaic place names. But the events themselves should be treated with a high degree of confidence unless demonstrated to be untrue or shown to conflict with most of the other evidence, just the same as with all other ancient histories.

However, regardless of whether *Historia Regum Britanniae* is a purely twelfth-century work or not, its account of history is generally accurate. This may seem like an odd statement to make, considering the book is very often described as complete fiction in reference works. These statements are grossly exaggerated. It corresponds to accepted history very well for most of the time – but in general terms, rather than specifics. When the *Encyclopaedia Britannica* says that its 'historical value is almost nil,' what it presumably really means is that nothing *new* that it contains is considered likely to be true, due to the idea that large parts of Geoffrey's history came from his own imagination. But the fact is, the general outline of *Historia Regum Britanniae* from the start of the Roman era onwards conforms to generally accepted history.

To demonstrate this, let us examine Geoffrey's account from the arrival of Caesar to the end of the Roman period in Britain, as this is the only era covered by Geoffrey's book that is well documented. Then, we will have a good idea of the level of accuracy we can expect for the Arthurian era itself. With that information, we will then be able to make an informed assessment of the tale of King Arthur's campaign into Europe.

Caesar's First Attack on Britain

Book Four of *HRB* describes the multiple Roman incursions into Britain. It begins with Julius Caesar having subdued Gaul, and then setting his sights on Britain. This is essentially accurate, though Caesar had not subdued the entirety of Gaul by this point.

The following detail that he then 'inquired of those about him what country it was, and what people inhabited it' is also correct, but the next sentence states that he was informed of the name of the kingdom and the people inhabiting it.[5] This latter part is in conflict with Caesar's statement that he 'could learn neither what was the size of the island, nor what ... were the nations which inhabited it'.[6]

HRB then reports that Caesar decided that the Britons would easily become subjects to the Roman state. However, he wished to offer them the opportunity to willingly submit themselves to the Romans, out of the desire to not shed the blood of their supposed kinsmen unnecessarily, both the Romans and the Britons being descendants of the Trojans according to this legend. He therefore sent a letter to Cassivellaunus, informing him of his intentions.

In the historical reality as given to us by Caesar, it was indeed he who made the first contact with the Britons. After not being able to discover much useful information about the island from merchants, he sent Gaius Volusenus to survey the south coast of Britain to look for useful harbours. However, he reportedly did not land, out of fear of 'entrusting himself to the barbarians'. Nonetheless, Caesar's intentions were conveyed to the natives by merchants from Gaul. This is not the same as Caesar having sent a letter to the Britons, but it is similar. His intentions were conveyed to them by messengers, albeit not purposely sent by Caesar, and they made a reply.

In *HRB*, the reply was a letter sent by Cassivellaunus, to the effect that Caesar's demand was harsh and unreasonable, and that the Britons were fully prepared to fight for their liberty if Caesar invaded. After receiving that reply, Caesar prepared his fleet to sail for Britain.

According to what Caesar tells us, after being informed of the potential invasion, 'ambassadors come to him from several states of the island, to promise that they will give hostages, and submit to the government of the Roman people'. This is the complete opposite of the message that Cassivellaunus sends Caesar according to Geoffrey of Monmouth's book, but the fact remains that the Britons sent a message to Caesar in response to hearing of his intentions. The details differ, but the general information is the same.

The third chapter of Book Four of *HRB* is quite lengthy, and describes the entirety of the first invasion. It commences by telling us that Caesar waited for a fair wind to execute his threats against Cassivellaunus. As a minor point of inaccuracy, it appears from Caesar's words that he was not aware of Cassivellaunus's existence or role until the second invasion. Still, the detail in *HRB* that Caesar waited for a fair wind is in agreement with the statement in *De Bello Gallico* that 'finding the weather favourable for his voyage, he set sail'.

The *HRB* records that Caesar arrived with his army at the mouth of the River Thames. This is a mistake, for Caesar initially attempted to land at Dubris, but finding that this was unsuitable, he took his ships about 7 miles north. His actual landing spot is generally thought to be at Walmer, where a small monument still marks the event. While *HRB* does not give the accurate location, it does place the event in the correct part of the country. The real landing site could be described as *near* the mouth of the Thames, so it is not hard to see how that could have become construed into '*at* the mouth of the Thames'. The error is present in Nennius as well, so it is certainly not a mistake that originated with Geoffrey of Monmouth.

Next, we are told by Geoffrey that as the ships were coming close to land, Cassivellaunus gathered all his army and arrived at a town called Dorobellum (probably either Canterbury, known to the Romans as Durovernum, or Durolevum, an obscure settlement around 12 miles away from Canterbury).[7] Here, he had a conference with rulers from all over Britain to determine how to deal with Caesar. As discussed previously, they decided to attack Caesar's camp, which by then had already been set up. Hence, the story skips past the initial opposition to the landing of Caesar's ships. It makes no mention of British ambassadors meeting with Caesar, submitting to him and agreeing to send him hostages. Nor does it mention how, soon after that, many of Caesar's ships were destroyed on the coast by a storm. It is necessary to remember that these omissions are just that: omissions. They are not errors.

Caesar's account tells us that after the British chiefs had discovered what had happened with the storm and the ships, they held a conference and decided to renew the war. This is evidently the conference described by Geoffrey. So while he does not include the detail that the British chiefs in question, according to Caesar, had been about to submit to Caesar's conditions, he is nonetheless accurate in writing about them holding a conference.

Androgeus – the spelling for Mandubracius used by Geoffrey – is called the duke of Trinovantum. While it is not, today, commonly accepted that a place by that name existed, the statement accurately identifies him as the ruler of the Trinovantes.

A person named Tenvantius is recorded as the duke of Cornwall. Elsewhere he appears as the father of Cunobelinus, identifying him as Tasciovanus, the historical father of Cunobelinus as revealed by coins minted in the latter's reign. However, he was historically the king of the Catuvellauni tribe, near London – nowhere near Cornwall. Historian Miles Russell suggests that the name 'Catuvellauni' became corrupted into 'Kerniw', or Cornwall. However, this is hardly convincing. Alternatively, it may well be the case that alliances existed between the Catuvellauni and the Silures, with their region of Cernyw in south-east Wales, considering that in the first century CE Caratacus seems to have immediately fled all the way over to the Silures when his tribe – the Catuvellauni – was defeated by the Romans. But whatever the reason for the error, it seems safe to conclude that Tasciovanus was not the duke of Cornwall.

The next three kings are referred to as being inferior to those just mentioned. The first is Cridious, king of Albania, which is Scotland. Needless to say, this is probably not true. The next two – Guerthaeth the king of Gwynedd, and Britael the king of Dyfed – are equally undocumented. It is highly improbable that kings from such distant places could have arrived in the south-east of England in such a short space of time.

To continue, *HRB* informs us that the British army marched toward the shore to attack Caesar's camp. The two armies engage in battle, and it is during this fight that Nennius, a British warrior, comes face-to-face with Julius Caesar. They exchange blows with one another, and the outcome is that Caesar's sword gets stuck in Nennius's shield, forcing Caesar to abandon it. Nennius then uses the sword to astonishing effect, and even kills a Roman tribune called Labienus. According to the book, after most of the day had passed, the Britons won against the Romans. The latter then retired back to their camp and ships. That same night, the Romans sailed back to Gaul.

Caesar's account is very similar, but it is remarkable to observe the distinct differences between them. That is not to say that they conflict, but it is evident that they are largely *independent* records of the same event. Caesar records two more battles with the Britons before he returns to Gaul, yet it is only the first that is described in *HRB*. Note that after the conference, *HRB* records that the Britons 'advanced towards the shore where Julius Caesar had pitched his camp'. Then, at the end of the battle, it says that 'by the blessing of God they [the Britons] obtained the victory, and Caesar, with his broken forces, retired to his camp and fleet'. What is clear from these quotes is that the battle just described did not actually take place *at* the camp – on the shore. Rather, it took place *near* the shore. This is in full agreement with Caesar's description. He describes how one legion had been sent from the camp to forage, but then 'they who were on duty at the gates of the camp reported to Caesar that a greater dust than was usual was seen in that direction in which the legion had marched'. So it was sufficiently close to the camp that those who were at the edge of the camp could see the dust created by the tumult. Caesar then says that 'when he had advanced some little way from the camp, he saw that his men were overpowered by the enemy and scarcely able to stand their ground'. This is clearly the battle described in *HRB*.

The next part of *De Bello Gallico* reports that upon Caesar's arrival – along with many other soldiers to assist those currently fighting – the Britons paused and the Romans recovered from their fear. However, what Caesar says next is particularly interesting. Without explanation, he decided that the time was 'unfavourable for provoking the enemy and coming to an action'. Therefore, he remained in his own quarter and then, after a short period of time, he withdrew the legions back to the camp. In other words, while Caesar did not describe it as the very decisive victory that Geoffrey wrote about, the battle did end with Caesar withdrawing his troops and retreating to the camp, just as the *HRB* describes.

According to Julius Caesar, a storm prevented the Romans and Britons from engaging again for several days, during which time the Britons were gathering warriors from all parts of the country to prepare to attack again. However, Caesar expected such a thing would happen, so he readied himself and his men. According to him, the Britons were quickly routed and many of them were slain. So this was a fleeting and wholly unsuccessful event for the British; hence, it is not recorded in the *HRB*. Once again, this is not an inaccuracy, but merely an omission.

However, there are some inaccuracies in Geoffrey's account of the final battle between the Romans and the Britons (which was actually the penultimate battle, as we have just seen). Though a certain amount of interpretation is possible, Caesar's statement, 'thinking the time unfavourable for provoking the enemy and coming to an action, he kept himself in his own quarter,' seems to imply that he did not personally engage in combat against the Britons. If this is the case, then the story of Nennius fighting Caesar and taking his sword cannot be true.

On the other hand, there is a possibility regarding the true nature of that event, which is revealed by examining another inaccuracy in the account. After Nennius acquires the sword of Caesar, he slays a great number of Romans, including a tribune called Labienus. This is generally taken to be a mistake for Laberius, the tribune who was killed during Caesar's second invasion of Britain. If this is correct, then the naming mistake is found as early as Orosius's *Seven Books of History Against the Pagans*, of the fifth century. Just why the death was moved from the second invasion to the first in the *HRB* is unknown. In any case, it is evident that details from this battle near Caesar's camp during 54 BCE were added to the account of the battle near Caesar's camp in 55 BCE.

With this in mind, it is conceivable that the entire story of Nennius and Caesar's sword, and not just the detail about Laberius dying, came from an event that occurred during the later battle and was grafted onto the earlier battle. But again, regardless of the reality behind the error, it is still an error as it appears in the *HRB*.

Additionally, Geoffrey says that the Romans sailed away from the island the same day that they were defeated, whereas we know from Caesar's account that they sailed away several days later. However, it was the same day that they had their last – and successful – battle against the Britons. In all likelihood, proud

British reports of the Romans fleeing the island the very same day that they last fought against them were grafted onto the much more detailed account of their last victorious battle against them.

To conclude, we have seen that the account given in *Historia Regum Britanniae* is very accurate. Plenty of information is excluded from the narrative, but that is simply the natural consequence of being written using detailed British sources, giving what is by and large the British point of view. The information that is contained in Geoffrey's book is far more accurate than not. In fact, there is a measly total of ten specific errors in the account:

1. Caesar finding out about the inhabitants of Britain before he set sail.
2. Caesar sending a letter to the Britons.
3. The Britons sending a reply of defiance to Caesar.
4. Caesar arriving at the mouth of the Thames.
5. Trinovantum being a place.
6. Tenvantius being the duke of Cornwall.
7. Kings from Scotland and Wales being present at the conference.
8. Nennius fighting Caesar during the battle near the camp.
9. Labienus being killed.
10. The Romans leaving Britain the same day that the battle near the camp was fought.

As can be seen from the list, many of the errors are minor details. Most of them have a very clear historical basis, such as the first three, and have simply been adjusted either towards simplicity (as in the case of the first two) or for the sake of nationalistic propaganda (as in the case of the third). Only points 5, 6, 7 and 9 are significant deviations from accepted history. In conclusion, the account of Caesar's first invasion of Britain as contained in the *Historia Regum Britanniae* is very accurate and is therefore by no means historically worthless.

However, *HRB* departs from recorded history in another fairly significant way when describing what happened to Caesar upon his return to Gaul. It tells us that the inhabitants of Gaul decided to take the opportunity (thinking that the Romans were sufficiently weakened after their expedition to Britain) to rebel against the Romans, wishing to drive them off their coasts. It includes the detail that the Gauls heard reports that Cassivellaunus was pursuing Caesar across the ocean, which is not attested to by any other historical account. The only event Caesar describes that may have been the basis for that statement is the fact that two British states sent hostages over to the Continent.

In any case, Geoffrey's account is correct in saying that the Gauls tried to rebel when the Romans returned. What is different is the outcome. While *De Bello Gallico* describes a battle being fought between the Romans and the natives, *HRB* reports that Caesar won over the natives by means of generous gifts. This is nothing like what Caesar himself wrote, but nonetheless, the general message of an attack on the Romans as soon as they returned to Gaul, which concluded with the Romans regaining control of the natives, is present in Geoffrey's book.

Caesar's Second Attack on Britain

Now that Caesar's first attack on Britain has been analysed and found to be largely accurate, let us see how well the account of Caesar's second attack agrees with the information provided by Julius Caesar himself.

The first error is the amount of time that elapsed between the two invasions. The *HRB* says that it was two years, whereas in reality it was only one year. The second major error, which is quite a substantial one, is the splitting of the second invasion into two distinct campaigns. The first is a description of an event that actually occurred quite far along in the invasion. This is the battle on the Thames. Geoffrey describes how Cassivellaunus gathered all the forces of the island and stationed them near the coasts in anticipation of the attack. He fortified the Thames, setting up stakes on the riverbed, concealed underneath the surface of the water. Caesar is said to have sailed up the Thames to Trinovantum (London). However, as the Britons had planned, the ships struck against the stakes and caused many ships to sink and thousands of men to be drowned. Caesar managed to flee with many of his men to dry land, whereon Cassivellaunus ordered his men to attack them. The Romans fought valiantly and slaughtered many Britons, but they were outnumbered and were eventually forced to flee back to their ships. Hence, the Romans returned to Gaul.

This completely skips past a considerable portion of the invasion as recorded by Julius Caesar. There are six chapters of narrative in *De Bello Gallico* before the battle on the Thames occurs. The first battle between the Romans and the Britons is not described in any marvellous way. The Britons were repulsed by the Roman cavalry and fled to a fortification in the woods. This was successfully besieged by the Romans and the Britons were driven out of the territory.

The next day, when Caesar had sent out some soldiers to pursue the Britons who had fled, news came to him that a great number of ships had been destroyed by storms. Caesar immediately recalled the soldiers from their march. He had his men working for many days to restore as many ships as possible. After this was accomplished, he returned to where he had been going previously, where the Britons had been driven from their fort, and found the armies of the Britons amassed there. This is the same event described in the *HRB* where Cassivellaunus gathered the forces of the island near the sea coasts in preparation for the Roman attack. The previous episodes with the Britons being defeated by the Romans and then the Romans returning to the camp to repair their ships have been skipped.

Regarding the hill fort that was used in the siege mentioned earlier, it is possibly significant that Caesar writes: 'they had secured a place admirably fortified by nature and by art, which, as it seemed, they had before prepared on account of a civil war; for all entrances to it were shut up by a great number of felled trees.'[8] Forgetting Caesar's personal speculation, this ties in with the information in the *HRB* that Cassivellaunus had 'everywhere fortified his cities' in preparation for the Roman invasion.

Returning to the narrative, Caesar describes the battle between his army and the armies of Cassivellaunus. From the description, it sounds as though it was more or less an equal affair, though it is the Britons who are said to have retreated. This is the fight during which Laberius was slain, so it seems that details from this battle were grafted onto the successful fight against the Romans the previous year. If so, then this may be at least partly why this battle is missing from Geoffrey's account of the second invasion.

The following day the Britons tried to attack the Romans once more, but this attempt was much less successful. According to Caesar, the Britons never again tried to attack them in large numbers. The reason for this event not being included in *HRB* should be obvious.

Finally, we arrive at the battle that is presented as the initial one in *HRB*. In the British account, as described previously, it is a victory for the British. But as Caesar describes it, it is a clear victory for the Romans. However, the *HRB* does report that the Romans 'made no small slaughter'. Nonetheless, the Romans are said to have fled back to their ships and sailed away from the island. This is a significant departure from history. Another error, of course, is the fact that the Roman army was already on foot by this point, so they did not sail up the Thames; rather, they forded it. Nonetheless, the Britons placing stakes in the riverbed is true.

After this event, according to Caesar, Cassivellaunus dismissed most of his army and was left with only 4,000 chariots. Perhaps it was this – the majority of the British soldiers returning to their homes – that led to false rumours among the natives that the Romans had been defeated. In any case, the error does not originate with Geoffrey, for it is present in Nennius as well.

A description of Cassivellaunus's celebration comes next in *HRB*, and if this has any basis in fact, then it must have occurred after the Romans left the previous year. An incident then occurred that is not recorded in any Roman account, for obvious reasons. The nephew of Cassivellaunus was killed by the nephew of Androgeus. This resulted in Cassivellaunus going to war with Androgeus, ravaging his country. With no other means to stop him, Androgeus sent a letter to Caesar asking for his help. This is corroborated by Caesar's account, which describes how Mandubracius had fled to Gaul to the safety of Caesar, to escape Cassivellaunus. However, that actually occurred *before* Caesar had returned to Britain, reinforcing the conclusion that Geoffrey's account of a celebration among the Britons is actually taken from after the Romans *first* left Britain, after the invasion of 55 BCE.

It seems that the compiler of this chronicle combined Mandubracius fleeing to Gaul with another event described by Caesar. The latter event is one where the Trinovantes (not personally Mandubracius, or Androgeus) sent ambassadors to Caesar with the message that they would submit themselves to him, and to ask him to protect Mandubracius. The confusion of these two events may well be an additional reason for why the Romans were thought to have returned to Gaul after the battle on the Thames, and only returned when the Trinovantes contacted them.

The compiler of the *HRB* mistakenly thought that Caesar was still in Gaul during the time of this summons, having fled from Britain after the battle on the Thames, but is nonetheless accurate in stating that Caesar demanded hostages from the Trinovantes. Caesar says he demanded forty hostages, whereas the *HRB* states that Androgeus sent his son Scaeva along with thirty others. Several other tribes then, in Caesar's account, surrendered themselves to the Romans and revealed the location of Cassivellaunus's stronghold, which the Romans proceeded to besiege. As discussed previously, this must be the event that is described as a mountain siege in *HRB*. Like in Caesar's account, the mountain is said to have been topped by a wood. However, it is unclear from Caesar's description of events whether or not Cassivellaunus was actually in his stronghold when it was being besieged. If not, then this conflicts with the information given in Geoffrey's account. However, because it is unclear, this will not be counted as an error.[9]

The events described immediately prior to the attack on the mountain are somewhat difficult to match up with the events described in Caesar's account, but the following scenario seems to be the answer.

The *HRB* says that Cassivellaunus was in the process of besieging Trinovantum when Caesar arrived for the third time in Britain. He then abandoned the siege and went out to meet him. However, Caesar had described how Cassivellaunus was engaging in guerrilla tactics against the Romans from the moment he dismissed the majority of his army and left himself with 4,000 chariots. He makes no mention of Cassivellaunus ceasing from this engagement with the Romans between then and the moment when the Trinovantian ambassadors came to Caesar, asking him 'to protect Mandubratius from the violence of Cassivellaunus'. This request might be taken as evidence that Cassivellaunus had, by this point, left the Romans and was attacking Trinovantian territory. However, after Caesar makes his demand for the forty hostages, his account says that he sent Mandubracius over to the Trinovantes. This shows that Mandubracius was actually with the Romans at the time, and therefore this seems to suggest that the meaning of the Trinovantes ambassadors' request is that they wanted Mandubracius out of harm's way of Cassivellaunus's ongoing attacks against the Romans. This would explain why Caesar then returns Mandubracius to his tribe. Hence, it seems that the *HRB* is wrong in stating that Cassivellaunus was besieging Trinovantian territory at this time.

Next, we are told that Cassivellaunus went to meet the Romans at a valley near Dorobernia, which is Canterbury. This is incorrect, for the Romans were north of the Thames by this point. However, Geoffrey's source is correct in saying that the Romans were preparing to assault the city; it simply got the name of the city incorrect. It seems that the battle that is henceforth described is the siege of Cassivellaunus's stronghold, which Caesar also describes. Very little detail is given by the Roman leader, but he tells us that he 'undertakes to attack it in two directions. The enemy, having remained only a short time, did not sustain the attack of our soldiers, and hurried away on the other side of the town'.[10]

That first detail is also contained in *HRB*, which tells us that Androgeus was hiding in a wood with 5,000 men, ready to assist Caesar. 'While they were thus engaged, Androgeus sallied forth from the wood and fell upon the rear of Cassibellaun's army.' Being attacked by both the Romans and the allied Britons, Cassivellaunus's army retreated. It is after this that Cassivellaunus flees to the top of a nearby mountain, which is paralleled by Caesar's words that the Britons fled away to the other side of the town. Since the town was almost certainly on the top of a hill anyway, the fact that the Britons were able to find some measure of safety on the other side of the town, as per Caesar's account, would imply that it had some sort of extra natural defences. A logical suggestion would be that it was significantly raised on that side. The account contained in the *HRB* is simply exaggerated in referring to it as a distinct mountain.

In the British account, the siege continued for several days until Cassivellaunus was depleted of resources, forcing him to surrender. Therefore, he sent a message to Androgeus and pleaded with him to make peace with Caesar on his behalf. Androgeus was understandably resentful towards Cassivellaunus, but he decided that he had suffered enough. Androgeus then went to Caesar and requested that Caesar cease the attack. After Caesar made no reply, Androgeus repeated the request and threatened to give Cassivellaunus his assistance if he did not comply. At this, Caesar was forced to comply and called off the siege.

This completely skips the event in Caesar's account where Cassivellaunus arranged an attack on the Roman camp on the shore, which ended up failing. Once again, this is a very understandable omission.

According to Caesar, it was after the loss of this battle was reported to him, combined with the fact that his territories had been laid waste and many British states had deserted him, that Cassivellaunus decided to surrender to Caesar. However, whereas in *HRB* he does this through Androgeus, in Caesar's account it is through the mediation of Commius the Atrebatian. *De Bello Gallico* makes it clear that Caesar did not agree to Cassivellaunus's surrender due to any threats, but it was due to his own contemplations about the general situation both in Britain and the Continent.

This does not agree with the details in the *HRB* regarding Androgeus's threat to Caesar, but the general message is the same. Cassivellaunus surrendered to Caesar through the means of one of the kings of a British state, and Caesar agreed to the surrender but imposed an annual tribute on the Britons. However, one significant error in Geoffrey's account is the information that Caesar stayed in Britain throughout the winter and only returned to Gaul the next spring. Caesar himself, on the other hand, informs us that he left immediately.

In conclusion, then, we can see that the account of Caesar's second invasion contained in *Historia Regum Britanniae* is less accurate than the account of the first invasion, but still follows the general outline of accepted history. The main reason for the apparent extreme dissimilarity between Geoffrey's account and

Caesar's is due to the omissions by the former, rather than actual contradictions. However, there are still many errors, and they are generally far more significant than the errors in the account of the first invasion. They are as follows:

1. Two years separating the invasions.
2. Caesar sailing up the Thames and having many ships sink due to the concealed stakes.
3. The Britons winning the battle on the Thames.
4. The Romans returning to Gaul after the battle on the Thames.
5. Cassivellaunus and the other Britons celebrating after this defeat of the Romans.
6. Androgeus himself sending a message to the Romans regarding submission and tribute.
7. The number of hostages imposed on the Trinovantes.
8. Cassivellaunus attacking Trinovantian territory immediately prior to the Roman attack on his stronghold.
9. The location of Cassivellaunus's stronghold.
10. Androgeus mediating between Cassivellaunus and Caesar.
11. Caesar being forced to comply with Cassivellaunus's surrender because of threats from Androgeus.
12. Caesar staying in Britain over the winter.

Unlike the errors in the account of the first invasion, most of these ones are significant departures from history. The most significant would probably be the record that the Britons won the battle on the Thames, causing the Romans to return to Gaul. Excluding that error, the general outline of events agrees with what we know from Caesar, though a considerable amount of information is not contained in Geoffrey's book, making it appear more inaccurate than it is.

A final bit of information in the *Historia Regum Britanniae* is this: 'At length he [Caesar] assembled all his forces, and marched towards Rome against Pompey.' This is accurate. In 49 BCE, five years after he returned to Gaul, civil war between Caesar and Pompey broke out.

Geoffrey's account tells us that Cassivellaunus died seven years later and was succeeded by Tenvantius. Androgeus had gone to Rome with Caesar. The Roman accounts say nothing of this, but they do not contradict it either. *HRB* then tells us just a little about Tenvantius, saying that he 'governed the kingdom with diligence. He was a warlike man, and a strict observer of justice'. Likewise, almost nothing is known of the historical Tasciovanus. However, it is known that he minted coins at Verlamion, which was in Catuvellauni territory, before then minting coins at Camulodunum, which was in Trinovantes territory. This seems to show that Tasciovanus had conquered that area, which agrees with the statement that Tenvantius was 'a warlike man'.

The next sovereign is Cunobelinus. He is described as a great soldier and is said to have been brought up by Augustus Caesar. There is no independent evidence for this, but according to Miles Russell, 'the system of bringing up the children of allied kings in the imperial capital was an old and established one.'[11] He then goes on to write: 'Having the offspring of barbarian aristocrats growing up under close supervision in Rome is something that emperors such as Augustus ... positively encouraged, and it is difficult to see why the Britons would have been treated differently.' So Cunobelinus may well have been raised in Rome, though there is no way of knowing this for certain.

The *Historia Regum Britanniae* then proceeds to tell us that Cunobelinus had an excellent, friendly relationship with the Romans and freely paid them tribute. This is borne out by the fact that trade with the Continent seems to have increased during his reign, certainly regarding luxury goods, and these seem to have arrived by means of the port of Camulodunum (modern-day Colchester), which was ruled by Cunobelinus. Additionally, the fact that he marked his coins with 'REX' and classical motifs also shows that he had good relations with the Romans. Furthermore, the following information is significant: Dumnobellaunus is a British supplicant recorded as visiting Augustus in *Res Gestae Divi Augusti*. This man was the king of the Trinovantes around 10–5 BCE, but his tribe was then conquered by Cunobelinus. The year in which Dumnobellaunus is described as being sent as a supplicant by a British king was around CE 7. Hence, it is very likely that the British king who sent Dumnobellaunus to Augustus was Cunobelinus. Strabo tells us that certain British chieftains had procured 'the friendship of Caesar Augustus by sending embassies'.[12] Therefore, this supports the concept of Cunobelinus having a good relationship with Rome.

Excluding the possibility of using modern archaeological techniques, it is very difficult to see how Geoffrey of Monmouth could have had any awareness of this good relationship between Cunobelinus and the Romans without the use of literary sources now lost to us.

The next statement in the *HRB* is that Jesus Christ was born in the days of Cunobelinus, which is correct.

The Claudius Invasion

According to the *Historia Regum Britanniae*, Cunobelinus reigned for ten years and then had two sons, Guiderius and Arviragus. According to generally accepted history, however, he had three known sons: Caratacus, Togodumnus and Amminius (or Adminius). It might initially be tempting to think of Arviragus as a corruption of Amminius due to hundreds of years of oral tradition and scribal corruptions, but Arviragus is mentioned by that name in a contemporary poem by Juvenal, so that is not possible. Additionally, the activities of Arviragus as recorded in *HRB* and the known activities of Amminius from Roman sources are polar opposites of each other. Hence, Arviragus must be someone different, and the fact that he is recorded in a contemporary source confirms that he did exist.

Many have speculated that he was actually a legendary version of the famous Caratacus. There are some reasons for believing this, but we will see over the course of this discussion that such a conclusion is without any strong basis.

Arviragus being an otherwise unknown son of Cunobelinus is certainly a plausible concept. We know that Caratacus had other brothers because, when he was defeated at the Battle of Caer Caradoc in CE 50, Tacitus mentions that his brothers surrendered. By this point, Togodumnus was dead, having been killed by the Romans at the battle of the River Thames years previously. It is unknown where Amminius was at this time, but considering he had fled to the Romans in around CE 40, it seems unlikely that he would have been fighting against them now. In any case, Caratacus must have had at least one more brother. The state of the Roman histories, therefore, is completely compatible with the concept that not every family member of Caratacus was named and identified. This allows for the possibility that Arviragus was a brother of Caratacus.

To return to the narrative, Guiderius, the elder son, succeeded to the throne after Cunobelinus died. Guiderius is evidently the historical Togodumnus.

Geoffrey's book makes the claim that Claudius invaded because Guiderius refused to pay tribute to the Romans. This is not what any Roman source says. Suetonius makes the claim that Claudius invaded for the sake of his reputation, whereas Cassius Dio informs us that it was for the purpose of reinstating a king who had been driven out of the country. Togodumnus may not have been paying tribute, but it seems certain that this was not the reason for the invasion.

The leader of Claudius's invasion is named in the *HRB* as 'Lelius Hamo', whereas in reality, the name of this individual was 'Aulus Plautius'. 'Lelius' is evidently just a corruption of 'Aulus'. The second part of the name has not been corrupted from 'Plautius' to 'Hamo', which corruption is plainly impossible, but 'Plautius' has been dropped entirely. Later in the account, Lelius Hamo is said to have been killed at Southampton, which was supposedly named after him. The names of some localities do derive from personal names, though records often make a false connection between a personal name and a place name. This is the case with Southampton. Thus, it seems that Aulus was given the name 'Hamo', not as a corruption of 'Plautius', but because Southampton was believed to have been named after him due to the belief that he died there.

The *HRB* states that Lelius arrived at Portchester. It has been widely believed that the Romans actually landed in Richborough, Kent; however, this view is challenged by many historians. There are good reasons for concluding that at least some of the fleet, if not all, landed much further west. The main reason for doubting the Richborough site is the fact that Cassius Dio informs us that the Romans were encouraged by a shooting star travelling in the direction in which they were going – east to west. Further, Suetonius informs us that Claudius sailed from Boulogne, and it seems reasonable – though by no means certain – that the Romans who had sailed under Aulus Plautius previously had left from the same location. If this is the case, then if they landed in Kent, the journey would have been from south to north, not east to west. However, a landing spot much further along the south coast of Britain would fit with the description of an east to west journey, as required by the account of the shooting star. This is made particularly likely by the fact that at least part of the reason why Claudius invaded Britain was to help reinstate the Atrebatian king, Verica. Since the Atrebates were in the Hampshire and Sussex area, it would be logical that this is where the Romans would have chosen to land.

For these reasons and others, Chichester and Portsmouth are commonly suggested as the landing site for the initial invasion of CE 43. It is important to note that the *HRB* does not say that Lelius landed at Portchester, but simply that he arrived there, with the implication being that this was soon or straight after the initial landing – though no actual timing is given. Portchester is a mere 6 kilometres from Portsmouth, so it entirely possible that the Roman army did march through there.

The British account then says that Lelius besieged the city. This is not mentioned in any Roman account. According to Dio, the Romans

...put in to the island and found none to oppose them. For the Britons as a result of their inquiries had not expected that they would come, and had therefore not assembled beforehand. And even when they did assemble, they would not come to close quarters with the Romans, but took refuge in the swamps and the forests, hoping to wear out the invaders in fruitless effort, so that, just as in the days of Julius Caesar, they should sail back with nothing accomplished.

Plautius, accordingly, had a deal of trouble in searching them out; but when at last he did find them, he first defeated Caratacus and then Togodumnus, the sons of Cynobellinus, who was dead.[13]

This does not seem to allow for the possibility of a siege of one of the first settlements they came to. Hence, it seems that the British account is incorrect in that regard. *HRB* does not mention the siege again, in any case.

The *HRB* then states that Guiderius gathered all the forces of his kingdom when he heard news of Claudius's coming attack. We now come to an event that is described by the Romans, though naturally in a completely different manner. Geoffrey's book makes no mention of the location, but simply says that Guiderius went out to meet the Roman army. Perhaps the implication is that he met them at Portchester, but the work never says this; no mention is made of the city in the description of the battle.

From a reading of Dio's account, it is evident that the British version only contains the last part of the encounter. The words of the *HRB* portray the event as if the fight between the Britons and the Romans, in which the Britons successfully held off the Romans, was the initial battle between them. In actual fact, according to Dio's words, Togodumnus was initially defeated by Aulus Plautius and fled. Battles by a river – generally thought to be the River Medway – and then by the Thames are described by the Roman writer. After relating how the Germans, who were on the side of the Romans, had lost a number of men while pursuing the Britons, we are told: 'Shortly afterwards Togodumnus perished.'

This implies that he was the one leading the Britons during this encounter, despite his previous defeat and flight. Certainly the Romans were the cause of his death, otherwise Dio could not then go on to say that the Britons tried to *avenge* his death by fighting harder against the Romans. However, his manner of death is not stated, so no certain claim can be made regarding the accuracy of Geoffrey's description of it. However, the *HRB* does claim that the Britons were successfully opposing the Romans just prior to Guiderius's death, so much so that Claudius was 'on the point of retreating'. This detail cannot be true, for Claudius was not yet in the country. However, we do know that at this point in the battle – shortly before the death of Togodumnus, or Guiderius – the Britons were managing to slaughter a large number of the German soldiers. Dio tells us: 'In pursuing the remainder [of the Britons] incautiously, they got into swamps from which it was difficult to make their way out, and so lost a number of men.'

This tactical blunder, which led to a loss of men worth noting by the Roman historian, evidently corresponds to the claims of success against the Romans in the British account. Exactly like in the accounts of Caesar's invasions, the Britons have simply omitted the unfavourable moments of the war from their own version of events. But an omission is not synonymous with an inaccuracy.

The *HRB* tells us that after Guiderius's death, Arviragus put on his brother's clothing and took his place at the head of the battle. The Britons, while not aware of Guiderius's death, fought powerfully under Arviragus and eventually caused the Romans to flee. Dio, similarly, informs us that the Britons 'united all the more firmly to avenge his death', though the latter part of that statement contradicts the British account inasmuch as the Britons must have known about Togodumnus's death to avenge it. Additionally, Dio's account merely says that Aulus became afraid and decided not to advance any further, but merely protected what he had already won. This is incompatible with the British account's claim that Arviragus pursued Lelius from place to place until reaching Southampton. The claim that Lelius was then killed by Arviragus is also incorrect, assuming that Lelius Hamo does indeed stand for Aulus Plautius, for Aulus continued living for several years after this initial invasion. The *HRB* also mentions Claudius retreating to his ships, but as has already been mentioned, Claudius was not yet in the country.

Geoffrey's account then goes on into a description of how Claudius besieged Winchester, where Arviragus was currently holding out. Arviragus then opened the gates and prepared to engage Claudius in a battle, but then the latter fearfully decided to sue for peace instead. The account says that he chose 'rather to reduce them by wisdom and policy, than run the hazard of a battle'. In Dio's account, the rest of the invasion of Britain is described in no detail whatsoever. However, he does say that Claudius 'won over numerous tribes, in some cases by capitulation, in others by force'. Geoffrey's description of Claudius's peaceful engagement with Arviragus would certainly be consistent with Dio's statement. However, the British story includes Claudius sending his daughter, Genuissa, to be married to Arviragus. This is generally viewed as fictitious.

Next, the founding of Gloucester is described. The book claims that it was named after Claudius, which is another inaccuracy – the 'Glou' element of the name originally derives from the Latin name 'Glevensium', which is transparently unrelated to Claudius.[14] Additionally, the archaeology suggests a date of *c.* 49 for the original construction of the Roman site, which is six years after Claudius had returned to Rome. The city could not have been built within his visit to the island either, as he only stayed for sixteen days. So in all, this brief section about Gloucester seems to be entirely inaccurate, though Gloucester was indeed founded about this time – still, in the specifics, Geoffrey's source is wrong.

After this, Arviragus is said to have grown arrogant and disdainful of the Roman subjugation he experienced. Due to his actions, Claudius sent Vespasian to deal with him. He first attempted to land at Richborough, Kent, but was prevented from landing by Arviragus. Therefore, he travelled all the way to Totnes, almost on the complete opposite end of the island. He then besieged Exeter, in Devon, and after seven days, Arviragus arrived and attacked him. The battle lasted one day, with no clear victor by the end. The next morning, Genuissa made peace between the two armies, who then – without explanation – sent their men over to Ireland. Vespasian returned to Rome once that winter was over.

It is commonly claimed that these events are entirely fictional, on the basis that if they really occurred there would certainly be records of them. However, such a conclusion is incorrect. What we know is that Vespasian was the head of the Second Legion, or the Legio II Augusta. This is the legion that fought at the Medway and the Thames against Togodumnus. Suetonius tells us that Vespasian, during his years in Britain, fought thirty battles against the Britons, yet, beyond the initial few against Caratacus and Togodumnus, not a single one of them is known to us. Additionally, he tells us that Vespasian 'reduced to subjection two powerful nations, more than twenty towns, and the island of Vectis [the Isle of Wight]'.[15]

The two powerful British nations, or tribes, that he reduced to subjection obviously had rulers, though Suetonius does not specifically mention these individuals – we do not even know their names. Therefore, there is nothing even the slightest bit remarkable about the fact that there is no independent corroboration for Arviragus's lone battle against Vespasian. While we do not know the names of Vespasian's enemies, we know that they existed. It must also be emphasised that Arviragus did not fight a *war* against Rome, as is commonly claimed. He was quickly subdued by Claudius by means of capitulation, and then after a period of doing nothing notable against the Romans, he fought a single battle against Vespasian. There is no need to exaggerate the events to make it seem improbable that he would not have received a mention from the Romans. He was merely one of the many leaders who Claudius subdued by means of capitulation, and his battle against Vespasian was merely one of almost three dozen about which we know nothing. Hence, there is no valid objection to the historicity of these events in Arviragus's life.

For various reasons, not least of which are archaeological ones, the two tribes subdued by Vespasian are commonly thought to be the Durotriges and the Dumnonii.[16] The first of these roughly corresponds to present-day Dorset and Somerset, while the latter corresponds to Devon and Cornwall. It is more than a little significant that Exeter, the site of Vespasian's battle against Arviragus in *HRB*, is in Devon. As already noted, the legend says that Vespasian left for Rome after the winter immediately following his encounter with Arviragus, so the battle at Exeter occurred almost at the end of his stay in Britain, which we know lasted from CE 43 to 47. According to *An Introduction to the Roman Legionary Fortress at Exeter* (Exeter Archaeology, 2005), the site was chosen for the new legionary fortress for the Legio II Augusta around 50–55, 'or perhaps a few years earlier'. Thus, the archaeological record is completely consistent with the idea that Vespasian was not just in Devon in general, but the Exeter area in particular during the last year of his British campaign.

One of the only apparent errors in this account, then, is that Vespasian and the Legio II Augusta were already in Britain before they were sent out to deal with Arviragus. They were, after all, the ones who fought at the battles of the Medway and the Thames against Togodumnus. Therefore, the attempted landing at Richborough and the subsequent landing at Totnes must be fictional. What seems to have happened is that records about Vespasian travelling all across the south coast of Britain, from the east to the west, were fumbled into records of him sailing from Richborough in the east to Totnes in the west.

A second error, though it concerns only an incidental remark, is that there is no evidence that the Romans went to Ireland during this time. However, there is both literary and archaeological evidence that the Romans did travel to Ireland under Agricola in the late 70s or 80s. Since Agricola was sent as governor of Britain by Vespasian, who was, at this point, the emperor, it seems that this detail was conflated with the information about Vespasian's earlier activities in Britain.

Geoffrey of Monmouth's book next says that Arviragus became more respectful towards the senate and increased in fame among the Romans, being both loved and feared by them. They are said to have written about him more than any other king in his time. This seems like an exaggeration, but as the text itself highlights, Arviragus was mentioned by the first-century, and therefore contemporary, Roman poet Juvenal; the mention being that Arviragus falling from his British chariot might be the glorious triumph that a certain omen was pointing towards. The poem was satirical, but the point remains the same. Arviragus was important enough to have been used for such an example, and all the way over in Italy, no less. The fact that he was evidently so well known that he *could* be used in such an offhand manner in a satirical poem directed at the emperor, without any introduction or explanation, is testimony to his fame.

Another accurate detail that should not be overlooked is the timing of the poem. It was apparently addressed to Domitian while he was emperor from 81 to 96.[17] The *HRB* includes this quote of Juvenal's in the context of Arviragus becoming famous across Europe, which, in turn, is in the context of him beginning to show respect to the senate and govern his kingdom in peace and tranquillity *when he grew old*. If he was in his twenties when he fought against Claudius and Vespasian in the mid-40s, then he would indeed have been old – though not unrealistically so – in Domitian's reign of 81–96. Thus, the information provided about Arviragus is logical and consistent with the evidence.

In summary, we can see that Geoffrey of Monmouth's account of the Claudian invasion does contain a number of errors, some of which are significant. Nonetheless, the general picture – as well as many specific details – is in line with accepted history. It also contains some remarkable details that seem impossible for Geoffrey of Monmouth to have known about without sources that are now lost to us, such as the presence of the Legio II Augusta in the Exeter area towards the end of Vespasian's stay in Britain. The errors contained in the account are as follows:

1. The invasion being caused by Guiderius (Togodumnus) refusing to pay tribute to the Romans.
2. The Romans besieging Portchester upon landing.
3. Claudius already being in the country when the battle on the Thames took place.
4. The Britons not immediately knowing about Guiderius's death.
5. Arviragus pursuing Lelius from place to place until Southampton.
6. Lelius Hamo (Aulus Plautius) being killed by Arviragus at Southampton.
7. Claudius giving his daughter in marriage to Arviragus.
8. Gloucester being named after Claudius.
9. Gloucester being founded while Claudius was in the country in CE 43.
10. Vespasian not being in Britain since the start of the invasion.
11. The Romans sending men to Ireland during Vespasian's stay in Britain from CE 43–47.

So there are eleven specific errors in Geoffrey of Monmouth's account of the Claudius invasion. This is similar to the number of errors for Julius Caesar's two invasions (ten and twelve, respectively). These errors tend to be more significant than the previous ones, but the general picture remains more or less the same as the picture we perceive from contemporary Roman sources and archaeology.

After the reign of Arviragus, his son Marius is described as succeeding to the throne. During his reign, the book tells us that the following occurred:

A certain king of the Picts, named Rodric, came from Scythia with a great fleet, and arrived in the north part of Britain, which is called Albania, and began to ravage that country. Marius therefore raising an army went in quest of him, and killed him in battle, and gained the victory; for a monument of which he set up a stone in the province, which from his name was afterwards called Westmorland after him ... He gave the conquered people that came with Rodric liberty to inhabit that part of Albania which is called Caithness ... And as they had no wives, they desired to have the daughters and kinswomen of the Britons. But the Britons refused ... Having suffered a repulse here, they sailed over into Ireland, and married the women of that country and by their offspring increased in number.[18]

There is no independent evidence for this event, and naturally the statement that they came from Scythia is viewed as erroneous. Perhaps 'Scotia', a Latin term that was used for Scotland, was misread or misunderstood by a Welsh scribe to mean 'Scythia'. It is almost certain that, Marius allegedly being a supporter of Rome, the origin of this story comes from one of the many real battles that were fought in the north of England and Scotland between the Romans and the Caledonians (the inhabitants of northern Britain). However, this event cannot be tied down to any one particular event, as there were many of these northern battles fought throughout this general time period. Nonetheless, what can be determined is that the *HRB* is almost certainly mistaken in the origin of these enemies of the story, and it is also mistaken in attributing the origin of 'Westmorland' to 'Marius'.

Marius is often considered to be a fictitious king, merely invented by Geoffrey to fill the gap between the Claudian invasion and the activities of Carausius, a later usurper who ruled Britain and Gaul. However, a consideration of his son could reveal that this may well be an incorrect conclusion.

His son is called Coilus in the *Historia Regum Britanniae*. The story goes that he began ruling after his father died, but also that he was brought up from his infancy in Rome and was taught the Roman manners. He was said to have had a firm friendship with the Romans, so much so that 'no king ever showed greater respect to his nobility, not only permitting them to enjoy their own with quiet, but also binding them to him by his continual bounty and munificence'. Other statements to this effect are given, such as him showing no opposition whatsoever to the Romans. Miles Russell makes the suggestion that Coilus was actually the governor of Britain in the late first century, Sallustius Lucullus. It is not difficult to see how Coilus could be a shortening and slight corruption of Lucullus.[19] Inscriptions bearing his name have been found in the Chichester area, one declaring him 'Lucullus son of Amminius'. The only Amminius of the time known to us is the third son of Cunobelinus, who had fled to Rome before the Claudian invasion. Therefore, Miles argues quite sensibly that Sallustius Lucullus was the grandson of Cunobelinus, his father Amminius being Cunobelinus's son of the same name.

Now, this is not a perfect match to the information contained in Geoffrey of Monmouth's book, as Coilus was said to have been the great-grandson of Cunobelinus. However, as we saw in the first chapter of this book, the Welsh records referring to someone as the son of someone else – that is, by the use of the term 'map' or 'ap' – do not necessarily mean it literally. For example, we saw that Galerius was not the son of Diocletian, yet he is still called 'Galerii map Diocletiani' because he succeeded him. So it may very well be the case that Amminius was termed 'ap Arviragus' simply because he succeeded him, despite actually being his brother. 'Marius', therefore, would be a corruption of 'Amminius'; this can mostly be accounted for by oral transmission, such as the dropping of the first syllable and the change from an 'i' to an 'a'. This would result in 'Manius'. The change of an 'n' to an 'r' would most likely be a scribal error, but it may be oral as well. Considering the extent of some of the other changes that we know took place, such as Tasciovanus to Tenvantius, this is not improbable.

Assuming Lucullus was not especially old when he was governor of Britain, and we have no reason to think that he was, then to have ruled in the late 80s and 90s, it is entirely possible that he was born after his father Amminius had fled to the Romans in *c*. 40, or had only recently been born. If we assume he was born *c*. 40, then he would have been in his late forties and fifties when he was ruling as governor, which is a reasonable expectation. If this is the case, then he would indeed have been 'raised in Rome from his infancy' like the Coilus of the legend. So, too, does his excellent relationship with the Romans fit, being appointed the governor of Britain by the Romans themselves.[20] So it could well be that the 'fictitious' King Marius was actually Amminius, and the 'fictitious' King Coilus was actually Lucullus, the governor of Britain.

No other details of Coilus are given by Geoffrey of Monmouth's work, other than that he was succeeded by his only son, Lucius. There is no contemporary evidence for this king, but his first known appearance predates the work of Geoffrey of Monmouth by several hundred years. This was in a sixth-century version of *Liber Pontificalis*, a collection of biographies about the popes. Here he is recorded as having sent a letter to Eleutherius, a pope in the latter half of the second century, requesting conversion. In the twentieth century, a theory came about that the story actually derives from the Christian king Lucius Aelius Megas Abgar IX of Edessa in the second century. However, despite how confidently it is often proposed as the origin of the legend, this is nothing more than a theory, and it is strongly argued against by David J. Knight in *King Lucius of Britain*. In any case, he is not an invention of Geoffrey of Monmouth's.

This concludes our analysis of Book Four of the *Historia Regum Britanniae*.

4

The History of the Kings of Britain: Book Five

Now we shall analyse Book Five of the *Historia Regum Britanniae*, which covers the period from the death of Lucius to the death of Magnus Maximus.

The Conquest of Septimius Severus

The *HRB* continues by claiming that dissensions arose among the Britons after the death of Lucius, which caused the senate to send 'Senator' Severus with two legions to subdue the country again. In reality, the senate could not have made Severus do this, as he was not a senator; he was the emperor. He did, however, travel to Britain, and this was correctly after the death of Lucius in *c.* 188 (see Appendix 2, 'The Thirty-three-year Error').

The text claims that Severus engaged in battle with the Britons as soon as he arrived in Britain. Some of these he was able to 'oblige to surrender to him', while the others were forced to flee from Deira to Albania (that is, Scotland).[1] Deira is roughly equivalent to modern-day North Yorkshire. It is not clear from the Roman accounts whether Severus really did engage with the Britons before quite getting to Scotland, so this passage – which is very brief, in any case – is suspect, but there does not appear to be any definitive reason to consider it fictional.

Immediately after this, Geoffrey describes how the Romans were severely opposed by the Britons under a certain Sulgenius. The commander of the northern Britons is not given a name in the Roman accounts, but we can be sure that he had one. What the contemporary account of Cassius Dio does confirm, however, is the fact that the Romans were indeed severely opposed by these Britons. He explains that there was never any open battle, but rather, the Britons used very effective guerrilla tactics to attack the Romans. He claims that 50,000 Romans died due to this, which is an obvious exaggeration, but it nonetheless agrees with the statement in *HRB* that the Britons frequently killed many of the Romans during this campaign of Severus's.[2]

The account then goes on to say that Septimius Severus built a wall from sea to sea between Deira and Albania. Given the geography, this is clearly Hadrian's Wall and not the Antonine Wall. Of course, we know that it was really Hadrian who had built the wall, and in the previous century. However, many ancient Roman writers held that it was built by Severus, and it is now widely accepted that Severus oversaw extensive repair work on the wall, which is what led to this mistaken belief among the ancient Romans. So, while Geoffrey's *HRB* is incorrect in saying that Severus actually constructed the wall, it is not too far from the truth. And it is interesting to note that Geoffrey did not describe it as a turf rampart, as Bede did, or even mention a rampart at all, as Nennius did. Rather than including this inaccuracy, Geoffrey merely describes it as a wall. Additionally, the *HRB* does not include the very inaccurate figure of 132 miles for the length of the wall, as Nennius did. Taking into consideration the various sources that describe Severus building the wall or rampart, Geoffrey's history is actually one of the least inaccurate.

While we cannot be absolutely certain about when exactly the extensive reconstruction of the wall took place, the sources are virtually all in agreement that the wall was 'built' *after* Severus had fought against the inhabitants of Scotland, not before. Thus, the available information is in agreement with the chronology in the *HRB*. However, the account then says that the wall 'for a long time hindered the approach of the enemy. But Sulgenius, when he was unable to make any longer resistance...' In reality, it seems that Severus had forced the Britons to surrender *before* he returned to the area of Hadrian's Wall and engaged in the repairs. Nonetheless, though the stated cause is inaccurate, the account is correct in associating the building (or repairing) of the wall with a cessation of hostilities between the Romans and the Britons.

Sulgenius is then said to have travelled to Scythia for reinforcements from the Picts. This is generally held to be fictional. It is almost certain that 'Scythia' is a mistake for 'Scotia', meaning either Ireland or Scotland. The fact that it was the Picts whom Sulgenius asked for assistance seems to confirm that this 'Scythia' was Scotland. So rather than travel on a sea voyage with a great fleet to and from Scythia, Sulgenius would merely have travelled around the nearby areas, raising support for a second rebellion against the Romans. From the Roman accounts, we know that the natives did indeed rebel at this time. Cassius Dio tells us that the Maeatae were the ones who 'again revolted', and after the Romans began attacking them in return, the Caledonians joined their revolt.[3] This matches Geoffrey's description: 'Upon this news [of the revolt] being spread through the country, the greatest part of the Britons deserted Severus, and went over to Sulgenius.'

Subsequently, in both the British account and the contemporary Roman account, Severus himself marches up to engage in the battle. One major error in this part of the British account is the fact that the battle is supposedly a siege of York. This cannot have been the case, for Severus was taken away to York after his illness got the better of him during this last campaign. Nevertheless, it is easy to see how such a confusion arose, for the British account goes on to say that Severus was killed in the fighting at York, while, in reality, he did die at York, but this was not where the fighting was taking place.

The *HRB* then goes on to say that Sulgenius was mortally wounded during the fighting; nothing is said of his fate in the Roman accounts. This essentially marks the end of the account of Severus's attempted conquest. One final detail, which is incorrect, is that Severus was buried at York. In reality, his ashes were taken to Rome. Geoffrey's book then states that Severus left two sons – Bassianus and Geta – which is correct. Bassianus was the actual name of Caracalla. However, an inaccuracy is the statement that the two children had different mothers, Bassianus's being British. While Geoffrey certainly did not invent the idea that they had different mothers, the claim that one had a British mother is widely agreed to be false.[4] The text then describes how the Romans made Geta king after Severus's death, but Bassianus was favoured by the Britons. This then led to a battle between them, in which Geta was killed and Bassianus became emperor. The implication is that Bassianus was not yet king before killing his brother, though it does not make this explicit. In reality, Geta and Bassianus became co-rulers after their father's death, and the latter did not kill the former in a battle, but had him assassinated. Whether the Britons really favoured Bassianus or not is unknown. Nevertheless, the essence of the account is correct.

In summary, we can see that this chapter of the *Historia Regum Britanniae* gives a generally accurate account of what really occurred in Britain between CE 208 and 211. There are some errors, but as with the previous sections, most of these are minor. Only a few, such as Sulgenius gathering support from Scythia, are in any way significant errors. Here are the specific errors made by Geoffrey or his source:

1. Septimius Severus being a senator.
2. Severus going to Britain by the orders of the senate.
3. Severus constructing Hadrian's Wall.
4. The wall being the reason for the cessation of hostilities between the Romans and Britons.
5. Sulgenius travelling to Scythia.
6. York being besieged.
7. Severus being killed in battle.
8. Severus being buried at York.
9. Bassianus having a British mother while Geta had a Roman mother.
10. Bassianus killing Geta in a battle.

These are all the errors in the account on Septimius Severus's invasion of Scotland and the aftermath. As can be seen, very few of these errors have any real significance. Arguably, only points 3, 5, 6 and 9 can be classed as 'major' inaccuracies in the account, the rest being largely inconsequential. Thus, the general accuracy of this event is consistent with that found in the previous events.

The Britannic Empire

The next major event in Geoffrey's account of the Roman era, which follows on immediately after describing Bassianus becoming emperor, is the usurpation of the empire by a soldier called Carausius. This account involves what is arguably the greatest historical blunder in Geoffrey's entire record of the Roman era. After describing Bassianus becoming the emperor, the account says that Carausius, 'a young man', was in Britain at that time.[5] In reality, Carausius did not usurp the empire until 286. For him to have been a young man at the time of Severus's death, he would have had to have been about ninety years old when he usurped the empire. Obviously, this is a gross anachronism. Carausius was undoubtedly born long after the rise of Bassianus.

Despite this major error, the rest of the account is largely correct. Geoffrey includes the detail present in more contemporary sources that Carausius was of humble origin. It is often stated that Geoffrey claimed that Carausius was a native Briton; however, in reality, such a claim is nowhere to be found in *HRB*. What the account does say is that Carausius proved his worth to the Romans in many engagements, which allowed him to secure the command of a fleet. This is indeed what happened. It was his conduct during a campaign against rebels in Gaul, at least in part, which led to him being given command of a fleet. Specifically, this was the Classis Britannica, a fleet that operated in the English Channel. Carausius was to protect against barbarian raids, which is exactly what the account in the *HRB* says.

Geoffrey's account says that Carausius then returned to Britain, which may be taken as a mistake, for Carausius was actually based in Bononia (modern-day Boulogne-sur-Mer, France). However, the statement that Carausius returned to Britain with his 'commission sealed' does not necessarily preclude the possibility that he was only in Britain briefly, before then moving more permanently to a base in France. What does appear to be a mistake is the claim that the purpose of Carausius's fleet was to protect the shores of Britain, whereas it was actually to protect the opposite shores – those of Belgica and Armorica.

Carausius is then said to have sailed around 'the whole kingdom', presumably meaning Britain, and heavily plundered the surrounding islands, acquiring great riches for himself. While the last part of this is true – he would allegedly keep some of the plunder for himself, pretending to give all of it to Rome – he fought in the Channel, not in the islands off the coasts of Britain, most of which are in the northern parts. While the plundering and acquiring of wealth does not seem to be exaggerated, this apparently took place in the sea, not on land.

It is unclear whether the description of people flocking to Carausius in the hope of plunder, leading to him acquiring an army – not a fleet – which no neighbouring prince was able to oppose is truthful or not. Contemporary knowledge of Carausius's activities on land is very limited, though obviously he did have the support of the Roman army in Britain, otherwise he would not have been able to withdraw to Britain and proclaim himself emperor there upon being summoned to Rome by Maximian. But we do not know for sure whether this support was based purely on respect or, as Geoffrey claimed, on Carausius's riches.

Having the support of the army, Carausius then decided to make himself the 'king', as Geoffrey terms it. This part of the account is peculiar, for it says that he was granted his request – that is, for the Britons to make him their king – but goes on to say that he *then* attacked Bassianus and took the government of the kingdom. This seems to be a contradiction, for how could Carausius take from Bassianus the government of the kingdom if he had already been made king? There are a number of possible explanations, but the most likely seems to be simply that there was not, at first, universal acknowledgement of Carausius as the king, and it was only after he slew Bassianus that he 'officially' took on the role. But whatever the case, this part of the history is significantly mistaken. Carausius could not have fought against Bassianus – that is, Caracalla – because Bassianus died around seventy years before Carausius proclaimed himself emperor. We do not know what exactly happened in Britain when Carausius retreated there, and it is entirely possible that he did fight and kill a person of significant authority soon after this, presumably with a very similar, if not identical, name; perhaps it was the currently unknown Roman governor who was in charge at the time. However, irrespective of the origin of the error, the Bassianus in question is unambiguously identified as the Bassianus of the previous account, making the *HRB* definitely inaccurate in this regard.

As a minor point, Geoffrey adds the detail that Sulgenius was the brother of Bassianus's 'British' mother. As we saw, Bassianus's mother was the same non-British woman as the mother of his brother, so we can confidently conclude that Sulgenius was not her brother.

The account goes on to say that when news of these events came to Rome, the Romans sent over Allectus with an army to defeat Carausius. It says that he fought and killed Carausius 'no sooner than he had arrived', subsequently making himself the ruler of Britain. In reality, Allectus was already in Britain as Carausius's treasurer, having been one of his supporters, though he did indeed kill him and then take over as the emperor of Britain. Additionally, Carausius's reign lasted for seven years, which is much longer than Geoffrey's account allows for. So while these details are inaccurate, the basic facts involved are correct.

Allectus ruled in Britain for three years. Virtually nothing is known of his reign, but Roman sources say that the Britons welcomed those who defeated Allectus as liberators, which seems to confirm Geoffrey's claim that he oppressed the Britons. However, a clear mistake is the stated reason for this oppression; that is, that Allectus was punishing the Britons for leaving Rome. Further, the account goes on to say that the Britons made a certain Asclepiodotus king in defiance of Allectus. Later, when the former is close to wiping out the remaining troops of the latter, the comment is made that if the rest of the Britons would assist Asclepiodotus, the Romans could finally be completely driven out of Britain. The obvious message behind all of this is that Asclepiodotus was not Roman, nor were his forces, but Allectus and his men were. As we have already considered, Allectus was just as 'British' and disconnected from Rome as Carausius had been. And in reality, Asclepiodotus was sent by the Romans to deal with the rebel Allectus – he was not the duke of Cornwall, as Geoffrey calls him, though he was well received by the native Britons. But regardless of how enthusiastically the natives may have received him, he was definitely the leader of Roman troops, and Allectus was definitely not representative of Rome, as he is portrayed in Geoffrey's history. In fact, what we have here is perhaps the only example of a complete role reversal in the entire *Historia Regum Britanniae*.

To return to the narrative itself, we are told that when Asclepiodotus began marching against Allectus, the latter was in London, celebrating a feast to the gods. This is impossible to confirm, but the account goes on to describe how, upon hearing that Asclepiodotus was coming, Allectus marched towards him and engaged him in battle. 'But Asclepiodotus had the advantage, and dispersed and put to flight Allectus's troops, and in the pursuit killed many thousands, as also king Allectus himself.'[6]

This is exactly what happened. The readers are then told that a certain Livius Gallus, along with all the rest of the Romans (as Allectus's forces are portrayed by Geoffrey), positioned themselves in the city of London. Asclepiodotus besieged him there, during which siege he called on all the dukes of Britain to come and support him. After the various British nations arrive, the city is successfully besieged and many of the Romans are slaughtered, leading to their desperate surrender. Asclepiodotus accepts this, but the men of Gwynedd take it upon themselves to massacre the remaining Romans. They behead them and then throw the heads into the stream now known as the Walbrook, though the account says that it was named Nantgallim, after Livius Gallus.[7]

This is quite accurate, though Asclepiodotus was not the one who led the force that defeated the remaining part of Allectus's army. In reality, those who defeated the remaining part of Allectus's army were merely a group that had been separated from the main force during the crossing of the Channel. There is no evidence that there was a prolonged siege, though the brevity of the contemporary Roman account that describes these events makes it difficult to say one way or the other. For the same reason, it cannot be said with certainty that native Britons from afar did not come to the aid of the invading Romans; the same source does claim that the Britons welcomed them as liberators, which suggests that they were willing to help.[8] Even so, it seems exceedingly improbable that Britons from as far away as North Wales and Scotland, as claimed in the *HRB*, could possibly have arrived within a reasonable time. In any case, the massacre of Allectus's army is credited to the Romans, not the Britons. And taking into account the fact that it is only the part of the army separated from the rest that is credited with the defeat of Allectus's remaining forces, it seems most unlikely that there was any sort of prolonged siege – surely the rest of the invading army would have had the time to come and assist in the defeat if there had been a prolonged siege.

Exactly what happened to the bodies of those slain is not revealed in any Roman account. In 1988, however, thirty-nine skulls were discovered in the Walbrook along with virtually no other bones. For archaeological reasons, this particular group has been dated to the mid-second century, but this is not the only group of skulls that has been discovered in the Walbrook. Many others have been found since the 1860s, which do not seem to have been dated. In all likelihood, throwing heads into the Walbrook was not an idea that the victors at London spontaneously acquired. Rather, it is probable that it was an established practice, hence the earlier hoard of skulls found in 1988.⁹

But whether it transpires that the skulls discovered in the nineteenth century are from the correct time period or not, there is nothing about Geoffrey's statement that is unbelievable. Regarding the last detail of this account, the true etymology of 'Walbrook', or 'Nantgallim', is simply unknown. And unlike Geoffrey's earlier statement regarding Gloucester, there is nothing about this claim that is particularly unlikely.

It is apparent that this account of the Britannic Empire once again provides a generally accurate picture of real history. However, as with the rest of the *Historia Regum Britanniae* considered so far, there are numerous mistakes in the details. Furthermore, this account contains a much larger error than any one previously considered – the completely anachronistic involvement of Bassianus, or Caracalla, in the story. The historical inaccuracies are as follows:

1. Carausius being a young man in Britain during the time of Bassianus the son of Severus.
2. His commission being to protect the shores of Britain.
3. Carausius engaging in battles outside the Channel.
4. The battles occurring on land.
5. Bassianus the son of Severus being slain by Carausius.
6. Sulgenius being the brother of Bassianus's mother.

7. Allectus being sent over by the Romans to deal with Carausius.
8. Carausius's reign only lasting a very short time.
9. The allegiances of Allectus and Asclepiodotus.
10. Asclepiodotus being the one who defeated the remaining part of Allectus's forces.
11. There being a long siege of London.
12. Britons from North Wales, Scotland and Deira assisting in the siege of London.

From the above list, we can see that there is a very similar number of errors in this account as there were in the previous accounts considered. However, errors 1, 5 and 9 are by far the largest mistakes encountered as yet in this consideration of *HRB*. These can probably be regarded as some of the outer limits of the boundaries of accuracy in Geoffrey's work, which will be particularly useful when analysing theories of Arthur's European campaign in the next chapter.

The Dynasty of Constantine

This next account immediately begins with the following historical error: 'The Romans being thus defeated...'[10]

As in the previous section, this account presents matters as if Allectus represented the Romans and his defeat was the Britons taking back their island for themselves, when in reality the opposite is closer to the truth. That being the case, this error is simply a continuation of the historical scenario as already described by Geoffrey of Monmouth, and therefore cannot be included as an additional error in the *HRB*, as it has already been counted.

We now come to what is arguably the largest deviation from known history in the entire Roman section of the *Historia Regum Britanniae*. This is not just a mistake, some major blunder in a description of an event that essentially really took place. This is a completely fictitious reign. The account claims: 'Asclepiodotus, with the consent of the people, placed the crown upon his own head, and governed the country in justice and peace ten years.'

This did not happen. There is no evidence at all that Asclepiodotus ever ruled Britain in any way. When he defeated Allectus in 296, he was merely one of the military commanders who served under Emperor Constantius. It should more properly be referred to as Constantius's invasion, though evidently Geoffrey's source did not include any mention of Constantius, attributing the entire event to Asclepiodotus. According to the *HRB*, the former only arrived and took over control of Britain after the end of the ten-year reign of the latter, with the very brief reign of a certain Coel separating the two.

It is unclear what exactly effected this major error. One possibility is that it arose due to a misreading of Bede's account, which states the following: 'The usurper [Allectus], having thus got the island from Carausius, held it three years, and was then vanquished by Asclepiodotus, the captain of the praetorian bands, who thus at the end of ten years restored Britain to the Roman empire.'[11]

In reality, this line is referring to the fact that the combined length of Carausius's usurpation and Allectus's continuance of it was ten years. Thus, when Asclepiodotus defeated the reigning usurper, Allectus, and restored it to Rome, it had been out of the empire for ten years. It does not mean that Asclepiodotus, after defeating Allectus, subsequently ruled for ten years before handing it over to Rome, but it may plausibly have been interpreted as such. However, an issue with this explanation is the fact that Bede's account says that Asclepiodotus 'handed over' the kingdom to the Romans, which is not what happens in Geoffrey's account. On the other hand, it is entirely possible that Geoffrey's source did not directly come from Bede, and that there were several intermediatory sources with more ambiguous wording, allowing this error to eventually develop.

There is an alternative possibility. It is self-evident that Geoffrey's source was not aware of Constantius's involvement in Allectus's defeat. The emperor is not mentioned anywhere until after Coel's brief rule. It is only Asclepiodotus who is mentioned in the account of Allectus's defeat, with the full implication that he was leading the invasion. This being the case, it is within reason to think that a source may have mentioned only Asclepiodotus arriving in Britain and defeating Allectus, and then had a record of Constantius coming to Britain roughly ten years later and fighting in Caledonia, which he did in 305. A chronicler who used such a source may well have assumed that Asclepiodotus had control of Britain for that period, with nothing to suggest otherwise. Therefore, Constantius's eleven-year reign was mistakenly described as having started after what was actually his *second* incursion into Britain. This explains the fact that the *HRB* describes the Diocletian persecution, which took place within the ten years after Allectus's defeat, as occurring during Asclepiodotus's reign rather than Constantius's reign. This latter explanation seems more likely to be correct, but in any case, the error is there nonetheless.

There does not appear to be any definite historical inaccuracies in the description of Diocletian's persecution of Christians, though few definite claims can be made about it because there are not many contemporary sources that describe the relevant events in Britain at this time.

The claim that 'King Coel' killed Asclepiodotus is possibly false, though we do not know what happened to him after the Romans recovered Britain. Perhaps he did stay in Britain as a military commander and was killed by a local ruler shortly before Constantius arrived in 305. In any case, it is certainly incorrect to say that Coel took the crown – that is, the rulership of Britain – after killing Asclepiodotus, for it was historically still under the control of Constantius. Even so, Constantius did arrive in Britain and make war on the Picts in 305. In the *HRB*, when he arrives in Britain, Coel – based in the south-east of Britain – immediately becomes fearful and sends ambassadors to offer terms of peace. The terms are that Coel would have the kingdom of Britain but would pay the standard tribute to Rome. These terms were granted, but then a month later Coel died and the kingdom went to Constantius.

Once again, the historical reality is that Britain was under the rule of Constantius for the entire period of 296–306. Coel may well have been a governor of part of Roman Britain, but even if that was the case, it cannot be said that he ever possessed Britain independently of Constantius. Therefore, Constantius taking over the rulership of Britain from Coel must be regarded as a fictional event.

The following event is a marriage between Constantius and Helena, a daughter of Coel. Constantius did have a wife called Helena, but according to much earlier Roman sources, she was a native of Asia Minor, not Britain. Additionally, Constantius was married to her long before his arrival in Britain, and had in fact been divorced from her for some time before heading to Britain. It might be argued that a completely different Helena is meant, but regardless of the unlikelihood of such a coincidence, that the same woman is intended in the account is shown by the fact that she is made the mother of Constantius's son Constantine, which fact the earlier records apply to the historical Helena of Asia Minor. Therefore, we have the error that Helena was with Constantius at this time in addition to the error that she was a native Briton. The description of Constantine being born during his father's reign in Britain cannot really be classed as its own inaccuracy, as it is just another manifestation of the aforementioned error of having Helena marry Constantius in Britain.

Geoffrey's account then tells us that after eleven years had passed, Constantius died and left the kingdom to his son Constantine. As noted earlier, the account contains the mistake that the full amount of time Constantius had control of Britain – that is, from 296 to 306, or parts of eleven years – was considered to have started from the *second* occasion he visited Britain, which was in 305. So in reality, just one year passed from the arrival of Constantius that is spoken of by Geoffrey and his death. However, the account is correct in saying that Constantius bestowed the kingdom upon his son Constantine. This new ruler is accurately described as attaining great fame and glory.

We next come to the war between Constantine and the Roman ruler Maxentius. Maxentius is described as being in Rome, which is true, and he is said to have 'oppressed the commonwealth with his grievous tyranny', which is largely subjective but is at least how he was presented after his death.[12] The Roman historians in Constantine's reign and afterward tell us that he severely oppressed the common people, taxing them highly and even ordering a massacre of his citizens. Geoffrey writes that Maxentius 'made it his endeavour to confiscate the estates of all the best of the nobility'. Indeed, the contemporary historian Eusebius claims that Maxentius had innumerable senators killed to seize their estates.

In the *HRB*, it is while Constantine is in Britain that he is encouraged to wage war against Maxentius. This too seems to be accurate, for there is evidence that Constantine was in Britain in 310, shortly before he started acquiring troops from several countries in 311 in preparation for the attack on Maxentius.[13] Constantine then proceeded exactly as Geoffrey wrote: 'Constantine ... made an expedition to Rome, and reduced it under his power, and afterwards obtained the empire of the whole world.'[14]

At this, Geoffrey claims that Constantine brought Helena's three uncles with him on this expedition. There is no clear evidence for this either way, but given that Helena was born around 250, or a few years earlier, it is very unlikely that her uncles would be serving as generals in 312. Even if they were very late siblings of her father or mother and were born at around the same time as her, they would have been in their sixties; more likely, though, they would have been in their eighties. Constantine may have had generals named Leolin, Trahern and Marius, but they were very probably not the uncles of Empress Helena. This is a similar mistake to the earlier claim that Sulgenius, the Pictish enemy of Septimius Severus, was the brother of Bassianus's 'British' mother. It is a false familial connection.

While Constantine is defeating Maxentius and 'obtaining the empire of the whole world,' a character called Octavius is introduced. He is said to be the duke of the Gewissei, a term that is rather elusive, but seems to denote the people living somewhere around what is present-day Gloucestershire or Whiltshire.[15] In the Welsh versions of the *HRB*, Octavius is called the earl of Ergyng and Ewias. This would denote a similar area, but more onto the other side of the Severn, where Gwrgan Fawr ruled in the sixth century. Geoffrey tells us that this Octavius rebelled against the Romans, killing the proconsuls and taking the throne.

There is no known contemporary text that clearly describes this specific event. However, that is not to say that there is no evidence of it. In fact, we know from the most contemporary of records – coinage evidence – that Constantine returned to Britain in around 314.[16] Eusebius records Constantine campaigning against the Britons, though it is unclear when exactly these campaigns took place. It has been suggested that they occurred in 311 when he was gathering troops to fight against Maxentius, though it has also been suggested that they refer to his subsequent arrival, in 314.[17] There is no way to know for sure, but what we do know is that in 315 he assumed the title 'Britannicus Maximus', which means 'the great victor in Britain'. This would strongly suggest that Constantine had come to Britain for a campaign, and that this campaign was successful.[18] This is so regardless of whether Eusebius's comments refer to this 314 arrival or not.

So how does this relate to the story of Octavius? Geoffrey tells us that Constantine sent Trahern to deal with the uprising of Octavius, which initially involved him retaking one of the cities in Britain. After this news had spread over 'the whole country', Octavius gathered his forces and went out to battle Trahern near Winchester. This battle was a victory for Octavius, causing Trahern to retire to his ships and then go to Scotland and cause 'great destruction' there, presumably referring to an attempt to bring the people back under Roman control. Octavius then travelled up the country and met Trahern in Westmorland, just below the Scottish border. This time, the battle went in favour of Trahern, causing Octavius to flee. Trahern pursued him and 'disposed him both of his cities and crown'. Octavius is then said to have sailed over to Norway to obtain assistance from a certain 'King Gombert', or Gunbert.

Needless to say, if Constantine did return to Britain in 314 by reason of an uprising, it did not start the moment he arrived. It would have begun some time prior to his arrival. In fact, the coins that proclaimed this upcoming arrival of Emperor Constantine started being minted in mid-313, showing that whatever it was that made him decide to visit had to have been something that had begun prior to this time.[19] This evidence is precisely in agreement with the account provided by Geoffrey of Monmouth. There is nothing unlikely about an uprising taking place while Constantine was going to war with Maxentius, and if it did, then logically Constantine would have sent someone else to deal with it, as he was occupied with his own troubles at the time. This was in 312. The war against Maxentius began in the spring and ended in the autumn. Octavius's uprising would have happened somewhere within this range.

From this starting range, we then need to allow time for news of the uprising to travel to Constantine, one of his generals to travel to Britain, the aforementioned events involving Trahern and Octavius in the south of Britain to take place, and then news of Trahern's defeat returning to Constantine. It would only have been after that point, when the general whom he had sent to deal with the situation had failed, that Constantine would have made the decision to deal with the rebellion himself. News of this intent would then have had to have travelled back to Britain for London to mint the coins proclaiming the upcoming arrival of the emperor. These events would comfortably cover the period between mid-312 to mid-313, which is when the coins started to be minted. The emperor then arrived in the first half of 314 and evidently took part in some campaign that resulted in him acquiring the title 'Britannicus Maximus' the next year, indicating a victory against the rebellion. This agrees with Geoffrey's description of Octavius's defeat at the hands of the Romans in the second half of the account.

Whether Octavius really did then travel to Norway or not shall be discussed shortly. For now, we can see that there is no reason to doubt, but every reason to believe, the account of Octavius's rebellion as described by Geoffrey of Monmouth.

In general, this section is similar to the previous one. There are fewer mistakes than in the earlier sections, but the mistakes it does possess are generally more significant than previously. The following is a list of all the errors in the account:

1. Asclepiodotus ruling Britain for ten years.
2. Coel taking over control of Britain.
3. Constantius taking over rulership of Britain from Coel.
4. Helena being the daughter of Coel.
5. Constantius marrying Helena in Britain.
6. Constantius dying eleven years after what was actually his second arrival in Britain.
7. Three uncles of Helena going with Constantine in his war against Maxentius.

It can also be seen that the majority of these errors would be classed as significant if found in any of the previous lists. This is unusual; evidently the source for this period was particularly unreliable for whatever reason.

Before we move on to the next section, we need to consider the later part of Octavius's career as told by Geoffrey of Monmouth and other sources. As with the legendary kings Marius and Coel, there is a theory as to the identity of Octavius. However, as it is a theory, and it may be that an alternative scenario is correct, it would be impossible to say exactly what is or is not accurate in the next part of Geoffrey's account. Yet it is at least worth considering as a possible explanation of the story.

Michael Walsh, researcher of British and Irish history, has suggested that Octavius was identical to an individual known to Irish history as Eochu. Consider the fact that 'Octavius' is actually Geoffrey's attempt at Latinising the Welsh name 'Eudaf', as it is spelt in *Brut Tysilio*. Immediately, it can be seen that Eudaf and Eochu are reasonably similar names. As 'Eochu' is a name that occurs several times through the Irish dynasties and was evidently a bona fide Irish name, it is plausible that the Irish chroniclers simply used the closest approximation to the foreign king's name. Furthermore, Eudaf held the epithet 'Hen', meaning 'the Old', while in the Irish records, Eochu is given the title 'Liathain', meaning 'the Grey'. So as well as having similar names, they also had similar epithets, and they both lived in the fifth century.

It must be admitted that this on its own would be quite a weak case. However, Geoffrey tells us that Eudaf Hen (or Octavius, as he calls him), had a nephew named Conan Meriadoc. Eochu, for his part, had a nephew named Crimthann Mor. These two names are not very similar, but Crimthann means 'fox', and Mor means 'the great', so this could just be a title. It is significant to note that in *The Dream of Maxen Wledig*, a Welsh tale about certain events in fifth-century Britain, this Conan – or Kynan, as his name is spelt there – is described as being 'auburn-haired'. This being the case, it is easy to see why he would have acquired the title of 'fox', or 'Crimthann' in Irish. But more significantly than that, there is a tradition recorded in the nineteenth century that Crimthann was buried in a spot called Ballykinnane, which translates to 'the place of Kinnane'. Given the plausibility of such a place being named after the person who was buried there, this may reasonably be taken as evidence that the real name of Crimthann was, in fact, Kinnane, or Kynan.

There is also evidence that Crimthann was more similar to Conan Meriadoc than in just name and description. The *Sanas Cormaic* claims that Crimthann was the king of all Ireland and Britain, yet it specifically mentions a fort in Cornwall. This is significant, for Conan was supposedly the heir to the throne of Britain next to Elen – and Elen became a Roman empress and moved out of Britain, so Conan should logically have become the high ruler of Britain. In fact, the *Jesus College MS 20* explicitly tells us that Conan became king after Maximus, Elen's husband, became the emperor of Rome, so this fits the evidence perfectly. Furthermore, Crimthann is said to have sailed to and subjugated part of Scotland, as well as gained territory in Gaul.[20] This matches the story of Conan, in which he sailed to Scotland and based himself there after becoming enraged at Maximus. Later, however, he travels with Maximus and helps him to conquer Gaul, being granted the area of Brittany to rule. At the same time, his descendants are recorded as the rulers of both Brittany and Dumnonia (which encompasses Cornwall, the area in which Crimthann's fort was said to be).

It must be admitted that there are some remarkable similarities involved in these individuals. Eochu Liathain and Eudaf Hen were contemporary, powerful kings, and were both known for being either old or grey. They both had a nephew who is recorded as becoming the high king of Britain, both of whom, it seems, were based in Cornwall. These contemporary high kings of Britain, both ruling from Cornwall at around the same time, both subjugated part of Scotland and fought and gained territory in Gaul. When this evidence is considered in conjunction with the fact that Conan was recorded as having auburn-coloured hair, while 'Crimthann' means 'fox', in addition to the gravesite evidence that Crimthann may well have had the birth name 'Conan', it must be admitted that the case is a convincing one.

If we conclude that Michael Walsh is correct in his identifications, does this really require Geoffrey to have been wrong when he wrote about them as British kings? Well, we must remember that, according to the story as recounted by Geoffrey of Monmouth, Octavius sailed away to Norway after being defeated by Trahern. Could this have been a mistake for

Ireland? Is there a plausible error, or series of errors, that could have changed 'Ireland' into 'Norway'?

Consider the following. One of the Latin names for Ireland was 'Scotia', meaning 'the land of the Scoti'. Starting in the early medieval period, the Scots (that is, the ancient inhabitants of Ireland) invaded and settled much of the north of Britain. This led to the term 'Scotia' being used for the Gaelic-speaking part of what is now Scotland; this became the case at least as early as the eleventh century. And as the designation was definitely ethnic, not geographic, then the fact that the Scots started inhabiting Scotland centuries prior to the eleventh century means that it is quite possible the term 'Scotia' was actually used for Scotland long before that. So if Octavius's destination was recorded as 'Scotia', then it is very reasonable to suppose that a later chronicler may have misunderstood this to be Scotland, rather than Ireland.

But could Scotland have plausibly become Norway? Surprisingly, the fact is that Welsh writers sometimes used the same word to refer to both locations. The Welsh word for Scandinavia was 'Llychlyn'.[21] But this was also used on occasion for Scotland, or parts of Scotland. It is used in this latter sense throughout *Brut Tysilio*. However, in that very same work, the word 'Llychlyn' is paired with 'Dennmark' several times. In these instances, the corresponding word appears as 'Norway' in Geoffrey's *HRB*. Therefore, it is a perfectly reasonable conjecture that Geoffrey simply misunderstood this instance of 'Llychlyn' to be Norway rather than Scotland, as he seems to have done on other occasions in his work.

In short, the change from Ireland to Norway could have resulted from a few very understandable steps. Firstly, Octavius's destination – Ireland – was written in a Latin text as 'Scotia'. Then, a Welsh writer understood this to be Scotland and therefore translated it using the Welsh word 'Llychlyn'. Geoffrey, who did claim to be translating from a Welsh book, took this to be 'Norway', as it does sometimes mean. Thus, Ireland was transformed into Norway.

That this is the correct understanding is indicated by the fact that the Welsh *Brut Tysilio* does in fact use the word 'Llychlyn' in the place of 'Norway' in this passage; furthermore, the passage explicitly terms

Gunbert, the king of Octavius's destination, 'the king of Prydyn', this latter word being a word specifically meaning Scotland. Therefore, the location is explicitly identified as Scotland, not Norway. It is thus clear that Geoffrey did mistranslate 'Llychlyn' in his source as 'Norway', when in reality it was intended to mean 'Scotland'. Therefore, it is only the first step in the suggested explanation – the confusion between Ireland and Scotland due to their common name 'Scotia' – which does not seem to have any direct support. Nonetheless, there is nothing implausible about this first step.

In the Irish records, Eochu is recorded as 'mac Dáire Cerbba' – that is, the son of Dáire Cerbba. However, this may simply be due to his having succeeded the king, without him necessarily being Cerbba's actual son. Perhaps Geoffrey's 'Gunbert', or 'Gombert', is a corruption of 'Cerbba'. The fact that Geoffrey's account specifically describes Eudaf as living in Britain when he was evidently very young – during 312 at the latest – while the Irish accounts do not seem to make a similar claim regarding Eochu and Ireland would suggest that the king did, in fact, live in Britain initially. His voyage away from Britain, as described by Geoffrey of Monmouth, would then have been how he ended up in the Irish records as a ruler of Ireland.

But how does this relate to the rest of Geoffrey's account? We are told that Eudaf encouraged his men to look for an opportunity to kill Trahern. After this had been successfully carried out and the news was taken to Eudaf, he returned to Britain, 'dispersed the Romans, and recovered the throne'. Then, significantly, we are told that he ruled the kingdom until the time of Gratian and Valentinian.

It is not entirely clear what is meant by 'the time of Gratian and Valentinian'. It might mean the co-rulership of Gratian and Valentinian II, which started in 375. Alternatively, it could mean the co-rulership of Gratian and his father, Valentinian I, which began in 367. Peter Bartrum accepted this latter understanding.[22] This being the case, we are being asked to accept that this British figure expelled the Romans and had control of Britain until, most likely, 367, starting from some point after 314. This seems like a ludicrous idea, as such an event would surely have been recorded in the Roman histories.

Geoffrey claims that the death of Trahern occurred not long after Eudaf's escape to Norway. However, he may have been wrong about this. Such a detail is not included in the *Brut Tysilio*, though it does say that the person who killed Trahern did so 'quickly'. A full reading of the line makes it clear that 'quickly' here is just referring to the actual act of killing, though, perhaps, if his Welsh source was sufficiently similar to the *Brut Tysilio*, Geoffrey saw this detail but misunderstood it. We also know that shortening the duration of events is within the *HRB*'s boundaries of accuracy; for example, the account of Carausius's reign claims that the Romans sent over Allectus as soon as news came to them of Carausius's uprising. It then says that Allectus killed Carausius 'no sooner than he had arrived'. This would mean that Carausius's reign was almost non-existent, whereas, in reality, we know that he ruled for seven years. Therefore, it is not unreasonable to speculate that Geoffrey made a similar error on this occasion, exaggerating how quickly the events transpired.

If we are granted the possibility that, in reality, a much longer period of time may have passed between Eudaf's defeat at the hands of Trahern and his repossession of Britain, and if we accept the identification of Eudaf as Eochu, a king of Ireland, then the reality of Geoffrey's account becomes self-apparent.

From Ammianus Marcellinus, a fourth-century Roman historian, we know that there were serious issues in Britain in the 360s. He tells us that in 360 the regions near the borders of the Roman territory were being devastated by attacks from the Picts and the Scots. A general named Lupicinus was sent to deal with the issue, though there is no record of what came of that attempt. Marcellinus then describes the Picts, Scots, Saxons and Attacotti as attacking Britain in the context of writing about the first year of Valentinian and Valens' joint reign – that is, 364 – but it has been suggested that this is simply a reference to an event described later.[23] However, the fact that the Saxons are mentioned as attacking Britain in this passage, whereas they do not feature in the later account (from the same writer, no less), throws this conclusion into doubt.

In any case, we know from Ammianus that by 367, Britain, from the southern coast to the northern border, had been overrun by 'barbarians' – that is, the Picts, Scots and Attacotti. A 'count of the seacoast region' named Nectaridus had been killed and another Roman, Fullofaudes, had been taken prisoner. News of this situation reached Valentinian in the summer of 367, and it was not resolved until well over a year later.[24] As has been mentioned, Gratian and Valentinian I began their joint reign in 367. Specifically, it began in the August of that year, towards the end of the summer. Thus, the takeover of Roman Britain by barbarian tribes began at least a little before Gratian and Valentinian's joint rule. Potentially, it may have begun in the north quite a while before, and only reached the south coast shortly before the news was delivered to Valentinian. Perhaps it was only when Nectaridus, on the south coast, was killed that the Romans decided the situation was severe enough to send word to their emperor. In any case, we can be confident that the situation started before Gratian and Valentinian's joint rule.

Ammianus refers to the event as a 'barbarian conspiracy', implying that it was an organised effort to overrun Britain. He does not tell us which tribe was at the head of the conspiracy, but we are confronted with the distinct possibility that it was the Scots (the Irish), with Eochu, or Eudaf, as the architect of the attacks. This being the case, Eudaf 'possessing the kingdom until the reign of Gratian and Valentinian' would simply be a reference to the Scots and others taking over Roman Britain from mid-367, if not a few years before, until late 367 or 368, partway into the joint reign of those two emperors.[25]

The Usurpation of Magnus Maximus

Now we arrive at a description of an event that is very well known to history – the usurpation of Magnus Maximus. Magnus Maximus was a general in the Roman army who was closely associated with Emperor Theodosius's family. He was a commander in Britain for several years, before being declared emperor by his army.

However, there is an apparent inconsistency at this point. Geoffrey tells us that Eudaf (or, Octavius) was 'at last, in his old age, willing to settle the government'.[26] He then arranged proceedings that resulted in Maximus being summoned over to Britain to marry his daughter and heir. The issue is that, historically, Maximus probably came to Britain in around 380. This was long after the quashing of the barbarian conspiracy. So how could Octavius still be in power?

Well, consider how the account is worded: '[Octavius] possessed the kingdom until the reign of Gratian and Valentinian. At last, in his old age, being willing to settle the government.'

Or, according to Thorpe's translation: 'He held the kingship of Britain in great content from that moment onwards until the days of Gracianus and Valentinianus. Years later, weakened now by old age, Octavius decided to make provision for his people.'

The way the second statement commences could easily imply that the following part of the story is actually meant to take place long *after* the end of his possession of the kingdom. In other words the 'government', which Octavius began making plans to settle, requiring him to invite Maximus to Britain to marry his daughter, was not the entire 'kingdom' of Britain, which he had lost years previously. Rather, we can imagine that it was some local area of Wales, neglected by the Romans. According to Nennius, the Uí Liatháin – Eochu Liathán's tribe – settled in the south-west corner of Wales some time before Cunedda drove the Irish out of the country in the first half of the fifth century. It is not impossible that the Irish, under the British king Eudaf, really did manage to maintain a foothold in this distant part of the country even after the barbarian conspiracy had ended. Perhaps it was even a case of the Romans allowing them to remain there as a friendly, quasi-independent tribe. That the Irish had at least some control over parts of the west of Britain before the Roman era had ended is claimed not only by the British sources but also by the independent Irish sources.

While it is possible that this is the reality behind the claim, later details of Geoffrey's account make it clear that Octavius is supposed to still possess the entirety of Britain (these details will be discussed when we come to them). Therefore, it is evident that Geoffrey's account does, strictly, make the claim that Octavius held the government of Britain from before the time of Gratian and Valentinian right up until he handed it over to Maximus. This, obviously, is a major error, though we can see that there are reasonable causes of it. Octavius may well have continued ruling in a small part of the country.

In any case, we can safely discount the claim that Maximus went to Britain because he had been invited there by a local chieftain. Nonetheless, it is entirely possible that Octavius and his people really were struggling to settle the issue of succession. The idea that they would have *wanted* to invite Maximus specifically is also possible. He was a powerful general in the service of Theodosius the Elder and had come to Britain with him to deal with the barbarian conspiracy in 367 or 368, so the natives may well have known of him. In fact, if the conclusion that Octavius was the leader of the conspiracy is correct, then it is definitely within reason to think that Octavius and his men knew of him. And if the Romans did subsequently permit Octavius to have some degree of control over south-west Wales, then we must conclude that they ended on reasonably peaceful terms. Therefore, the recommendation by Caradocus of Cornwall to invite Maximus is not totally implausible.[27]

An inaccuracy in the account is the fact that Maximus is referred to as a senator, whereas he was actually a military general. Next, in describing Maximus's worthiness as a husband to Octavius's heir, it is claimed that Leolin, one of Helena's three uncles mentioned earlier, was the father of Maximus. We have already addressed the point that any uncle of the real-life Helena would have most likely been in their eighties by 312, though perhaps in their sixties at a stretch. As Maximus's birth is generally placed in the mid-330s, this would require Leolin to have been in his eighties at best when he fathered him, though more likely he would have been over 100 years of age.

On the other hand, if we take the view that Leolin was unrelated to Helena but was still a brother of Coel, the tentative governor or possible rebellious tribal leader who was met by Constantius in 305, then the chronology is more realistic. If Coel was about thirty years old in this year, then a younger brother might have been born in *c.* 280 or so. He may have been significantly younger, though if he went with Constantine to fight against Maxentius in 312, then he is unlikely to have been born later than *c.* 290, as this would make him twenty-two in 312. If this is the case, then this would mean that he was probably in his mid-forties at the time of Maximus's birth. This would be an unlikely age to father a child, though it is by no means impossible.

Pacatus's panegyric of Theodosius, composed just one year after Maximus was killed, mentions that Maximus boasted of his kinship with the emperor. Other early information about Maximus shows that he was from a Spanish household, which is consistent with this claim. If the Coel whom Constantius encountered was, in fact, the governor of Britain, or had some similar office, then it is quite reasonable that a person of this rank may have been a member of the Theodosian dynasty. We cannot say for certain either way. Thus, this claim that Maximus was the son of Leolin the brother of Coel will not be counted as an error. Of course, we have already established and counted the error that Coel, Leolin and Trahern were brothers of Helena, the wife of Constantius.

The account in the *HRB* then goes on to describe Mauricius, the son of Caradocus, being sent to Rome to invite Maximus to Britain. As already noted, this is certainly a mistake. Or at least, the idea that any invitation sent over by a quasi-independent tribe in Wales could have had any effect on Maximus's assigned position in the Roman Empire is certainly an error.

An interesting detail at this point that the account gets right is the remark that there was, at this time, 'a great contest between Maximian [Maximus] and the two emperors, Gratian and Valentinian, on account of his being refused the third part of the empire, which he demanded'. There is no reason to take this 'contest' to refer to actual fighting; the next line refers to Maximus being 'ill-treated' by the emperors. It may simply refer to strong contentions between the men. In this case, Geoffrey gets this exactly right, as Zosimus, a writer of the late fifth century, tells us the following: '[Maximus] was offended that Theodosius should be thought worthy of being made emperor, while he himself had no honourable employment. He therefore cherished the animosity of the soldiers towards the emperor.'[28]

Theodosius was made the effective eastern emperor in 379 by Gratian, while Gratian and Valentinian had already been ruling as co-emperors of the Western Roman Empire since 375. Theodosius, then, had received the 'third part of the empire' in 379, which was shortly before Maximus was assigned to Britain. Furthermore, according to Zosimus, Maximus was offended by this – and this is self-evidently not something that he kept to himself, as Zosimus was able to write about it. Therefore, Geoffrey's description of contentions between Maximus and the two western emperors due to Maximus not receiving the third part of the empire is perfectly correct.

The account then goes on to say that Maximus left for Britain. However, on the way, it says that he subdued the cities of the Franks, amassed a great quantity of silver and gold, and 'raised men for his service in all parts'. There is no record of this, though there does not seem to be any record of Maximus's whereabouts at all during the time immediately prior to his appointment in Britain. It is possible that Maximus served as a military commander in Gaul during this time, but there does not appear to be any record of a rebellion that needed to be dealt with then. And even if this was the case, the idea that he amassed a great treasure for himself by subduing these Frankish cities would not be consistent with his position as a military commander (unless he was keeping treasure illegally, like Carausius). Such a conclusion would also force us to accept the statement that this happened 'on his way to Britain' as an error.

On balance, the most probable explanation would appear to be that this is a misplaced record of Maximus's 383 invasion of Gaul. The information in the statement accords very well with this later event, aside from the chronological placement within Maximus's career.

The entire remainder of this section presents a semi-plausible account of Maximus's arrival in Britain. Geoffrey says that Octavius's men were frightened that this was a hostile invasion, so they 'raised all the forces of the kingdom' and went out to meet the landing party. Maximus was not prepared to deal with such a force. So, after discussing the issue with some councillors, he and his men approached Octavius's men (led by Conan Meriadoc, the nephew of the king) and insisted that they came in peace, merely being 'sent by the emperors upon an embassy to Octavius'. Eventually, this was accepted and Maximus was brought to London to meet Octavius. After a speech by Caradocus of Cornwall, arguing for Maximus to become Octavius's heir by marrying his daughter (in which speech he repeats a number of errors already noted), the king accepted. Thus, Octavius's people came to be 'under the protection of the Roman state'.

It must be remembered that there is absolutely no contemporary account of Maximus's arrival in Britain – we do not even know for sure in which year he was appointed there – so we can only try and deduce how accurate this account is.

Firstly, the claim that Octavius viewed the arrival of Magnus Maximus as a hostile invasion is not unlikely. In fact, if there really was a sizable group of settled Hiberno-Britons acting independently in Wales to which the Romans had turned a blind eye for an extended period of time, it is quite possible that Maximus was specifically told to deal with this issue when he was to be made governor of Britain. However, we must question the claim that Octavius sent an army to confront Maximus. If Octavius, historically, only had control over part of Wales, then would he really have marched an army through the Roman-controlled areas to confront the person he expected was sent to put an end to his rule? That would be quite ambitious, as the Roman armies stationed in the areas through which his army would have had to have travelled would surely have attacked and put a stop to them long before they got to the coast. Yet here, in the *HRB*, Octavius is brazenly behaving as if he controls all of Britain. For similar reasons, Maximus could not have been taken to meet the king in London.

It is not totally clear just what the errors in this account are, but the *Brut Tysilio* points toward a particular solution. In this Welsh version, the location in which Maximus meets Octavius (or 'Eudaf') is not London, but Caernarvon in North Wales. This is far more plausible. In *The Dream of Maxen Wledig*, an independent tale in the *Mabinogi* about Maximus (Maxen Wledig) meeting Eudaf, the king is also placed in Caernarvon. It seems likely that Geoffrey, when translating his source into Latin, somehow misidentified the said location for London.[29] Furthermore, the location at which Maximus arrived in Britain is not Southampton, as in *HRB*, but 'Kent'. Perhaps this was originally 'Gwent', which would confine the entire incident to Wales. There is definitely some confusion of geography in this account, so it may be that the events themselves are entirely accurate but simply incorrectly located, making them appear impossible. We can only speculate. Therefore, we will count Octavius sending an army to Southampton as an error, as well as the placement of Octavius in London.

The idea that Maximus, as the newly appointed governor of Britain, would have tried to deal with this Hiberno-British issue peacefully is quite possible. It would be similar to Claudius subduing certain tribes in Britain 'by means of capitulation' in the first century. But then there is the matter of the actual marriage between Maximus and Octavius's daughter. If Octavius had indeed decided that Maximus was a suitable husband for his heiress, it would make perfect sense that he would hand over full control of his government in exchange for Maximus marrying her. This new Roman governor would surely have been all too eager to reconsolidate the Roman provinces.

However, is there any evidence at all that this actually took place? Well, we know that Magnus Maximus had been in Britain for at least a few years before he was declared emperor in 383. His son, Victor, whom he appointed as Augustus of Gaul in 384, is referred to as an 'infant' by the majority of reference works. These two things being true, we must arrive at the conclusion that Maximus had relations with a woman – presumably his wife – within the relatively short period of time in which he had been stationed in Britain. The more contemporary Roman sources do not provide any information about her that contradicts the story in the *HRB*, and the story of her marriage to Maximus during his relatively short stay in Britain is consistent with the fact that Maximus and his historical wife had only recently had relations by 383, during the time in which he was stationed in Britain. This marriage was accepted by Peter Bartrum, saying concerning *The Dream of Maxen Wledig*: 'This romance is evidently woven about the tradition that Maximus, while in Britain, and probably before he was actually proclaimed emperor, married Elen the daughter of Eudaf, a prince of Arfon [Caernarvon]. There is no reason to doubt this tradition.'[30]

After these events, Geoffrey tells us that Conan Meriadoc, out of rage over not receiving the kingdom himself, travelled to the north of Britain and raised an army of Picts. With this army, he devastated the border regions. Maximus then travelled up to that part of the country and fought against him. After some time, Maximus was eventually able to subdue Conan. There is, in fact, a record of this. The *Gallic Chronicle of 452* records a victory over the Picts and the Scots by Magnus Maximus in 381 or 382, a year or two before he was proclaimed emperor.

Geoffrey next claims that Maximus remained in Britain for five years after this. In reality, if we take the *Gallic Chronicle* at its word, then only two years separated this event from Maximus's invasion of Gaul. This is reminiscent of Geoffrey extending the gap between Caesar's two invasions of Britain.

Then, Maximus is said to have invaded Gaul and arrived in Armorica, or Brittany. This is possible. He is then said to have conquered that region and given it to Conan, after which it was populated with the British soldiers, as well as regular Britons brought over from Britain specifically to populate that area. There is no evidence that Armorica was extensively populated by Britons prior to Maximus's usurpation, while it is very well documented that it had become extensively populated by them by the mid-fifth century at the latest. There is no contemporary record of what actually happened, and there continues to be much debate about the historicity of this event. Therefore, nothing certain can be said here concerning it.

One minor error is involved with the statement that Maximus 'suspended his arms for a time' between conquering Armorica and moving on to the rest of Gaul. It is *during* this rest period that he is said to have peopled the region with Britons. After this, Maximus is described as subduing the rest of Gaul and Germany by many battles, establishing the seat of his government at Trier, killing one emperor and causing the other to flee from Rome. In reality, Gaul was not made subject to him by the conquest of cities, but merely by the swift killing of the western Roman emperor, Gratian. Germany, too, does not seem to have actually been invaded by Maximus, though it did come under his power, as the *HRB* claims. But to return to the issue of timing, there was, historically, only a relatively short gap between Maximus arriving in the country and Gratian meeting him in the battlefield. Perhaps a few weeks or months is all that is meant by Geoffrey's description of Maximus suspending his arms 'for a time'. In which case, the error would be that the peopling of Armorica by the Britons did not take place during this short period of time, though it may well have *started* then. This might be comparable to the earlier claim that Gloucester was built during Claudius's stay in Britain, when Claudius was actually only in Britain for sixteen days.

As with the other parts of the *HRB*, there are errors of detail scattered throughout this passage. Maximus's seat of government is correctly placed at Trier, and he did kill one emperor, Gratian, and cause the other, Valentinian, to flee, though Valentinian fled from his seat in Milan – the then capital of the Roman Empire – not Rome. The first of these incidents happened in 383, while the second took place when Maximus invaded Italy in 387. Evidently, this description serves as an overview of Maximus's reign.

The very next sentence claims that 'in the meantime' the Gauls and Aquitanians frequently harassed the Britons in Armorica. Since the previous sentence covers almost the entirety of Maximus's reign, this event could have occurred at any point between 383 and 387. This incident is another one for which we must simply accept that we have no definite evidence either supporting or refuting its historicity. In any case, not much is made of it, as Conan is shortly said to have entirely vanquished them. Next, the account tells us that Conan decided to send for British wives for his men living in Armorica, so that they would not have to mix with the Gauls.

The ruler of Britain at this time is said to have been a certain Dionotus. He is described as a noble and powerful prince who succeeded Caradocus to the throne of Cornwall (possibly Cerniw in Wales). In the British genealogies, there is a son of Maximus by the name of Dimet, or 'Dunod' in some records. This latter form is what is used in place of 'Dionotus' in the Welsh version of the *HRB*, so there is a distinct possibility that 'Dionotus', to whom Maximus had 'committed the government' while he was occupied with affairs on the Continent, was 'Dunod', the son of Maximus of the genealogies. The reference to Caradocus as 'his brother' is commonly taken to mean that he was the brother of Dionotus. This would be inconsistent with the conclusion that Maximus was Dionotus's father for it would mean that Mauricius, the son of Caradocus, would have been the grandson of Maximus. It is impossible for Maximus, if he was born *c.* 335, to have had a grandson old enough to engage in political assignments in *c.* 380, when Maximus arrived in Britain. However, the passage that refers to Caradocus as 'his brother' might actually mean that Caradocus was the brother of *Conan*, who is also involved in this passage. In any case, Geoffrey is consistently unreliable in terms of familial relationships, so the speculation that this Dionotus is the Dunod ap Maxim of the British genealogies is by no means definitively excluded by this reference. Indeed, Dunod appears as the ancestor of the kings of South Wales, so his placement as the king of Cerniw in Geoffrey's account would fit perfectly.

The subsequent account of the arrival of these wives-to-be is just Geoffrey's version of a legend that long predates him. It is the legend of Ursula – the titular individual being a daughter of Dionotus, according to Geoffrey of Monmouth, and the focus of Conan's passion. In earlier versions of the legend, it is simply the intended marriage between her and the son of a pagan king that appears. Her thousands of companions are simply portrayed as her handmaidens, or the handmaidens of her and several others. Geoffrey's version – that the reason there were thousands of them is because they were being brought over to be the wives of the new British inhabitants of Armorica – is clearly more plausible, and though it is not the earliest version that exists, the version it contradicts was still written hundreds of years after the events in question, so there is no guarantee that it is the most accurate.

In Geoffrey's account, which now agrees broadly with the others, the women begin to sail from Britain to Armorica. However, a storm hits, destroying most of the ships. Those that are not destroyed are driven off course and land on islands apparently off the coast of Germany.[31] There, many are taken as slaves and others are simply killed. The army that committed these cruelties was a joint one, composed of the Huns and the Picts. The account claims that they were, at that time, ravaging Germany and the nations on the seacoasts by the command of Gratian. In fact, it is claimed that Gratian sent them specifically to attack Maximus's men who were stationed there. Historically, though, Gratian had been killed by Maximus long before he could have stationed any men in Germany. Therefore, the portrayal of Gratian as if he were still alive at this point is another error in the account.

We know that the Huns had not advanced this far west by Maximus's reign, so it is tempting to think that this account has been misplaced in time. Indeed, the Huns under the famous Attila attacked Germany in the 450s – another common date claimed for this event. However, the inclusion of the Picts in this area is surely mistaken whatever time period is concerned. Either this is simply a case of Geoffrey or his source imposing a name on a previously unidentified tribe, as with the nations of the kings at the conference upon Caesar's landing in 55 BCE, or it is an honest mistranslation of a tribe that really was active in that area. Whatever the case, there is no obstacle to the same logic being applied to the use of 'Huns' in this account (as well as in the sources for this legend that predate Geoffrey). Therefore, we have two options – either this is a real account and Geoffrey has simply misplaced it in time, which would necessitate many other errors, due to how interconnected it is with Conan Meriadoc and Magnus Maximus, or he is simply incorrect in claiming that it was the Picts and the Huns who massacred the virgins. The weight of evidence supports the earlier, rather than the later, date. One piece of evidence that specifically points to Maximus's reign is the mention of a certain 'Pope Cyriacus' of Rome in one version of the legend. The pope in Rome at the time of Attila's raid on Germany was Leo, while the pope from 384 to 399 was named Siricius. Of the two, the latter is clearly the closest to 'Cyriacus'. While we would have to accept his actions in the legend as being fictional, such as his stepping down from his office and being killed with Ursula and her companions, Siricius is the only pope of Rome from the second century down to the time of Attila the Hun who possessed a name this similar to 'Cyriacus'.

If we accept that the legend rightly takes place in the time of Magnus Maximus, then the inclusion of the Huns in this account cannot be any more accurate than the inclusion of the Picts. Therefore, the nationalities of the enemies in this account are mistaken – though the mistake of the Huns clearly did not originate with Geoffrey of Monmouth.

It has been claimed that this entire event receives no mention by Gregory of Tours, a sixth-century writer in France. However, this is most likely not the case. While he does not mention Ursula or any other virgins, he does describe a major attack on Germany by the Franks. Their leaders were Marcomer, Sunno and Genobaud. Several details indicate that this is the event that features in the *HRB*.

Firstly, the timing. In the *HRB*, immediately after the massacre of the virgins, the Picts and the Huns are said to have travelled to Scotland and ravaged the country there. An army is sent by Maximus to deal with this, and then the confrontation between them is described. Here, Maximus is said to have been killed 'in the meantime' – that is, while the Picts and Huns were being defeated in Scotland. We know that the emperor was killed in 388, so the attack on Germany should have taken place not long before this. It so happens that this was the very year in which the Franks attacked Germany.

Secondly, the nationality of the raiders. While it is true that the *HRB* identifies them as Picts and Huns, we have already established that this cannot be true. Therefore, it is significant to note that *Brut Tysilio* refers to Melga, the leader of the Picts in Geoffrey's account, as the king of 'Paittio'. This is surely Poitou, France, whose citizens are mentioned in a later section of the *HRB* and are named 'Pictavians'. It was concluded earlier that Geoffrey's 'Picts' in this Ursula story must derive from a mistranslation of a tribe that really was active in that area. We can now see that the Pictavians, or the Pictones, as they were originally called, are the tribe in question. Of course, in the time of Magnus Maximus, the Franks did not live in the area of Poitou. This would require the inclusion of the Pictavians to have derived from a later, incorrect, selection of a base for the enemy in the story. The mention of the Pictavians would then, even later, have been corrupted into something that Geoffrey rendered as 'Picts'. It nonetheless provides evidence that the enemies were originally associated with France, which points towards the invasion by Marcomer.

As mentioned, the army of Huns and Picts – led by their respective leaders Guanius and Melga – are next said to have travelled to Britain to ravage the defenceless country of Scotland. In this context, the account makes the claim that Maximus had depleted the kingdom of its soldiers, its 'warlike youth'. This claim is found as early as Gildas, in the sixth century, and the archaeological evidence does support the claim that all or most Roman forces were withdrawn from Wales in *c.* 383. However, the idea that the northern frontier had been totally depleted of its forces is contradicted by the archaeological evidence. So Geoffrey is wrong, but no more so than Gildas, who was simply exaggerating.

Obviously, the idea that an army that was raiding Germany would sail all the way over to Scotland is quite unlikely, whether that army was meant to be composed of Huns or Franks. Therefore, it is likely that a source along the line of transmission up to the *HRB* simply assumed a connection between two events that happened very close together. That the Picts ravaged northern Britain during Maximus's reign, causing him to intervene, is a conclusion that was reached by P. J. Casey several decades ago on the basis of coinage evidence.[32] However, the conclusion he reached is inconsistent with Geoffrey's account in several regards. Firstly, the account says that Maximus sent an officer to Britain to deal with this situation, whereas the coinage evidence that Casey refers to requires Maximus to have returned to Britain personally. While it would normally be possible for both to be true, we have already observed that the *HRB* specifically says that Maximus was killed 'in the meantime' – that is, while the situation in Scotland was being dealt with. Therefore, there is no allowance in the account for Maximus to have returned to the country himself. Secondly, Casey concludes that the year in question was 384, yet Geoffrey's account, for reasons already discussed, must have taken place in 388. Therefore, the weight of evidence does not support the conclusion that Geoffrey's account is here talking about the Pictish campaign whose existence was speculated by Casey.

Nonetheless, the idea that there was a later Pictish campaign is quite reasonable. There do not seem to be any records of what was happening in Britain during Maximus's rule of 383–388. If a visit to Britain by Maximus himself to deal with an uprising of Picts could have gone unmentioned by Continental accounts, as seems to have happened in 384, then an uprising of Picts that required no personal visit by Maximus certainly could have gone unmentioned too.

One final definite error in this part of the *HRB* is the claim that Maximus was killed in Rome. In truth, he was executed at Aquileia, which is still in Italy but far from Rome. Again, this illustrates the unreliability of the geography presented in the *HRB*.

In summary, we must acknowledge the unfortunate fact that this portion of Geoffrey's book, while about an event that has a lot of contemporary documentation, focuses on moments, such as the time between Maximus's landing and the defeat of Gratian, and locations, such as Britain, that were simply not well recorded by these sources. Therefore, it is perhaps not as useful an analysis as would have been hoped, but here is the list of errors nonetheless:

1. Octavius ruling over the entirety of Britain until the arrival of Maximus.
2. Maximus going to Britain because he was invited there by Octavius.
3. Maximus being termed a 'senator'.
4. The cities of the Franks being raided and subdued by Maximus on his way to Britain.
5. Octavius sending an army to confront Maximus at Southampton.
6. Octavius being stationed at London.
7. There being five years between Maximus's victory over the Picts and his invasion of Gaul.
8. The regions of Gaul and Germany coming under the control of Maximus by means of the conquest of cities.
9. The peopling of Armorica by the Britons being completed before Maximus had gained control of Gaul.
10. Rome being the location from which Valentinian fled.
11. The attackers of Germany being Picts and Huns.
12. These attackers being sent by the command of Gratian.
13. Gratian still being alive after Maximus had stationed men in Germany.
14. Maximus having taken all the military forces from Britain.
15. The army that was attacking Germany sailing over to Scotland and being the cause of the raiding there.
16. Rome being the location in which Maximus was killed.

As can be seen from this list, the account of Maximus's invasion of Britain has the largest number of errors out of all the major Roman-era events that feature in the *HRB*. However, it must be borne in mind that it is also the longest passage. As with the other accounts, there are minor errors – such as points 3, 7, 10, and 16 – and much more significant ones – such as points 1, 4, 11, 13 and 15. Yet, despite the errors, we can also see from this analysis that the general outline of this event as presented by Geoffrey closely follows the historical reality of the late fourth century. There is a considerable amount of factual material to be found in this account. The accusation that the *HRB* is historically worthless has, once again, been shown to be false.

This brings us to the end of the analysis of the Roman era of the *Historia Regum Britanniae*. It is true that this is not quite the end of Roman Britain (it is generally held to have ended in *c.* 410, approximately twenty-two years after Maximus's death), but the truth is that the surviving sources are simply too unreliable and confused to make any kind of beneficial analysis of the final years of Roman Britain. Any attempt at this would be almost as speculative as an analysis of post-Roman, Dark Age Britain.[33] It would certainly not contribute to determining with confidence the accuracy of Geoffrey's account, which is what this analysis of the Roman era in Geoffrey's book is supposed to do. Therefore, we will end the analysis here. Now, armed with this information, we can finally begin analysing theories about Arthur's European conquest.

5

Proposed Theories

As mentioned in an earlier chapter, there is no record of any sixth-century British king mounting an invasion of Europe against Roman forces. The majority of Arthurian speculations do not address this major part of the legend, but simply focus on the war against the Saxons. Still, there have been a few theories. This chapter will discuss several of the most prominent theories that address this part of the legend.

Riothamus

Several decades ago, a theory was developed by British scholar Geoffrey Ashe, which has since become quite popular. Like this book, he acknowledged that it was conspicuously inconsistent for Geoffrey of Monmouth to have simply invented such a large portion of his history. Hence, he did the logical thing and looked for a historical basis for the story.

The theory is that King Arthur was really the historical figure known as Riothamus, who was employed by the Romans to fight the Visigoths in Gaul in the fifth century. Very little detail is known about the war concerning Riothamus, but then, very little seems to have happened. The source for the event is the writings of Jordanes, writing *c. 551*. He tells us:

> Now Eurich, king of the Visigoths, perceived the frequent change of Roman Emperors and strove to hold Gaul by his own right. The Emperor Anthemius heard of it and asked the Brittones

for aid. Their King Riotimus came with twelve thousand men into the state of the Bituriges by the way of Ocean, and was received as he disembarked from his ships. Eurich, king of the Visigoths, came against them with an innumerable army, and after a long fight he routed Riotimus, king of the Brittones, before the Romans could join him. So when he had lost a great part of his army, he fled with all the men he could gather together, and came to the Burgundians, a neighboring tribe then allied to the Romans. But Eurich, king of the Visigoths, seized the Gallic city of Arverna; for the Emperor Anthemius was now dead.[1]

This is all that is heard of Riothamus. According to this theory, that is the reality behind King Arthur's mighty European campaign.

One of the more notable aspects of this theory is the fact that the activities of Riothamus occurred in 470, whereas King Arthur is firmly rooted in the mid-sixth century by most other sources, as was established earlier in this book. However, Ashe noted that the names of the characters involved in this particular tale point much more towards a fifth-century setting – the main indicator being the name of the emperor: Leo. According to Ashe, this can only be the eastern emperor Leo I, who ruled from 457 to 474. Since Riothamus, a king of the Britons, came to Gaul and fought a battle there during the reign of Leo I, it is easy to see how the idea that he was the original Arthur is a tempting suggestion. Additionally, almost at the end of Leo's reign, there was a western Roman emperor called Glycerius, whom Ashe thought could have been the basis for Arthur's Roman enemy 'Lucius' in the legend. In the *Chronicle of Sigebert of Gembloux*, written just over two decades before Geoffrey of Monmouth wrote, Glycerius is called 'Lucerius' and is placed in the years 469–470, rather than 473–474, when he actually ruled. Thus, this chronicle gives him a name that is very similar to 'Lucius' and places him earlier in the reign of Leo, precisely in the time when Riothamus is estimated to have fought the Visigoths.

Furthermore, 'Riothamus' seems to be composed of 'Rigo', meaning 'king', and 'tamo', which is apparently a superlative suffix. If true, then this appears to be a title meaning 'Highest King', rather than a personal name. This both fits the rank of Arthur and allows for the possibility that his true name was Arthur. Ashe also brought to attention several factors that he felt closely paralleled the Arthurian tale. One of these is the fact that they were both betrayed in a sense, which is what led to their downfall (Arthur by his nephew Mordred, and Riothamus by a praetorian prefect named Arvandus). A more notable piece of evidence provided is the fact that when Riothamus was defeated, his probable escape route would have led him near a village called Avallon, which is virtually identical to the name of the place where Arthur was said to have been taken to be healed of his wounds at the end of his life, after his final battle at Camlann.

The evidence in some respects is quite compelling, but there are significant problems that make it extremely unlikely to be the truth behind the stories. The main issue is that it is not nearly accurate enough for what we should expect from *Historia Regum Britanniae*. We have seen the level of accuracy that is manifest throughout the Roman-era portion of the book, so we have clear boundaries of accuracy to work with. While it is true that Geoffrey's work features some gross inaccuracies, the idea that Riothamus's activities were the basis for the Arthurian story stretches the inaccuracies too far from provable levels. To demonstrate this clearly, let us examine both events step by step and see how exactly they compare:

Arthur travels across to Roman Gaul and begins subduing the country.
Riothamus was invited over to Gaul by Emperor Anthemius and arrived in the state of the Bituriges.

The ruler of Gaul, the Roman tribune Frollo, comes to meet Arthur to fight against him.
Euric, the king of the Visigoths, came to meet Riothamus to fight against him.

Most of the Gallic army switches sides to join Arthur, causing Frollo to flee to Paris with a small number of men.
There was a long fight between the British and Visigothic armies, eventually ending in Riothamus's defeat. A great part of his army having been lost, Riothamus fled to the Burgundians.

Arthur pursues Frollo and besieges the city of Paris, until eventually Frollo agrees to have a formal, one-on-one fight with Arthur. They do this, and Arthur slays Frollo.
Nothing more is known of Riothamus.

Arthur then proceeds to subdue all of Gaul over a period of several years and becomes its ruler. He then returns to Britain.
Nothing more is known of Riothamus.

After several more years, King Arthur receives a letter from the Romans condemning him for his actions and demanding tribute. This incites Arthur to attack Rome.
Nothing more is known of Riothamus.

Arthur's men have a fight against the Romans, who are under a military commander called Petreius. Arthur's men capture him as well as many other Roman soldiers and take them back to Arthur's base in Paris.
Nothing more is known of Riothamus.

Arthur's men position themselves in a valley at a place called Siesia, where they wait to meet the coming attack of Lucius, who has summoned kings of various different nations to join him in defeating Arthur.
Nothing more is known of Riothamus.

The battle between Lucius and Arthur's men is crushing for both sides. Eventually, Arthur himself arrives and his army manages to overcome the Roman forces and kill Lucius. Arthur then continues on his way to Rome, but has to abandon the attack when he is forced to return to Britain to deal with Mordred.
Nothing more is known of Riothamus.

If the nominal connections of the theory are left to the side for the moment and we just focus on this comparison of the patterns of events, it can be seen that there is very little similarity between the two accounts. The first major flaw is the fact that Riothamus did not subdue any Gallic territory; he was invited over by the emperor and merely arrived there. Then, Arthur's fight with Frollo would have to have been Riothamus's fight with Euric, but the account clearly states that Frollo was a Roman tribune. Conversely, Euric – who would have to occupy the position of Frollo in the story – was the king of the Visigoths, enemies of the Romans. What is more, Riothamus himself was not fighting against the Romans but was fighting *for* them. This is a complete role reversal. Admittedly, such an error does have a precedent in Geoffrey's book, for it occurred in his account of Allectus and Asclepiodotus. Therefore, though being a major difference between the Arthurian story and the reality of 470, this cannot be classed as outside the provable boundaries of accuracy of Geoffrey's book. Nonetheless, there would have to be substantial reason to actively support the similarity of the two events, just as there is in the account of Allectus and Asclepiodotus.

One difference between the two events that does not appear to have any parallel within the rest of the *HRB* is the nature of the battle. In Geoffrey's account, it was essentially a non-event. The battle itself is not even described – all that is said is that most of the Gallic army (Frollo's army) switched to Arthur's side. This is hardly in line with the 'long battle' fought between Riothamus and Euric. Furthermore, the outcome of the battle is completely different. In fact, it is essentially the reverse. Rather than Arthur's easy victory in the legend, Riothamus lost and fled, leaving Euric to continue on his conquest of Gaul. And after this, the identification of Riothamus with Arthur does nothing at all to explain all the subsequent events in the Arthurian story, as can clearly be seen by the list of comparisons.

All in all, this attempt at an equation between Riothamus's activities and those of Arthur falls short on virtually every count. In the legend, the Romans were not allies but were the enemy, and there was not a lengthy battle between the opposing armies, but rather, the battle was easily, decisively won by Arthur with no great conflict, causing his enemy to flee and ultimately perish at Arthur's hand. The only real similarity in the patterns of events is that Riothamus was a British king who fought in Gaul, and so was Arthur.

However, it seems that Geoffrey Ashe prefers to connect the two events by supposing that the battle against Euric was the origin of the *second* of Arthur's Gallic invasions. Hence, the connection between the patterns of events according to Geoffrey Ashe's version of the Riothamus theory can be seen by the following:

Arthur travels to Gaul and begins subduing the country.
Nothing is known of Riothamus from this period.

The ruler of Gaul, the Roman tribune Frollo, comes to meet Arthur to fight against him. Most of the Gallic army switches sides to join Arthur, causing Frollo to flee to Paris with a small number of men.
Nothing is known of Riothamus from this period.

Arthur pursues Frollo and bieseges the city of Paris, until eventually Frollo agrees to have a formal, one-on-one fight with Arthur. They do this, and Arthur slays Frollo.
Nothing is known of Riothamus from this period.

Arthur then proceeds to subdue all of Gaul over a period of several years and becomes its ruler. He then returns to Britain.
Nothing is known of Riothamus from this period.

After several more years, King Arthur receives a letter from the Romans condemning him for his actions and demanding tribute. This incites Arthur to attack Rome.
Roman Emperor Anthemius appealed for Riothamus's help against the Visigoths, causing him to come to the state of the Bituriges.

Arthur's men have a fight against the Romans, who are under a military commander called Petreius. Arthur's men capture him as well as many other Roman soldiers and take them back to Arthur's base in Paris.
Riothamus was in the state of the Bituriges.

Arthur's men position themselves in the valley of Siesia, while Lucius, the Roman procurator, heads toward Arthur with a large army, assisted by the kings of various nations.

While Riothamus and his men were in the state of the Bituriges, Euric, king of the Visigoths, headed towards him with an innumerable army.

The British and Roman armies battle against each other in a lengthy battle which ends up crushing for both sides. Eventually, Arthur himself arrives and his army is able to overcome the Roman forces and kill Lucius.

There was a long fight between the British and Visigothic armies, eventually ending in Riothamus's defeat. A great part of his army having been lost, Riothamus fled to the Burgundians.

These connections show somewhat more promise. Just as Arthur was incited to cross over into Gaul due to receiving communication from the Romans, so Riothamus went on his expedition due to receiving communication from the Romans. However, the rest of the account of Riothamus's invasion that eventually made its way into Geoffrey of Monmouth's hand should have made it clear that it was the Visigoths, not the Romans, who were Riothamus's enemy. The fact that, after the battle, Riothamus fled to a tribe allied to the Romans should also have made it clear which side Riothamus was on.

Next, the activities of Riothamus do not explain the major event in the legend between Arthur arriving and the battle at Siesia, in which Arthur's men have a significant fight against the Romans and end up taking many of them captive. If the Riothamus theory is right, then two whole chapters of *HRB* in this Common Era setting have no historical basis at all. This is without precedent.

There is also no evidence that Euric came against Riothamus with the help of other nations, as Lucius did against Arthur. Previously, Geoffrey of Monmouth had included some apparent errors in his account of Caesar's first invasion, giving otherwise unknown names and improbable territories to the kings at the conference. But the fact remains that there was a conference of various different kings, regardless of their names and territories. While it would be reasonable to suppose that the names and territories of Lucius's allies might be inaccurate, there does not seem to be a precedent for the idea that the *HRB* would simply produce non-existent foreign allies from nowhere.

When we use this second attempt at equating the two events, we can see that the battle itself is fairly similar. It was a lengthy battle, like in the Arthurian tale, and Riothamus lost a lot of men, as did Arthur. However, once again, the battle was a defeat for Riothamus, in direct contrast to Arthur's victory in the legend. It must be admitted that changing the outcome of a battle is within the *HRB*'s boundaries of accuracy. But even so, arguing that this change must have taken place would only be admissible if there were sufficient reason to believe, from the rest of the tale, that the Riothamus event led to the Arthurian legend.

As it is, the only notable similarities between the two is that both Arthur and Riothamus were British kings, they both journeyed to Gaul by reason of communication with a Roman emperor, and they fought a long battle in which many of their men were lost. Plenty of members of the royal families of Britain moved over to Gaul during the fifth century, and battles that were long and ended in a great loss of life were common. The only one of these three similarities that is in any way peculiar to Riothamus and Arthur is the second – the fact that their journeys to Gaul were a result of communication with a Roman emperor. In fact, it is entirely possible that Riothamus was already in Gaul when this communication took place. The source in which Riothamus is described simply terms him 'king of the Brittones', which could apply either to the inhabitants of Britain or the inhabitants of what is now Brittany. The fact that Jordanes felt the need to specify that Riothamus travelled to the state of the Bituriges 'by way of the ocean' would suggest that Riothamus was already on the Continent, for if he was based in Britain then he would have no choice but to travel to the state of the Bituriges – or anywhere in Gaul, for that matter – by way of the ocean. Though it does not prove the matter decisively, it makes it the more likely conclusion. If we accept this as the case, then the similarities between Riothamus and Arthur become even weaker than they already were.

In addition to the fact that an entire two chapters of the account must be dismissed as errors if the Riothamus theory is correct, we are also left facing the obvious lack of any known historical reality behind the first invasion of Gaul. The initial encounter with Frollo, the slaying of the ruler of Gaul, and the subsequent conquest and subjugation of the whole of Gaul must all be historical errors, or inventions from Geoffrey of Monmouth's own mind. Surely, according to Ashe's own logic as well as the analysis of *HRB* presented in this book, such a conclusion is unacceptable.

But what of all the other evidences used by Geoffrey Ashe to support this theory? Regardless of the pattern of events, it is claimed that the names of those involved point unmistakably to Riothamus's invasion. There is Emperor Leo, who corresponds with Leo I; the procurator Lucius Tiberius of the story may be the historical Glycerius; a Pope Supplicius is mentioned immediately prior to the invasion of Gaul, and that would fit Pope Simplicius of 468–483; then finally there is Mordred, Arthur's betrayer, who fits as Arvandus.

On careful analysis, however, only the first of those identifications could possibly hold any weight. Glycerius, a Roman who would become emperor several years after Riothamus's fight with Euric, never fought against Riothamus. There is no precedent for Geoffrey changing the identity of the enemy of a story into a different historical figure who never fought against the person in question.[2] Additionally, the idea that Geoffrey acquired Glycerius's modified name and position as emperor in 470, the year Riothamus fought in Gaul, from the *Chronicle of Sigebert of Gembloux* is highly improbable for at least two reasons.

Firstly, the *Chronicle* makes him the co-emperor of the Roman Empire, along with Leo I. It is often claimed that some passages of *HRB* make Lucius an emperor, but this is incorrect. After receiving Lucius's letter, the account says that Arthur sent word to 'the emperors' by their ambassadors. This does not say that Lucius himself was one of 'the emperors', though it does reveal that Leo was not the only one. The only other mention of an emperor who is not explicitly Leo is in the account of a dream Arthur has in which a dragon fights a bear. He speculates, in the story, that this dream represented his fight against 'the emperor', but the emperor in question is not named. So in reality, there are no passages that call Lucius an emperor or even suggest that he was one. He is only ever called a procurator or a general and is shown to be taking orders from the senate. Yet if Geoffrey had got the character of Lucius from 'Emperor Lucerius' of 469–470 in Sigebert's account, then there is no reason at all for Geoffrey to have called Lucius a procurator.

Secondly, if Geoffrey had used Sigebert's *Chronicle* to find additional details for his story, then he must have known that the account was set in 470. Yet he says that Arthur gave up the kingship to Constantine after being mortally wounded at the Battle of Camlann in 541 – this took place straight after Arthur got back from fighting in Gaul. Regardless of when the Battle of Camlann actually took place, if Geoffrey *thought* that Arthur abdicated in 541, then it is illogical in the extreme to suppose that he took information from a chronicle regarding the year 470.

These two objections to the idea of the *Chronicle of Sigebert of Gembloux* contributing to the account in the *HRB*, as well as the fact that Glycerius had no connection to Riothamus historically, should suffice to show that this supposed piece of evidence cannot be used as such.

The connection between Pope Simplicius and Pope Supplicius seems convincing enough at first sight, but quickly becomes impossible when the evidence is looked at in context. The pope is mentioned as being the one to whom Walgan, as a twelve-year-old, was sent for instruction. Yes, this line occurs just prior to Arthur and his army setting out to invade Gaul, but the line itself puts it within its own context. That context is Walgan, otherwise known as Gawain, the nephew of Arthur. The line in full is: 'Walgan, the son of Lot, was then a youth twelve years old, and was recommended by his uncle to the service of pope Supplicius, from whom he received arms.'[3]

This is the one and only line in which the pope is mentioned, and he is clearly, firmly attached to the context of Gawain. Ashe may put Arthur in the mid-fifth century, but the family of Cynfarch is unambiguous as to its general temporal position. Gawain ap Llew ap Cynfarch would have been a cousin of the mid- to late sixth-century Owain ap Urien ap Cynfarch. The chronology of this family was discussed in Chapter One, and it was shown that Mordred, Gawain's brother, must have been born *c.* 545 or later. With no better information to assist the calculations, we can only conclude that Gawain was born within a few years of this. Therefore, he was almost certainly twelve years old at some point in the late 550s, or perhaps the early 560s.

Obviously, this can have nothing whatsoever to do with Simplicius of the fifth century, regardless of the origin of the story of the Gallic conquest. We find, instead, that the pope from 556 to 561 was a certain Pope Pelagius.

To see how 'Pelagius' could have become 'Supplicius', consider the fact that 'Gwrgan' in the Latin of the *Book of Llandaff* is written 'Gurcan'. Notice the change from a 'g' to a 'c' in the middle of the name. So it may be that a Latin scribe, somewhere along the line of transmission leading up to the book that Geoffrey possessed and translated, wrote this name as 'Pelacius'. It is also a well-attested phenomenon in language in general that an unstressed syllable has a tendency to be dropped over time.[4] If the 'e' in 'Pelagius' was unstressed, then this would be reduced to 'Plagius'. If we apply both changes, this becomes 'Placius'. From this stage, we must note from a consideration of the *Brut Tysilio* and, indeed, other records (such as the Llancarfan charters) that vowels were not always used consistently. It is therefore fair to suggest that 'Placius' may have sometimes found itself written as 'Plicius'.

Therefore, there is really nothing improbable about oral and scribal transmission changing 'Pelagius' into 'Plicius'. What is harder to determine is where the prefix 'Sup' came from. It is possible, though admittedly unlikely, that his name was written down as 'S. Pelagius' – the 'S' standing for Sanctitas, which was a common way of addressing popes, though it was not commonly written down. Alternatively, his name could have been written that way with the 'S' intended for 'Sanctus' or 'Saint'. A document written in 1670 records him as 'S. Pelagius' apparently with that meaning, and at least as early as the thirteenth century (in *Legenda Aurea*, by Jacobus da Varagine) he was considered to have been sainted.[5] This was the century after Geoffrey wrote. If he was considered to have been sainted prior to the compilation of Geoffrey's source, then the name may well have been written

Above: St Illtyd's Church in Llantwit Major, Glamorgan. It stands on the site of the ancient college of Illtud, where numerous sixth century individuals studied, such as Gildas, Maelgwn, and Athrwys's nephew Samson. It has been said that this college is the oldest in the world. (Author's collection)

Inset: An ancient inscription of the name of Illtud. The monument on which this inscription is found is currently kept in St Illtyd's Church in Llantwit Major, Glamorgan. This sixth-century individual was a very prominent character and was likely the teacher of Gildas. He was also, apparently, the cousin of Arthur. (Author's collection)

Below: A view from the top of Arthur's Seat in Edinburgh. One of Arthur's battles was said to have been at Edinburgh, and it may well be the case that Arthur's Seat really is named after King Arthur. (Author's collection)

Above: A view of the Severn, at the border of England and Wales. It was into this river that Twrch Trwyth was forced by Arthur's men, before 'regaining the ground with his feet' and rushing towards 'Kernyw', likely nearby Cernyw in Gwent. (Author's collection)

Left: The tomb of Teilo inside Llandaff Cathedral in Cardiff, Glamorgan. This sixth-century bishop of Llandaff is very important for establishing the correct dating of Athrwys, for Teilo's nephew Oudoceus was contemporary with great-grandsons of Athrwys. (Author's collection)

Below left: A list of the bishops of Llandaff found inside Llandaff Cathedral in Cardiff, Glamorgan. This puts Oudoceus's tenure as bishop between the years 570–600, a close match with the estimate of 570–630 presented in this book. This shows that local tradition supports the early chronology, not the late chronology that is commonly proposed. (Author's collection)

Above: A modern carving of Merlin's face on the cliffs of Tintagel, Cornwall. The character of Merlin originated with Myrddin Wyllt, a bard whose grandfather is said in one record to be 'Meurig of Dyfed', likely Meurig ap Tewdrig. (Author's collection)

Below: A view of Hayle Beach, Cornwall, where Gwinear and his men landed before being attacked by King Tewdrig. Gwinear was probably the historical origin of Gorlois, the 'duke of Cornwall' who was killed by Uthyr according to Arthurian legend. (Author's collection)

A modern statue of King Arthur at Tintagel in Cornwall. According to legend, Arthur was conceived here at Tintagel by Uthyr and the wife of Gorlois while Gorlois himself was being attacked by Uthyr's men. In reality, it appears that the association between Arthur's conception and this battle between Gorlois and Uthyr originated simply because Arthur was born shortly after the battle between Gwinear and Tewdrig. (Author's collection)

Above left: Pont y Saeson at Tintern, Monmouthshire, where Tewdrig fought his last battle against the Saxons after years of retirement. This is likely the historical origin behind the story of Uthyr Pendragon coming out of retirement and fighting one last battle against the Saxons, as found in *Historia Regum Britanniae*. (Author's collection)

Above right: A modern statue of Tewdrig, the grandfather of Athrwys, outside St Tewdric's Church in Mathern, Monmouthshire. Tewdrig was very probably the historical Uthyr Pendragon, Arthur's father in the legends. (Author's collection)

Above: The ruins of Margam Abbey in Margam, Glamorgan. According to one tradition, this was named after and is the burial place of Morgan ap Athrwys. This Morgan was likely the origin of Geoffrey of Monmouth's enigmatic 'King Margadud of south Wales' and also Morgan the Black, son of King Arthur in *Le Petit Bruit*. (Author's collection)

Below: Some of the ruins of the sixth-century royal residence at Tintagel, Cornwall. In these very rooms may have walked Geraint, Cador and Constantine, the kings of Dumnonia during Arthur's time and all of them his allies. (Author's collection)

A section of the defensive earthworks of Cissbury Ring in Worthing, West Sussex. This hill fort was in the territory of the Atrebates, and thus may have been used by Commius, the king who allied himself with Julius Caesar, and Verica, the king who allied himself with Claudius. (Author's collection)

An area of the floor of Fishbourne Roman Palace in Chichester, West Sussex. According to Miles Russell, this was the residence of Sallustus Lucullus, the governor of Britain in the late first century. Lucullus was likely the historical origin of Coilus, a 'king' of Britain in the early Roman period in *Historia Regum Britanniae*. (Author's collection)

Above: A view of Paris, the city that Arthur besieges after his Gallic enemy Frollo takes refuge there in *Historia Regum Britanniae*. (Courtesy of Hermenegildo Santamaria under Creative Commons 2.0)

Below: The ancient ruins of the Roman Forum. Rome was the home of the majority of emperors who feature in *Historia Regum Britanniae*, and it is this city that Arthur sets out to attack near the conclusion of his mighty European campaign. (Author's collection)

Above: St Michael's Mount, Cornwall. According to local folklore, Jack slew a giant living here named Cormoran, likely a distant memory of Count Conomor of Brittany. The correlation between this folktale and the account of Arthur slaying a giant on Mont-Saint-Michel in Brittany indicates that the giant of the Arthurian tale was also Conomor, and this helps to establish the chronology of Arthur's life. (Author's collection)

Inset: According to local folklore, the grave of the giant Cormoran slain by Jack on St Michael's Mount, Cornwall. It is very likely that Cormoran had his origin in the real sixth-century Count Conomor of Brittany and Cornwall. (Author's collection)

Below: The Adriatic Sea. It was in this sea that Andragathius, Magnus Maximus's cavalry commander, was said to have killed himself by jumping overboard. There is, however, reason to believe that Andragathius faked his death. (Courtesy of Breta Valek under Creative Commons 2.0)

as 'S. Plicius'. If so, then one can see how this may have been misread or inferred as 'Suplicius'.

Whatever the case, Pope Simplicius cannot be the pope of the story. Regardless of the origin of the Gallic conquest, the pope is mentioned in the context of Gawain, whose lifetime cannot be pushed back to the fifth century by any stretch of logic. In fact, the connection is doubly inadmissible, for Simplicius became pope in 468, yet the mention of 'Pope Supplicius' occurs immediately prior to Arthur's *first* Gallic campaign, putting it at least fourteen years before the final battle against the Romans.[6] Yet it is this final battle that Ashe would require to be Riothamus's battle of 470. Therefore, according to this Riothamus theory, the 'Supplicius' of the story should be a pope of 456. The pope of that time was named Leo, which is completely dissimilar to 'Supplicius'.

In all, the connection between Pope Supplicius and Pope Simplicius must be rejected. The two are not a chronological match even according to Ashe's own theory, and the pope of the story is firmly linked to Gawain, of the historical family of Cynfarch and would have been twelve years old around 556–562. The pope at this time was named Pelagius, and he seems to be the Supplicius of the story.

The supposed connection between Mordred and Arvandus is equally weak. The activities of the two bear virtually no similarities whatsoever. The two are made to seem more similar than they really are by merely referring to them as 'betraying' Arthur and Riothamus, respectively. In reality, Mordred usurped the throne of Britain while Arthur was away. It is then Arthur who goes and attacks him to reclaim his kingdom, leading to the Battle of Camlann. Arvandus, on the other hand, encouraged the Visigoths to attack Riothamus's army rather than pursuing peace with the Romans. He played no larger role than that. True, he was arrested for treason, which may be likened to Mordred's role, but it was treason against the Romans, to whom Riothamus and his army were merely allies. Additionally, Arvandus's actions led to the battle against Euric; this is the battle that is supposed to correspond to the battle at Siesia, *not* the later Battle of Camlann.

The concept that Riothamus's flight to Burgundy, probably through the town of Avallon, led to the story of Arthur being taken to Avalon after the Battle of Camlann is flawed for much the same reasons as the Mordred-Arvandus connection. The battle between Riothamus and Euric must be the one at Siesia, but Arthur was said to have been taken to Avalon after the later Battle of Camlann, not Siesia. The battles of Camlann and Siesia are manifestly not the same.

An additional argument that Ashe uses to support this theory is the fact that several chronicles place Arthur's reign around the 470s, which is a match for the reign of Riothamus. There is the statement of Albericus Trium Fontium, of the second quarter of the thirteenth century, that Arthur reigned from 459 to 475. Then there is a thirteenth-century version of the *Salzburg Annals*, which records that 'Arthur, of whom many stories are told, reigned in Britain'. This statement appears in the entry for Hilarius's accession in 461, agreeing with the dates given by Albericus Trium Fontium. Next, Martinus Polonus, of the second half of the fourteenth century, believed that Arthur reigned during the pontificate of Hilarius, which was from 461 to 468. Jacques de Guise is the next source; he says that a part of Belgium experienced oppression in the time of Arthur and the Huns, Goths and Vandals. As the Huns stopped being a significant threat after Attila the Hun's death in 453, Ashe reasoned that the start of Arthur's reign cannot have been much later, which also conforms to the previously stated dates. The same writer, Jacques de Guise, also stated that Arthur was the ruler in Britain at the time when Aegidius ruled northern Gaul, which was from 461 to 464.

The main flaw in all these supposed pieces of evidence is the simple fact that they all post-date *HRB*. Ashe claims that these sources cannot originate with *HRB*, for they mention Arthur in conjunction with figures not mentioned by Geoffrey (such as Hilarius and Aegidius). However, this does not follow. Despite giving his year of abdication as 541, Geoffrey does place Arthur's reign in the time of Emperor Leo. As this Leo is mentioned both during Arthur's first and second Gallic campaigns, this can only be Leo I.[7] It would not have been a mystery to Albericus as to when Leo I reigned; it was from 457 to 474. This, of course, conflicts with the date given for Arthur's abdication. Any historian would have to choose between following the explicit date given and the information regarding the reigning Roman emperor. It is not surprising that, over the course of a few hundred years after Geoffrey of Monmouth wrote his very popular book, several people gave greater weight to the information regarding the reigning emperor.

While no one can say for sure where Albericus acquired his sixteen-year reign for Arthur, its placement during the reign of Leo I is easily explained as coming from Geoffrey of Monmouth. Exactly the same can be said for the next source used by Ashe – the later, thirteenth-century *Salzburg Annals*. The compiler would have known when Leo I reigned, so he would have known that Arthur's rule 'must' have been contemporary with Hilarius's accession. Potentially, he may have acquired this 'fact' from the dates provided by Albericus, if not from *HRB* directly. Similarly, Martinus Polonus's claim that Arthur ruled during Hilarius's pontificate could have been based on exactly the same logic, or it could even have been derived from the entry in the *Salzburg Annals*. Jacques de Guise, who explicitly noted the fact that Arthur's reign is set in the time of Emperor Leo, should not have been unfamiliar with the dates of Aegidius's reign.

The reality is, unless any of the people whose statements place Arthur's reign around the 460s and 470s claimed to be translating or working from an ancient source that predated *HRB*, there really is no basis for believing that any of these statements do not simply originate with the *HRB* itself.

Nonetheless, the fact remains that Geoffrey of Monmouth does set the Gallic campaign in the reign of a Roman emperor called Leo. Since there are at least two emperors involved at the time of the story, it cannot be any of the later Byzantium emperors by that name, as there were no longer two emperors of the Roman Empire after the fifth century. And as Leo II's reign was not long enough to be the Leo of the tale, Leo I is the only emperor who fits the profile. However, as we have seen from this section, the only event to occur during his reign that is even remotely similar to the Arthurian legend is not nearly enough like the story to be the origin behind it. Certainly, a conquest of Gaul and the slaying of its leader would be noted, as would a battle against the combined forces of many nations. Since, historically, nothing similar enough to the Arthurian legend occurred in the reign of Leo I, the inescapable conclusion is that whatever reality is behind the tale must have occurred in the reign of a different emperor. Either 'Leo' is a rendering of an epithet of some sort – perhaps a Welsh epithet or title meaning 'the Lion' – or it is a corruption of the emperor's real name.

Lucius Artorius Castus

Another attempt to connect the Arthurian legend to a known historical figure is found in a theory that originated in the 1920s and has since been developed by several others. This claims that a Roman officer known as Lucius Artorius Castus was the basis for King Arthur. To be clear, this is not merely an attempt to explain the European campaign. The proponents of this theory think that Lucius Artorius Castus explains the greater part of the Arthurian legend, including Arthur's activities in Britain.

It is not known exactly when Artorius lived, but his life is generally placed between the second and third centuries CE. Obviously, he cannot have had any interactions with Dubricius, Budic of Llydaw, Cadoc, Illtud, Gildas, the family of Cynfarch, and many other individuals with whom the legendary King Arthur was said to have interacted. We have already identified the historical figure behind those legends – Athrwys ap Meurig. Likewise, Arthur's family can be clearly identified as members of Athrwys's family. So the idea that Artorius could in any way be the primary figure behind the Arthurian legends is completely untenable. Nonetheless, the idea that the stories of Athrwys's life could have been unintentionally combined with legends of Artorius is a reasonable suggestion. The similarity of their names would easily have allowed such a confusion to take place. This would eliminate the problem of Artorius being hundreds of years removed from the Arthurian period. Therefore, could the origin of the European campaign lie with Artorius?

Pertinent information about Artorius's career is found on his memorial plaque in Croatia. It lists the various positions he held during his life, noting that he was the prefect of the *Legio VI Victrix*, which was based in York during the time when Artorius was active. Therefore, we know that he was in Britain for a time, so it is not unreasonable to suppose that tales of his activities would have continued to have been told among the Britons, provided he was sufficiently noteworthy. Furthermore, the same inscription also informs us that he took two legions from Britain to fight against the 'Arm____s'. Unfortunately, the inscription has been broken in half, with some material missing from the space between the two halves. The 'm' is on the very end of the first half; the 's' begins the same line on the other half on the plaque.

It has been speculated that the word was 'Armoricos', as a shortening of 'Armoricanos'. This would mean that a high-ranking officer in Britain named Artorius led a campaign into Gaul to fight against the Armoricans. The proponents of the Lucius Artorius Castus theory consider this to be evidence that his career has significant similarities to that of the legendary King Arthur.

By itself, this might just seem like a vague similarity. However, some of the theory's main pieces of evidence involve the Sarmatians. About 5,500 of these Iranians were, having been defeated by Marcus Aurelius in 175, sent to Britain. The theory goes that Lucius Artorius led a band of these warriors across northern Britain when fighting the Caledonians. The significance of this is that several researchers (notably Covington Scott Littleton, Linda A. Malcor and John Matthews) have pointed out perceived similarities between Sarmatian legends and the Arthurian legends. For example, there is a legend of a warrior-king known as Batraz who displays several similarities to the legends of King Arthur. As a young man, he pulls a sword from the roots of a tree, which is reminiscent of the stories of Arthur pulling a sword from a stone as a youth. Furthermore, after being mortally wounded, Batraz is said to have asked his companion to throw his sword into the ocean. At first, the companion only pretends to do this, yet eventually is persuaded to actually do it. When he does this, the sea turns blood-coloured and turbulent.

There are clear similarities between this legend and the story of Arthur getting his companion Bedivere to throw his sword into a lake after being mortally wounded. There are supposedly many more similarities between Sarmatian legends and the Arthurian legends, all of which apparently provide convincing evidence that these aspects of the Arthurian legends, excluding the ones that obviously have a later historical basis, may indeed come from Sarmatian mythology. There is really nothing unexpected about this, given that we know several thousand Sarmatians were brought to Britain and evidently stayed there for a long time, if not indefinitely – it is easy to imagine that their mythology would have influenced, to one degree or another, the local legends and even stories of historical figures.

At first, this seems like an appealing theory. Artorius was a military officer in Britain who led a campaign into Gaul and was associated with a group of Iranians who had legends that are very similar to the Arthurian tales. A sensible idea could be that the Britons combined the tales of Athrwys ap Meurig (*the* King Arthur of the sixth century) with tales of Artorius, whose own life story had accumulated legends from his warriors, the Sarmatians. The result of this would mean that the stories of Arthur were a fusion of the life of Athrwys, Artorius and Sarmatian legends.

But, regardless of all the connections to the Sarmatians that can be found, however numerous they may or may not be, this does not mean that Lucius Artorius was King Arthur. If Artorius was the only military officer in Britain to have led the Sarmatians, then the conclusion laid out in the previous paragraph would, indeed, be a logical theory. However, the Sarmatians stayed in Britain long after Artorius left. Numerous other officers would have had interactions with them, leading their cavalry into battle across Britain. Why would they be more strongly associated with Artorius than with any of the other officers who led them? In fact, it is not the Sarmatians themselves who show a link to the stories of King Arthur, but it is their myths and legends. These would likely have become absorbed into the local legends of the Britons – perhaps with the story of Batraz being linked to the known Celtic custom of throwing swords into lakes – and could quite easily have become attached to Athrwys ap Meurig. The Roman officer Artorius can be removed from the equation entirely.

Really, the only reason to even consider Lucius Artorius Castus as having anything to do with the Arthurian legends is the fact that he supposedly led a campaign into Gaul. As with Riothamus's campaign into Gaul, it is vitally important to actually assess just how similar the two events are, and whether Artorius's campaign could realistically have led to the stories of Arthur's European conquest.

In truth, this theory suffers from many of the same downfalls that impact the Riothamus theory. Firstly, the campaign is on much too small a scale. The Armoricans inhabited modern-day Brittany, so Artorius's campaign would logically have been confined to that small part of Gaul. Arthur, meanwhile, is not said to have engaged in a small area of the country, but is said to have killed the very ruler of Gaul. The extent of both the first and second conquest goes far beyond the area of the Armoricans. In fact, even the seriously flawed Riothamus theory is superior in this regard, as that warrior made it much further into Gaul than Artorius would have.

Another flaw – one that is common to both theories – is the fact that Artorius did not fight against the Romans. Rather, he fought *with* them. In fact, this flaw is even more damning to the Lucius Artorius Castus theory, as Riothamus was an independent king, albeit assisting the Romans. Artorius, however, was actually a Roman officer. It is exceedingly difficult, even more so than with the Riothamus theory, to see how this could have been corrupted into Arthur battling *against* the Romans. Due to the severely limited information about the details of Artorius's activities, it is very hard to compare them with the legendary activities of Arthur. However, what little information we do have is completely incompatible with the legend. There is simply no reason to believe that Artorius's European campaign had anything at all to do with King Arthur's.

This analysis has allowed the theory all the favour that can be granted it. In reality, it is entirely possible that the inscription did not read 'Armoricos', but actually read 'Armenios' – that is, the inhabitants of Armenia. The first known drawing of the inscription recorded a ligatured 'ME' before the edge of the plaque, and presumably the stone has weathered since then, in the mid-1800s. This reading is normally preferred now, particularly in conjunction with the lack of evidence of disturbances among the Armoricans in this period. In contrast, there were many known disturbances among the Armenians in this period; notably, the Roman–Parthian War of 161–166. If this is correct, as is supposed by most modern scholars, then there is no evidence that Lucius Artorius Castus had anything whatsoever to do with the Armoricans. Hence, when he left Britain, he did not fight in Gaul, but travelled all the way over to Armenia. Therefore, this theory really would be utterly baseless. There is no need for an alternative insular Arthur, as Athrwys fits that identification, and Artorius cannot be the Continental Arthur, as he did not fight in Gaul.

If Artorius went to Armenia during the war of 161–166, as some researchers think, then he would have left Britain before the Sarmatians came in 175, thereby nullifying any supposed connection between him and the Sarmatian mythology. Even if this were not the case, many researchers have rejected the strength of the similarities that Littleton and Malcor claim to have found between the Sarmatian mythology and the Arthurian legends. One major criticism is the fact that most, if not all, of the information about 'Sarmatian legends' actually comes from Ossetian legends, recorded in the nineteenth century. It is assumed, by the proponents of the theory, that these accurately reflect the legends that the ancient Sarmatians would have had, though this is an enormous assumption. It is certainly within the realms of possibility that certain motifs or details in these legends actually come *from* the famous, widespread Arthurian literature, rather than the other way around. Or alternatively, it is possible that the legends did come to Britain from the land of the ancient Sarmatians, but much later in history. For example, it may have happened during the time of the Crusades. It need not be related to the presence of the Sarmatians in Britain in the second century.

But regardless, even if the legends in all their relevant details truly do date back to the time of Lucius, really were part of the Sarmatian culture specifically, really do contain the strong similarities that Littleton and Malcor claim they do, and the Sarmatians really were in Britain at the same time that Lucius Artorius was there, and Artorius really did travel to Armorica, there is still no valid basis for connecting him to King Arthur. As we have seen, there is already a clearly identified insular Arthur, and any engagement by Artorius on the Continent was either much too small scale or in the wrong place. The 'Sarmatian legends', for their part, may or may not have found their way into the Arthurian mythos, but there is no basis to conclude that they would have found themselves attached to Artorius as opposed to the sixth-century Athrwys ap Meurig directly.

Llenlleawg Wyddel

This is a theory that is supported by Arthurian researchers Barber and Pykitt, though it was suggested much earlier in the twentieth century by Roger Sheerman Loomis. This is based on several characters mentioned in early Welsh tales of Arthur. For this reason, it does not connect the European conquest with any known historical event, but it develops a hypothetical scenario on which the legend was supposedly based.

In *Culhwch ac Olwen*, there is a character in Arthur's court list called Llenlleawg Wyddel, this latter word meaning 'the Irishman'. He is said to have 'seized Caledfwlch [Excalibur] and brandished it' while with Arthur on an expedition to Ireland. This expedition involved retrieving a magical cauldron. In *Preiddeu Annwn*, another Welsh tale about a voyage, there is also a mention of a cauldron. Near to this reference, there is the line: 'Cledyf lluch lleawg idaw ry dyrchit.'

The first part of this is sometimes rendered: 'The sword of Llwch Lleawg.' This is taken to be related to the episode in *Culhwch ac Olwen*, involving Llenlleawg grasping Arthur's sword. If this is a valid connection, then Llwch Lleawg and Llenlleawg Wyddel would logically be alternative names for the same person, 'Lleawg' being a shortening of 'Llenlleawg'. Therefore, if he was known alternatively as Llwch Lleawg and also Llenlleawg Wyddel, this opens up the possibility that the character may, in some stories, have been known as 'Llwch Wyddel'. Llwch could quite easily be Latinised into Lucius, and Wyddel may have been Latinised into Hibernus, from the Latin name for Ireland, 'Hibernia'. From there, it would be a fairly simple corruption from Hibernus to Hiberius. The result of this would be the name of Arthur's Roman enemy in the European conquest: Lucius Hiberius (also recorded as 'Lucius Tiberius' in various manuscripts).

The theory then claims that Arthur's attack on the Gauls was actually an attack on the Gaels – that is, the Irish. Hence, rather than travelling to Gaul and fighting on the Continent, he travelled to Ireland, remaining in the British Isles.

In its entirety, the theory claims that Llwch Lleawg, Llenlleawg Wyddel, another character from *Culhwch ac Olwen*, known as Llwch Llawwynnyawc, and the hypothetical 'Llwch Wyddel' are all the same person, all deriving from the Irish god Lugh. Barber and Pykitt evidently consider these to have originated with a real Irish person who simply shared a name with the Irish god. Llawwynnyawc is then considered to be identical to Lleenog, the father of a king of the North known as Gwallog. These two historical kings are then considered to be the origins of Lancelot and his son Galahad, respectively.

This historical Lleenog, then, would be Llwch Wyddel – the Lucius Hiberius of the 'European' conquest – and Lancelot. This idea is supported by the fact that Lancelot does occupy the position of Lucius in the later romances. Lancelot is the one whom Arthur fights when he travels to Gaul (in fact, it is for this very reason that Arthur travels there) in these tales, rather than Lucius.

However, this theory relies on a great deal of assumptions. Firstly, the line in *Preiddeu Annwn* that supposedly mentions a 'Llwch Lleawg' probably does no such thing. Patrick Sims-Williams points out that *'lluch* is probably the adjective "flashing", since *cledyf lluch* [as it appears in the poem] is an attested collocation'. Therefore, the line would mean 'The flashing sword of Lleawg', rather than 'The sword of Llwch Lleawg', erasing that piece of evidence for Llenlleawg Wyddel having 'Llwch' as part of his name. Additionally, the name 'Lleawg' apparently means 'death-dealing', so while it could be a name, it could also easily be an adjective.[8] This would mean 'The death-dealing flashing sword'. If this reading is correct, then the line would have nothing whatsoever to do with Llenlleawg.

The primary reason to give Llenlleawg Wyddel the additional name 'Llwch' actually seems to be by reason of identifying him with the god Lugh, along with Llwch Llawwynnyawc. However, while there is a perceivable reason for identifying this latter person with Lugh, equating either of them with Llenlleawg Wyddel is utterly without any basis whatsoever.[9]

Setting Llenlleawg aside from this point on, it is notable that Llwch Llawwynnyawc is described, in *Culhwch ac Olwen*, as being 'from beyond the raging sea'. Perhaps this means he came from Ireland. If so, then it is plausible that he would have been recorded as Llwch Llawwynnyawc Wyddel on occasion, or even just Llwch Wyddel. This being the case, we return to the possibility of Llwch

Wyddel becoming Lucius Hibernus and then Lucius Hiberius. This is valid only if one accepts that 'from beyond the raging sea' means 'from Ireland', which may or may not be correct, and that Llwch Llawwynnyawc was recorded with the epithet 'Wyddel', which is only a possibility if the previous assumption is correct.

So if we accept these hypotheses, then there would, according to the available sources, have been a person living in Arthur's time whose name could have been translated into Lucius Hibernus. It is admittedly not too difficult to see how 'Hibernus' could become 'Hiberius' through a scribal error. All things considered, this is by far the best theory considered so far to account for the name of Arthur's enemy in the story.

This theory continues to surpass the previous two in that there is a record of an invasion and conquest that is reasonably similar to Arthur's Gallic invasion and conquest. The account reports how Arthur set out to conquer Ireland, and was met by the king there, Guillamurius. However, the Irish king's army fled and then the king himself was captured. After this, Arthur conquers all of Ireland. This is superior to the previous two theories in that this actually involves the conquering of a large area. Nonetheless, it diverges from the European account in several ways. Firstly, the majority of Frollo's army was said to have switched to Arthur's side, whereas here, the opposing army flee from Arthur. Secondly, Frollo is killed, whereas Guillamurius is just captured with no mention of his death. Still, these are relatively minor differences, and one can see the attraction in the theory. This account of Arthur subduing the land of the Gaels could conceivably have been corrupted into an account of Arthur subduing the land of the Gauls, with various minor errors being introduced during the course of transmission.

However, the theory is not without its difficulties. One such difficulty is the fact that the aforementioned account that describes this conquest of Ireland is actually contained in Geoffrey's HRB itself. It is separated from the actual Gallic conquest by twelve years of peace. Thus, to accept this as the origin of the Gallic conquest, one would have to accept the notion that the account has been duplicated.

Additionally, it only explains the first half of the European campaign. It does not explain the subsequent attack against the

Romans, after Arthur received a letter from them condemning him for the conquest of their territory. This is the part of the story in which Lucius is introduced. But there is no record of any warfare or even animosity between Arthur and Llwch Llawwynnyawc or any of the other men who are supposedly identical. This being the case, the idea that the second part of Arthur's European conquest comes from an attack on Ireland relies on a completely hypothetical scenario for which there is no actual evidence. It also disregards the fact that, in the account of this second expedition to Gaul in the *HRB*, Arthur assists the niece of Hoel of Brittany, clearly showing that the story is taking place on the Continent. Further, in the prelude to this second expedition, Arthur's court was said to have received a letter from Rome. Even if the Gauls and the Gaels were confused, placing the campaign in Gaul rather than Ireland, it is very difficult to see how Rome could have become involved in the story. How would Llwch have become a Roman senator? By Arthur's time, Gaul had long since ceased to be governed by the Romans.

It might be argued that the evidence of conflict between Arthur and Llwch Llawwynnyawc is the fact that, according to the theory, Llawwynnyawc can be identified as Lleenog, who can, in turn, be identified as Lancelot. As Arthur was demonstrably said to have fought Lancelot in Gaul, then by extension, it is evident that there was a tradition of Arthur fighting Llwch Llawwynnyawc, regardless of *how* that ended up being transferred to Gaul.

So is there good reason for accepting these two identifications? Well, let us first consider the identification of Llwch Llawwynnyawc with Lleenog. This spelling of the latter character's name is the modern, commonly used spelling. In the *Harleian MS 3859*, his name is spelt Laenauc. The 'auc' ending is simply the antiquated version of 'awc', so this is equivalent to the ending of Llwch's second name. However, Llwch's name ends, in full, with 'yawc', which has two syllables, not one. Additionally, it seems improbable that the initial 'Llawwy' could have become 'Llae', 'Lyey', 'Llei', or 'Llee', as the name is variously spelt. One would expect the initial 'aw' to be reduced to 'o', as has happened on the end of Lleenog's name. However, it must be acknowledged that, as mentioned in a previous chapter, a certain historical individual called Rhun ap

Nwython appears in *Culhwch ac Olwen*, while his father's name is spelt 'Neithon' in the Harleian genealogies. This supports the idea that 'Llawwy', as it is spelt in *Culhwch ac Olwen*, may have been spelt 'Llawei' in other records. With the 'aw' becoming 'o' and the 'wy' becoming 'ei', the full development of the name might be expected to be something like 'Lloeiniog'. Though the value of the vowel is different, the 'Lyey' spelling found in the *Jesus College MS 20* supports the idea that Lleenog's name could have originally had an extra vowel between the 'L' and the 'e'. With sufficient transmission, it is fairly plausible that Lloeiniog could have been reduced to Lleinog, or Lleenog, as it is now commonly spelt. However, the Harleian genealogies are roughly contemporary with *Culhwch ac Owlen*, making it unlikely – though not impossible – that one would have a spelling that is far older than the other.

Therefore, while it might just about be possible for Llawwynnyawc to have become Lleenog, is there really any reason to believe that they were the same person? One significant reason to believe that they were not is the fact that Llwch Llawwynnyawc was said to have come from 'beyond the raging sea', whereas Lleenog is listed as the son of Mar or Maeswig, the grandson of Coel Hen of the North. His son, Gwallog, is explicitly listed as one of the 'Men of the Old North' in the Harleian and Jesus College genealogies. Hence, Lleenog was not Irish, and there is no reason to believe he ever spent any time in Ireland.

Given the unlikelihood that Lleenog's name would have ever been spelt 'Llawwynnyawc', especially in a tale contemporary with a record that spelt it 'Llaenauc', and the fact that there is every reason to think that he lived in Britain, the balance of probability is that Lleenog from the North and Llwch Llawwynnyawc 'from beyond the raging sea' are not the same person. They were simply two people living at about the same time with vaguely similar names. Certainly, Lleenog would not have been termed 'Wyddel' – the Irishman – as he was not Irish. There is, therefore, no basis for giving Lleenog any title that could have become Hibernus or Hiberius, nor is there any reason to associate him with the name Llwch or Lucius.

With this identification invalidated, there is no reason whatsoever to believe that Lleenog had anything to do with Arthur's European conquest. Even if there is good reason for believing that Lleenog was the origin of Lancelot, there is no reasonable explanation for the invasion of Gaul. Even if the two kings fought each other, Arthur would not have been fighting against the Gaels, as Lleenog was a king of the northern Britons, not the Irish. The theory that the Gaels were confused with the Gauls is not a possibility if the Gaels were never even involved. Consider that Lucius first appears in *HRB*, while Lancelot does not appear in his role as Arthur's enemy in France until quite some time after this. Lucius is also never described as a companion of Arthur's before this European war, in contrast to Lancelot. It thus seems far more likely that, whatever the origin of Lancelot, he was a separate character who simply came to take on the role that Lucius originally held. Hence, even if Lleenog was the origin of Lancelot and he really did fight Arthur for whatever reason, it is most unlikely that this has anything to do with the origin of the Gallic conquest.

In truth, there is no evidence that Lleenog was the origin of Lancelot. This theory relies on the identification of Lleenog with Llwch Llawwynnyawc, and in turn with the Irish god Lugh, as it is based on perceived similarities between Lugh and Lancelot.[10] If either of these identifications are wrong – and, as we have seen, they are both unlikely – then the theory falls apart.

Even if Lleenog were removed from the equation altogether and Llwch Llawwynnyawc (Wyddel) were claimed to be a derivation of Lugh and the origin of Lancelot, this theory is still not an acceptable explanation of the European conquest. Notice that the association, now, is between Lancelot and the tales of the Irish *god* Lugh, not any hypothetical Irish ruler of the sixth century by the same name. Thus, this explanation of the European conquest relegates it to the land of myth, not confused history. But as we saw in the previous chapter, Geoffrey of Monmouth's boundaries of accuracy are much narrower than is normally claimed – there is no precedent, after the start of the Roman era, for an entire event of the scale of Arthur's second European invasion to be completely unhistorical, as this theory would require. To make the point clear, this second European invasion is the subject of more or less the entirety of Book Ten of *Historia Regum Britanniae*. To claim that this entire section is fictional is totally at odds with what has been established about the *HRB*. Further, as has already been mentioned, it seems far more probable that Lancelot was an independent character who simply took on the role of Lucius in later legends, which means that the tale of Arthur fighting Lancelot cannot possibly be the origin of the much earlier tale of Arthur fighting Lucius.[11]

In summary, there is no good reason to believe that Llenlleawg Wyddel (the Irishman) had the first name 'Llwch'. There is no evidence whatsoever that he should be equated with the Irish god Lugh. Llwch Llawwynnyawc, meanwhile, might have been from Ireland and therefore could plausibly have had the epithet 'Wyddel', though this is uncertain. Regardless of whether or not Llwch came from Lugh and whether Lugh was the origin of Lancelot, the tale of Arthur fighting Lucius greatly predates the tale of Arthur fighting Lancelot in Gaul. It is therefore much more likely that Lancelot simply took on the role of Lucius as Arthur's pre-Camlann Gallic enemy and that Lucius has a totally separate origin. Further, even if Lugh's Gaels were confused with the Gauls, this does nothing to explain Rome's involvement or how Lugh became a Roman, rather than a Gaul. It also does not account for the fact that the episode involving the family of Hoel of Brittany immediately prior to the engagement with the Romans clearly shows that the story is set in Gaul, not Ireland. Additionally, by making Arthur's European campaign a mythic war against an ancient god, the theory completely disregards the boundaries of accuracy that are clearly set by the rest of Geoffrey's book from the Roman era onwards.

Conclusions

As Geoffrey Ashe noted, any consideration of *Historia Regum Britanniae* from the start of the Roman era onwards makes it glaringly obvious that *something* must have been the origin of Arthur's Gallic campaign. The *HRB* may contain many inaccuracies, but the idea that such a major portion of this record of Arthur's life could be fundamentally based on a fiction is completely at odds with the rest of the book – it is without precedent.

Furthermore, the consideration of the Roman era specifically has helped to make it clear that none of the theories discussed in this chapter could have been the origin of the story of the European conquest. It must be made very clear that the story is fundamentally a *conquest* of Gaul, not simply a minor battle there, and it was *against* the Romans. While it is not impossible for the sides to have been switched, such a conclusion would only be permissible if there were active reason to equate the two pertinent events. With both Lucius Artorius Castus and Riothamus, this is not the case. The extreme dissimilarity of the patterns of events involved makes such equations invalid. If the patterns of events were sufficiently similar, then the argument that the enemies could have been turned into Romans, and the allegiance *with* the Romans could have been lost somehow, might be acceptable. However, the fact that this fundamental aspect would have to be mistaken according to these theories *in addition* to the fact that the patterns of events bear no similarity to each other makes it virtually impossible for these to be the origin of Geoffrey of Monmouth's account.

The case gets even worse for these – and similar – theories when Welsh material is taken into account. In the early Welsh tale *Culhwch ac Olwen*, Arthur's porter lists numerous locations to which he has been; the implication is that these are all places in which Arthur has fought, his porter merely travelling to those locations due to this fact. Therefore, it is significant that the porter mentions how he has been in Europe, Africa, the islands of Corsica, Greece, and even India. If no candidate thus far could match the events described in *HRB*, then for any of them to account for this far greater conquest indicated by *Culhwch ac Olwen* is instantly inconceivable.[12]

But even setting this Welsh record aside for the moment, we are still left with the lack of any historical origin for King Arthur's Gallic conquest as found in *HRB*. There is evidence that the sixth-century Arthur did travel to and fight in Gaul, and this evidence will be considered later, but this still cannot come close to accounting for the majority of the events in the story. The legendary King Arthur of Geoffrey of Monmouth's *Historia Regum Britanniae* simply must be a composite figure, otherwise the Arthurian section contains a complete deviation from the established boundaries of accuracy in the book. It is purely a matter of being able to identify the second individual. We have seen in this chapter that it cannot have been Riothamus, nor can it have been Lucius Artorius Castus.

We have also seen that, since the account refers to Arthur sending a message to the Roman emperors, the historical origin must be found somewhere before 476, which marked the end of the western Roman emperors. For the same reason, the events must have taken place after 284, which is when the empire split in two.

Who, then, of the 284–476 period was the second figure who came to compose such a significant part of the famous legend of King Arthur?

6

The Man Who Conquered Europe

One of Geoffrey Ashe's claims is that Riothamus is the only person who is known to have done anything Arthurian. But, as shown in the previous chapter, Riothamus's activities were hardly Arthurian at all. In the *Historia Regum Britanniae*'s account, Arthur conquered Gaul, personally killing its ruler, and then, after several years of peace, he fought a fierce and bloody battle against a united force of Romans and other nations. If there was a figure known to history who did this, *then* they could be said to have done something Arthurian.

In view of the forgoing, and the fact that the event must have taken place between 284 and 476, it is quite obvious that the origin of this Arthurian legend lies, not with a minor incursion into Gaul such as by Riothamus or Lucius Artorius Castus, but with one of the usurpations within the Roman Empire during this period. Naturally, it is most likely that the usurper in question would have been based in Britain, or otherwise was strongly associated with it.

The Men Who Seized the Empire

One notable example is Constantine the Great. He became emperor in Britain and was even believed to have been born in Britain by some later historians, such as the writer of Geoffrey of Monmouth's source. He achieved great fame and power, which accords with the description of Arthur in *HRB* before he sets out to conquer Gaul. Additionally, both Arthur and Constantine fought against the inhabitants of northern Britain before leaving for Gaul. Constantine then marched from Britain to Rome and fought against the Roman emperor, Maxentius. However, it is at this point that the similarities between Constantine and Arthur end. The latter, as has been repeatedly stated, conquered Gaul and killed its ruler. On the other hand, Constantine received Gaul essentially as an inheritance upon the death of his father, Emperor Constantius. He did not have to conquer it, nor kill its Roman ruler, for he *was* its Roman ruler before he had even arrived. Additionally, there was no period of peace between arriving on the Continent and departing to attack Rome. Furthermore, Constantine's journey towards Rome was characterised by the progressive capture of cities, whereas there is no indication of this in the Arthurian account. Another dissimilarity between the two is the fact that there is no record of Maxentius coming against Constantine with an army composed of various non-Roman allies.

Really, the similarities between Constantine and Arthur are rather generic, and there are just as many differences as there are similarities.

There are some interesting similarities between the Arthurian legend and the historical usurpation of Constantine III. He was a soldier in Britain who was proclaimed emperor by his troops in 407. He invaded Gaul and seized it from the legitimate Roman government. He did this by means of two prominent generals, one of whom was a Briton. This British general's name was Edobichus. He, along with a general named Gerontius, was sent to battle Sarus, the general of the legitimate western emperor Honorius. Just like Frollo in the Arthurian legend, Sarus fled. And interestingly, Gerontius's name is equivalent to 'Geraint', one of the companions of the sixth-century Arthur.

Another similarity is the fact that, some months later, Constantine sent Gerontius to Spain to attack several cousins of Honorius before they could attack him. Gerontius succeeded in defeating them and actually captured two of them. This is reminiscent of the first conflict between Arthur's men and the Romans during the second campaign into Gaul. The outcome of this skirmish is that many Roman soldiers were captured and taken back to Arthur, who was not with his men for this incident. This ties into the idea that Edobichus was 'Arthur', inasmuch as he was not present for the incident involving Honorius's cousins.

Finally, at the end of Constantine's reign, Edobichus marched to the rescue of Constantine, who was being besieged by a certain Constantius, one of Honorius's generals. However, his army was defeated and Edobichus fled the scene. He was then found by someone who desired the favour of Honorius, and was thus executed.

So we see that the activities of Edobichus reflect a number of parallels with the activities of Arthur as described by Geoffrey of Monmouth. Upon an initial invasion of Gaul, both Edobichus and Arthur confront a Roman leader of some kind and cause that ruler to flee. Their men are then subsequently involved in the fight with and capture of a number of supporters of the enemy side. Then there is a final battle against the Romans.

Though there are some parallels, there is no real case to be made here. The differences are too severe for the few, mostly generic, similarities to outweigh. Sarus was merely a general for the Romans who happened to fight against Edobichus in Gaul. He was not the ruler of that territory. And he was in the middle of a siege against Constantine when Edobichus arrived to defeat him. There is no mention of this siege in Geoffrey's account. Rather, Frollo is said to have gone out with his army to meet Arthur upon news of his arrival in Gaul. Most of his army is said to have switched sides before he fled, which is not something for which there is any evidence in the case of Sarus. Furthermore, Sarus was not killed, but completely escaped the clutches of Constantine's forces. This is in contrast to Frollo, who found refuge in a city that was besieged for a time before eventually engaging in a jousting battle against Arthur, resulting in his death.

Regarding the capture of Honorius's cousins, this event took place very shortly after the defeat of Sarus, and there was a gap of several years, with no meaningful connection, between this and the final battle between Edobichus and Honorius's forces. In contrast, the capture of Roman soldiers by Arthur's men occurs at the start of their second expedition into Gaul; it commences the march toward Rome, which culminates in the final battle against the Romans at Siesia. The final battle involving Edobichus, for its part, was an engagement to save Constantine from another siege. But again, no mention is made of a siege in the Arthurian account.

In short, while being the closest match considered so far, there is still no real reason to conclude that this event had anything to do with the legend of Arthur's European conquest. But what should be clear is that it is a serious mistake to say that Riothamus is the only person known to have done anything Arthurian. He is not. Both Edobichus and Constantine the Great are superior in their similarities to the legendary Arthur, and it is likely that similarities to Arthur that are far more substantial than those that Riothamus can lay claim to can be found in many other Britain-based usurpers or their generals.

However, there is one particular individual connected to a famous usurpation whose activities bear more than a few passing similarities to the activities of Arthur. The usurpation is that of Magnus Maximus, and the individual is his cavalry commander, Andragathius, to whom 'the general direction of the war' was given, according to the Roman historian Orosius. Consider the following comparison:

King Arthur arrives in Gaul and is met by Frollo, a Roman tribune in control of Gaul. Most of Frollo's army switches sides, and he is thus forced to flee to Paris. Arthur besieges the city for a number of months, and then he and Frollo agree to have a formal, one-to-one fight. They do this, and Arthur slays Frollo.
Andragathius, in the service of Magnus Maximus, arrived in Gaul and was met by the army of Western Emperor Gratian near Paris. After several days with small skirmishes, the majority of Gratian's army switched sides and Gratian was forced to flee. Andragathius was sent in pursuit of him. He caught up with Gratian at the city of Lyons and killed him.

King Arthur then proceeds to subdue all of Gaul over a period of several years and becomes its ruler. He then returns to Britain.
With his slaying of Gratian, Andragathius essentially won the majority of the Western Empire for Maximus, and soon afterwards Maximus was officially recognised as the joint Western Emperor with Valentinian II by the Eastern Emperor Theodosius, who was too occupied with difficulties in the East to oppose Maximus.

After several more years, King Arthur receives a letter from the Romans condemning him for his actions and demanding tribute. This incites Arthur to attack Rome with a large army composed of various nations.

Maximus remained emperor for several years. Finally, in 387, Andragathius returned to war with a large army of Britons, Celts, Gauls, and others, when Maximus decided to attack Italy.

Arthur's men have a fight against the Romans, who are under a military commander and senator called Petreius. Arthur's men capture him as well as many other Roman soldiers and take them back to Arthur's base in Paris.

Maximus attacked Italy, whose Praetorian prefect was Petronius Probus, and took Milan, the capital at the time, causing Valentinian to flee. He then besieged Rome and took it after about a year.

Arthur's men position themselves in a valley at a place called Siesia, where they wait to meet the coming attack of Lucius, who has summoned kings of various different nations to join him in defeating Arthur.

Andragathius set up his men all across the Alps to prevent Theodosius from getting through, while part of his army went ahead to meet Theodosius by a place called Siscia. The Eastern Emperor, for his part, had employed various peoples to join him in defeating Maximus, such as the Huns and the Goths.

The battle between Lucius and Arthur's men is crushing for both sides. Eventually, Arthur himself arrives and his army manages to overcome the Roman forces and kill Lucius. Arthur then continues on his way to Rome, but has to abandon the attack when he is forced to return to Britain to deal with Mordred.

Andragathius's men were beaten at the battle of Siscia, while Andragathius himself removed his army from the Alps and sailed in the Adriatic in pursuit of Theodosius, having received misinformation about his whereabouts. Theodosius marched west and defeated and executed Maximus.

Many researchers have acknowledged that Maximus's usurpation may have contributed to the story of Arthur's European campaign. However, the extent of the 'contribution' does not seem to have ever been fully realised. In actuality, it is clear from this step-by-step comparison that the Arthurian story in the *HRB* was not merely influenced by Maximus's usurpation, but it is a bona fide account of it. But Geoffrey had already described that historical event earlier in his book, so is it really plausible that it could have also featured here, in Arthur's life?

Perhaps the majority of British accounts spoke about Maximus performing this invasion, but the more military-focused accounts may have described the same events with Andragathius as the hero of the story. An example of this is the account of Allectus's defeat as it appears in *HRB*. Even though Constantius, the emperor, was actually leading the invasion, he is never mentioned. Instead, one of the generals, Asclepiodotus, is portrayed as the leader of the invasion. Thus, it is perfectly plausible for a similar thing to have taken place within accounts of Maximus's usurpation.

This division of these historical events into two appears to be reflected in the way in which Geoffrey's account of Maximus is written. The two most notable events of the invasion – the encounter with Gratian and the takeover of Italy – are virtually unmentioned. The account mentions in passing that Maximus killed one emperor and caused the other to flee, but aside from that, these major events are left unspoken of. Nor does the story tell us what happened to Maximus's army further east. All that is said about the conclusion of the event is that Maximus was killed by Gratian's friends. Nothing is said of the battle at Siscia.

The Welsh story known as *The Dream of Macsen Wledig*, on the other hand, gives a significant amount of detail to the siege of Rome, though it does not relate any of the events that occurred in Gaul, such as the defeat and death of Gratian, nor does it mention the final defeat of Maximus's army in the east. Given that there are such significant omissions in both surviving Welsh accounts of Maximus's usurpation, it seems reasonable to propose that the missing events (which, incidentally, are all related to battles) were recorded primarily under the name of his military leader, Andragathius.

To see how the historical events involved in Magnus Maximus's usurpation of 383–388 could have developed into how they appear in Geoffrey of Monmouth's Arthurian story, and to consider more specific evidence for the connection, we will examine each event in greater detail.

The Fleeing Roman

The name given to the Roman leader of Gaul is not Gratian, nor is it anything like Gratian. Instead, he is named Frollo (some manuscript variants spell this 'Flollo', but 'Frollo' is more commonly used). 'Frollo' could be a title that comes from the Welsh words 'fro', meaning 'foreign', and 'llu', which could mean 'man of war'. It is a possibility, though there is no way to confirm it. In any case, there is a precedent for a character in Geoffrey's history being recorded under a name which was not actually theirs. This precedent is found in the person of Aulus Plautius, who is recorded in *HRB* as 'Lelius Hamo'. While 'Lelius' is undoubtedly just a corruption of 'Aulus', the 'Hamo' element is clearly unrelated to 'Plautius'. It serves to explain a place name in the story. But throughout the account he is most often referred to simply as 'Hamo', thus demonstrating how a historical figure could become known by a fictional name, as would have to be the case with Gratian and Frollo.

Regarding the difference in rank – Gratian was an emperor, while Frollo is described as a tribune – this also fits within Geoffrey's boundaries of accuracy. The ranks given for Severus and Maximus in the *HRB* are both incorrect, being made lower than they really were. Therefore, there is nothing implausible about the rank given to Gratian, or 'Frollo', being incorrect as well.

To return to the actual events, Maximus's army sailed over to Gaul from Britain. As already explained, they were led by Andragathius, so the events shall be described here with a focus on him, rather than on Maximus.

Gratian marched across Gaul with an army to attack the invaders, just as Frollo was said to have done. The opposing historical armies met up in the north of France, in close proximity to Paris. This is roughly the same area in which King Arthur fought Frollo (the account does not say exactly where it was, but since Frollo fled away from Arthur and managed to arrive in Paris shortly afterwards, it must have been in more or less the same area as the battle with Gratian). Here is how Geoffrey of Monmouth described the event:

> The province of Gaul was then committed to Flollo, a Roman tribune, who held the government of it under the emperor Leo. Upon intelligence of Arthur's coming, he raised all the forces that were under his command, and made war against him, but without success. For Arthur was attended with the youth of all the islands that he had subdued; for which reason he was reported to have such an army as was thought invincible. And even the greater part of the Gallic army, encouraged by his bounty, came over to his service. Therefore Flollo, seeing the disadvantages he lay under, left his camp, and fled with a small number to Paris.[1]

In 383, there was a brief period of small skirmishes, until the majority of Gratian's army switched sides and he was forced to flee along with a small number of remaining forces. In both cases, it was not a major battle. It did not last long and there were no great losses on Arthur's side. It was a decisive victory for Arthur, just as it was for Andragathius. The loss is so severe from the Roman's point of view that he is left with no choice but to flee, and that statement is equally true for both events. Additionally, the detail that the majority of the Roman leader's army switched sides is present here in the Arthurian account (the 'Gallic army' being Frollo's army). In fact, in both the Arthurian story and the historical event, there is the minor detail that the British army was notably composed of individuals in their youth, for Gildas informs us that Maximus went into Gaul 'with the flower of [Britain's] youth'. With the names removed, the quoted extract from *HRB* could easily be describing Maximus's invasion.

In addition to Geoffrey's *Historia Regum Britanniae*, another source that contains information regarding Arthur's European conquest is the Welsh Triads. Regarding the battle between Arthur and Frollo, one Triad says: 'Three Elens who went from Ynys Prydain [Britain]: Elen ferch Coel, Elen ferch Eudaf, and Elen sister of Arthur, who is said to have gone with Arthur when he went to fight Frollo, and she did not return.'

Maximus's wife, Elen ferch Eudaf, is known to have gone to Gaul when Maximus invaded, as revealed by the references to her made by the contemporary Roman writers. So there was both an Elen who accompanied Maximus (and therefore Andragathius) when he went from Britain to invade Gaul, and an Elen who accompanied Arthur when he went from Britain to invade Gaul. It is also noteworthy that the Triad says that the Elen who accompanied Arthur did not return, because exactly the same thing is said about Elen the wife of Maximus in another Triad.

The only dissimilarity is the fact that Elen is called Arthur's sister, whereas there is nothing to indicate that Andragathius was the son of Eudaf Hen. However, the King Arthur of the sixth century had – or was believed to have had – a sister called Elaine. It is easy to see how the associate of Andragathius called Elen could have been confused for the sister of Arthur called Elaine.

So, to summarise, in both the Arthurian account and the reality of 383, the powerful war leader from Britain arrives in Gaul with his army, which is notably composed of individuals in their youth, and sets out to conquer it, being accompanied by a woman named Elen who is later known for having never returned to Britain. The Roman ruler of Gaul becomes aware of this invasion, gathers an army of his own, and meets the invading army near Paris. The attempt at war is unsuccessful and the majority of the Gaulish soldiers switch sides to join the British force. The Roman leader flees with a small band of remaining soldiers. The similarities are striking.

After this point in the narrative, Frollo reaches Paris and takes refuge in the city. This is where the two events begin to diverge in terms of similarity. Gratian fled to Lyons, which is not near Paris. While this is certainly a difference, it is perfectly in line with other mistakes demonstrably made in the Roman-era part of *HRB*. For example, as noted in Chapter Four, Geoffrey claims that Valentinian fled from Rome, whereas he actually fled from Milan. Similarly, Severus's last battle is said to have taken place at York, whereas in reality he was taken to York after being mortally wounded at the final battle – evidently, the clash itself was not at that city. Likewise, Caesar is described as landing within the mouth of the Thames, which is inaccurate. Additionally, the location of Cassivellaunus's stronghold is mistaken. There is no doubt that a mistaken location is well within Geoffrey of Monmouth's boundaries of accuracy. Thus, the fact that Frollo's destination is not the same as the actual destination of Gratian is not an obstacle to equating the two events.

To continue with the Arthurian story, Frollo hides away in Paris for a month as Arthur besieges it. Eventually, Frollo and Arthur communicate and they agree to have a jousting battle. It ends with them both falling off their horses and having a fight on foot, during which Arthur manages to kill his opponent.

There are differing accounts of how Andragathius killed Gratian, but almost none claim that it was a simple matter of him catching up with the emperor and slaying him. Most accounts claim that he sent word ahead that Gratian's wife was coming to meet him in a cart, when in reality it was Andragathius. This allowed him to get close enough to kill the emperor. Another account claims that Andragathius caught Gratian but did not kill him immediately. Instead, he led him away – apparently with the promise of survival – and the two men had a meal together, after which Andragathius murdered Gratian.

Regarding the siege, it is possible that something like this did happen in 383 and it was simply grafted onto the story of the killing of Gratian. Or it could simply be a fictional addition to the story. From the analysis of Geoffrey of Monmouth's book up until the Arthurian era, we know that there are at least several sieges described that did not really occur. One example is Cassivellaunus's siege on the Trinovantes, and another is the Roman siege of Portchester in CE 43. Therefore, the fact that there was no siege of Lyons is not an obstacle to this explanation of Arthur's European campaign.

One significant, fundamental point of similarity between the two events is that this slaying of the ruler of Gaul was not in the context of a battle. Arthur and Frollo do have a fight, but it is a personal fight and is arranged between them. It is not a case of Frollo being killed on the battlefield, and the same applies to Gratian. While there is no record of any jousting match between Andragathius and Gratian, this is easily explained as a later embellishment. It has to be, because jousting was not invented until hundreds of years after Arthur's time.

This discrepancy in the actual manner of death may be likened to Carausius being mistakenly described as gaining wealth and prestige from many victories on land, whereas in reality, his victories were fought in the Channel. Therefore, while he did have many victories, the manner in which they occurred is incorrectly described in the *HRB*. Similarly, after the first invasion of Britain in 55 BCE, Geoffrey describes the fact that the Gauls rebelled, but the Romans were quickly able to regain control of them. Caesar's first-hand account describes how this was achieved by means of a battle fought between his men and the Gauls, while the *HRB* says that it was achieved by Caesar bestowing many gifts on the natives. Thus, the manner in which this event is said to have occurred is totally different from its historical reality. So despite the difference in how Arthur and Andragathius are portrayed as killing their respective enemies, this type of error would not be without its precedent in *HRB*. Importantly, both Arthur and Andragathius entered a city to find their enemy and personally killed them in a one-to-one setting.

Also, it may be significant that the account says that Arthur came upon Frollo unawares while he was holding out in the city. This statement may have its origin in the fact that Andragathius took Gratian by surprise by sending out the story that his wife was coming to see him.

The Subjugation of Gaul and the Interregnum

One inconsistency between the Arthurian legend and the reality of Andragathius's invasion is the number of years involved. In Andragathius's case, there were five years between the initial attack on Gaul and the defeat at Siscia. In *HRB*, it is said that Arthur subdued Gaul over a period of nine years, and then when they are at Siesia after having come to Gaul the second time, Arthur remarks that it has been five years since they last fought. Therefore, we arrive at a total of fourteen years for Arthur's Gallic campaign, while Andragathius's only lasted five years. This seems very inconsistent.

The reason that this apparent problem with the theory arises is simply due to the fact that Andragathius's campaign is not based in some abstract, undefined time during the reign of Arthur ap Meurig.

Rather, it is specifically, intentionally placed where it seemed most logical to the confused chroniclers. It is placed during the time in which King Arthur really did travel to Gaul. Understanding the timing involved in this real sixth-century event is vitally important to understanding how it relates to the chronology found in the *Historia Regum Britanniae*. Therefore, consider the following information regarding sixth-century events.

There are several sources, such as the *Life of St Teilo* and the *Life of St Oudoceus*, which describe a great plague ravaging Britain. It is said that Teilo and Oudoceus, along with those left of the nation that had become largely destroyed, left for Brittany, staying there for seven years and seven months. These accounts also claim that Maelgwn Gwynedd, the king of North Wales at the time, was killed by this plague. The *Welsh Annals* also report this same event, saying that Maelgwn Gwynedd was killed in the great plague. The date given for this is traditionally understood, based on the *Welsh Annals*, to be 547. This is about the actual time of the Battle of Badon. The obvious issue with this is that Maelgwn was still alive when Gildas was writing, forty-three years after Badon, for he was one of the kings to whom Gildas directed his comments.

An immediate thought would be that the chronicler who added the entry regarding Maelgwn's death did so based on a statement that dated it relative to either Badon or Camlann, thus meaning it was accidentally backdated as a natural consequence of the backdating of Badon and Camlann. It is placed ten years after Camlann, so this would mean that Maelgwn's death actually took place in *c.* 580. However, even this does not solve the issue, because this would only place it a little over thirty years after Badon, yet Gildas was writing forty-three years after.

An explanation presents itself in the form of Maelgwn the Monk. This is a character who appears in a sixteenth-century manuscript concerning 'Curig Lwyd'.[2] This Maelgwn is made a contemporary of Maelgwn Gwynedd, though is shown to be a distinct figure. Therefore, whether the entry for Maelgwn's death really belongs to 547 or 580, it was almost certainly not Maelgwn Gwynedd who died, but Maelgwn the Monk. A likely explanation for how this confusion arose is that there was an entry that said something like: 'Maelgwn died of the great plague.' A later chronicler simply mistook this for the great king Maelgwn, who was certainly more well known. If the 'Maelgwn' of the record was not qualified, then it is very likely that the reader would have assumed the king of Gwynedd was intended. It is a required conclusion that the scribe must have been confused in some way, and rather than pushing the date of the event even later than it already is with the thirty-three year adjustment – and additional adjustment does not have any obvious basis – a case of mistaken identity seems more reasonable here.

Even with this being the case, the problems with the dating of this event do not end there. Let us consider the possibility that the plague, resulting in Maelgwn the Monk's death, took place in 580. The problem with this is that this would mean it broke out ten years after the Battle of Camlann, yet Arthur either died or disappeared soon after that battle. His death was most likely in 579, with his abdication most likely in 574. The reason this is an issue is because, in the *Life of St Oudoceus*, Athrwys is there as a witness to Oudoceus's appointment as the Bishop of Llandaff *after the end* of the great plague. The plague was supposed to have lasted seven years and seven months. In truth, some scribal liberty has probably been taken with this time span, as seven was a holy number to those Christian writers.[3] Still, it shows the rough length of time involved. Eight years from 580 brings us to 588. How could Arthur, or Athrwys, be a witness to an event that occurred after the end of the plague, or in 588 at the earliest, if he had died about ten years previously?

Furthermore, Meurig is also a witness to this event; he is, in fact, shown to still be ruling as king. Yet we know from one of the charters in the *Book of Llandaff* that Athrwys spent some period of time – though we do not know the length – ruling as king after his father's death. From this information, we gather that Meurig died some time prior to 574, the year of Arthur's abdication.[4] Therefore, the end of the plague cannot have been any later than this, meaning the beginning of the plague (and Maelgwn's death) cannot have been any later than about 565.

Idnerth is also a witness to Oudoceus's appointment. Yet, his death is recorded in the *Life of St Cadoc* as occurring before the deaths of Cadoc himself and Illtud, both of whom are believed to have died around 580. If these two individuals were dead by *c*. 580, then Idnerth's death must have occurred earlier still. So his being recorded as still living after the end of the plague supports the conclusion that it did not end as late as 588.

What about the date of 547 for the outbreak of the plague? This is more plausible, though it is not without its issues. This is about the time of the Battle of Badon. How could it be that this major event took place in the middle of Arthur's reign without so much as a mention in the *HRB*? In fact, after subduing Scotland and Ireland soon after defeating the Saxons at Badon, Arthur is said to have ruled the kingdom in peace for twelve years. If Badon took place in *c*. 548, how can this plague have been devastating the land from 547 to 555? This is especially significant considering that Teilo and Oudoceus, two individuals who are identified as fleeing the plague, are specifically from Arthur's personal kingdom of Glamorgan, Gwent and Ergyng. Surely Arthur himself would have needed to flee?

Consider one of the events that Geoffrey places at around the time of Arthur's special coronation: Teilo's appointment as archbishop of Dol in place of Samson. This, in the *Life of St Teilo*, takes place while Teilo is living in Brittany to escape the plague. Geoffrey places this after the twelve years of peace after Badon, but before Camlann. Therefore, this appointment of Teilo's should have occurred some time between *c*. 560 (twelve years after Badon) and *c*. 570 (when the Battle of Camlann was fought). The conclusion that the great plague broke out around this time fits in with other information. For example, as we have already noted, two of the people who are confirmed as having fled from Britain are Teilo and Oudoceus, both of whom were active in Glamorgan. Therefore, it is extremely probable that Athrwys and his family would have taken refuge in Brittany as well. But there are only two trips to the Continent recorded for Arthur in *HRB*, and both of them are placed between the twelve-year period of peace and the Battle of Camlann. A conclusion that is slowly but firmly developing is that one of the occasions when Arthur and his army travelled to Gaul in Geoffrey's *HRB* was actually effected by the great plague.

Now consider the fact that Geraint, the king of Dumnonia, was said to have died at the end of the plague, just as Teilo was returning to Britain. Yet, in the Welsh poem *Geraint son of Erbin*, Geraint is described as dying in battle at Llongborth under the command of Arthur the emperor. Llongborth is on the Ceredigion coast, on the west of Wales. So if we combine these two sources, we must conclude that this coastal battle at which Arthur was the commander and at which Geraint died took place at the end of the great plague, when Teilo was about to return to Britain. Considering that this would mean this was a coastal battle fought by Arthur at around the time people started to return to Britain, the natural conclusion would be that this was a battle fought by Arthur to get back into Britain, after being away for many years. Who would have been opposing him?

In Geoffrey of Monmouth's account, when Arthur returns to Britain the second time, he is opposed by his usurping nephew Mordred. The two are said to have met and engaged in battle upon Arthur's landing at the port of Rutupi. This is in Kent, and there is no reason at all why Arthur would have landed there, which in any case was deep in Saxon territory at this time. As we have repeatedly noted, Geoffrey's geography is terribly unreliable. It is sufficient to note that this was a coastal battle and it takes place upon Arthur's return to Britain after having been away for a period of time. Additionally, this battle against Mordred is said to have resulted in a great loss of Arthur's men, resulting in the death of some of his allied kings. This certainly fits the Battle of Llongborth, in which Arthur's allied king Geraint was slain.

Despite the losses, Arthur's army is said to have won the battle against Mordred and caused his nephew to flee. The idea that this battle between Arthur and Mordred was actually the Battle of Llongborth is supported by the fact that a route plotted from Llongborth back up to Mordred's home territory around the border of Scotland takes one very near a location called Camlan, by the modern town of Dolgellau in North Wales. Certainly not by coincidence, this location shares a name with the location of the final battle between Arthur and Mordred.

To summarise so far, we have seen from the evidence concerning Teilo and Oudoceus that the great plague must have happened between the end of the twelve years of peace after Badon, in *c.* 560, and the Battle of Camlann, in *c.* 570. From the evidence concerning

Geraint's death at the end of the plague and the information about Llongborth and Arthur's coastal battle against Mordred, Arthur's return to Britain in *c.* 570 must correspond to the end of the great plague. Thus, the beginning of the plague must have occurred in roughly 562. In the entry for Camlann in the *Welsh Annals*, it says that there was plague in Britain and Ireland. What seems to have happened is that the entries for Maelgwn's death and the Battle of Camlann were originally recorded in connection with each other, marking the beginning and the end of the plague, with a rough 'decade' separating them. Then, somehow, through some misreading or careless copying, the entry for the beginning of the plague was accidentally misplaced *in front* of the entry for the end of the plague. Thus, the entry for the beginning of the plague pivoted around Camlann and ended up ten years (or nine, according to the B-text of the *Annals*) in front.

To gain a more accurate understanding of the chronology involved in this series of events, we must look beyond the normal corpus of Arthurian literature. One understandably commonly overlooked source is the folktale of Jack the Giant Killer. This is based in the time of King Arthur, giving it a clear historical setting, and there is active reason to believe that the story does reflect real events of the period. The first giant slain by Jack is a certain Cormoran, a tyrant of Cornwall who lives on St Michael's Mount. It has already been observed by previous researchers that this is very probably Conomor, the historical tyrant of Brittany and Cornwall in Arthur's time. The natural conclusion, then, is that the 'Jack' who killed Cormoran in the story is Judwal, the person who killed Conomor in real life.[5] This event is known to have happened in 560 from Gregory of Tours, a contemporary source.[6] Interestingly, in the *Historia Regum Britanniae*, Arthur is said to have killed a giant on Mont-Saint-Michel upon arriving in Gaul, which strikingly resembles Jack's slaying of a giant on St Michael's Mount. The difference is that Mont-Saint-Michel is in France, whereas St Michael's Mount is in England. However, they are essentially the same name, so it is easy to see how there could have been confusion as to where the 'giant' lived and was killed. In any case, we know that Conomor was killed in Brittany, not Britain, so the much earlier Arthurian story is correct in placing the death of the giant in that country.

If Arthur killing the giant on Mont-Saint-Michel is indeed a recollection of his hand in helping Judwal defeat the infamous Count Conomor, then we can confidently assert that he travelled to Gaul in 560, for we know from a contemporary source that this is the year in which Conomor was killed.

This information ties in with the evidence regarding the start of the great plague. From the contemporary Gregory of Tours, we know that there were several plagues in France in the mid-sixth century that were preceded by the appearances of comets. One particularly significant comet, allegedly visible for a whole year, appeared in 563. As concluded earlier, if the end of the plague was in 570, then the start must have been around 562. The comet of 563 was said to have caused a devastating plague in Auvergne and, given the timing, it is quite likely this is the same comet that caused the great plague in Britain.[7]

Earlier in this book, it was explained that the appearance of a great star with the likeness of a dragon at the time of Ambrosius's death was evidently a comet – the comet recorded in one document as having been seen in 499. Well, in Geoffrey's account, as Arthur is sailing towards Gaul, he sees a dragon in a dream that 'enlightened the country with the brightness of its eyes'. A bear also appears in this dream, which is defeated by the dragon. The account itself explains this as a vision of the future, representing either Arthur defeating a giant, according to his men, or Arthur defeating the emperor, according to Arthur himself. It is very likely that this vision of a future event, involving a dragon 'enlightening the country with the brightness of its eyes', is actually a reference to the devastating comet of 563. While this admittedly takes place *before* the fight against the giant on Mont-Saint-Michel, the fact that it was supposed to have been a vision of the future explains this.

So, in reality, rather than Arthur fleeing to Brittany to escape the devastation left by the comet, it seems that he was already in Brittany at the time. As the giant was said to be holding the niece of Hoel, whose family had close marital connections with the family of Athrwys – and as Hoel had assisted Arthur in his battles against the Saxons according to legend – it is most logical that Arthur would have offered his assistance in defeating Conomor. This explains the inconsistency between the amount of time Arthur spent in Gaul according to Geoffrey of Monmouth and the amount of time Teilo spent in Gaul according to his *Life*. Arthur was already in Gaul when the plague commenced in 563, having arrived there in 560 – specifically towards the end of 560, as Conomor was killed around November or December. Then everyone else fled to Brittany after the comet of 563. This means that Arthur and his army spent nine years in Gaul, while everyone else (such as Teilo) spent only some seven years there.

'Nine years' from December 560 brings us to December 569, or, more likely, some time during 570. This is exactly when all the other evidence indicates the Battle of Camlann took place.

However, there is one detail that seems to conflict with this interpretation. In the *Historia Regum Britanniae*, the nine years that Arthur spends in Gaul is placed *before* the fight with the giant. The latter event (along with the vision of the dragon) is said to have occurred when Arthur went to Gaul the second time, after receiving the letter from the Roman emperor regarding Arthur's illegal subjugation of Gaul.

The reason for this issue becomes apparent when comparing the data Geoffrey of Monmouth provides with the data from other sources. In the A-text of the *Welsh Annals*, there are twenty-one years between the Battle of Badon and the Battle of Camlann. In the B-text, there are twenty years between them. The *Red Book of Hergest* gives twenty-two years. However, in *HRB*, there are the nine years spent in Gaul initially, and then the five years between that and the final battle at Siesia. That gives us fourteen years. In addition to that, we are told that Arthur resided in his kingdom for twelve years in peace before heading out to conquer Europe. A number of events and at least parts of two years pass between the Battle of Badon and this statement. Therefore, it seems that there were thirteen or fourteen years between the Battle of Badon and Arthur going to Gaul. This gives us a total of at least twenty-seven or twenty-eight years between Badon and Camlann according to Geoffrey's account.

Using the highest number of years between Badon and Camlann from the independent sources, which is twenty-two, we can see immediately that there are an extra five or six years in Geoffrey's chronology that simply should not be there. This, in itself, is strong evidence that much of the Gallic campaign has been taken from somewhere else and inserted into the reign of King Arthur. Five or six years' worth, to be precise. Needless to say, from 383 to 388 is five years. It is even more significant to note that Cador of Cornwall actually says it has been 'nearly five years' since they last fought when they receive the letter from the emperor – that is, there were four years between them completing their subjugation of Gaul and receiving the emperor's letter. It is only later, when they are at Siesia, that Arthur remarks that a full five years have passed since they last fought.

Magnus Maximus was officially acknowledged as the joint western Roman emperor in early 384, but Andragathius may have returned to Britain even before this, soon after killing Gratian in August 383.[8] Presumably, Andragathius would have been recalled when Maximus set out to invade Italy in 387, which would be about four years after leaving Gaul – or at least, four years since the previous engagements. Then, the final battle at Siscia occurred the following year, in 388 – five years after Andragathius and his men last fought.

This explains why there are too many years in Geoffrey's chronology. The extra five years are from Andragathius's activities having been attributed to Arthur ap Meurig. But more relevant to this section, we can now understand why the nine years in Gaul were placed before the slaying of the giant in 560. Because Arthur evidently did not travel to Gaul twice, but Andragathius did. Hence, information about Arthur's *one* stay in Gaul became distributed between Andragathius's *two* stays in Gaul. The thirteen or fourteen years from the Battle of Badon – which occurred in the late 540s – to travelling to Gaul would bring us to around 560, when Conomor was killed. Therefore, the narrative in *HRB* clearly *should* jump straight to the 'second' trip to Gaul, when Arthur kills the giant on Mont-Saint-Michel. The first attack on Gaul is a phantom, taken from Andragathius's first campaign of 383. The detail about Arthur's nine-year stay in Gaul has been incorrectly placed within that first campaign. In reality, this, perhaps along with some other details, should be placed in the 'second' campaign of the legend, which began with the events of 560.

The Attack on Italy

In the story, the letter that Arthur receives is from Lucius, a Roman procurator, and is a complaint against Arthur's invasion of Gaul. Lucius insists that the Britons pay Rome tribute. This greatly angers Arthur and his men and they are compelled to return and attack Rome.

This probably originates in brief accounts of Arthur – that is, Andragathius – receiving a letter from the Roman emperor – that is, Magnus Maximus – which caused him to set out to attack Rome. As the accounts developed and became part of the Arthurian legend, this would have become misunderstood to mean that the letter from the emperor was offensive and angered Arthur so much that he decided to make war with the emperor. Nonetheless, the essential elements were probably correct. If Andragathius did return to Britain after killing Gratian, then he really would have received a message from an emperor, which really did cause him to attack Rome. The detail of the letter specifically coming from this man called Lucius, rather than the emperor directly, can merely be attributed to a detail that developed along the course of transmission. It is, after all, the emperors to whom Arthur is said to have sent his reply, not Lucius. So the account does indicate that it was the emperors who originated the letter, while Lucius was simply the person they assigned to compose it.

At this point, Arthur begins making preparations for his war with the Romans. He organises an army composed of virtually all the nations of Britain, as well as several Scandinavian nations (probably actually meant to be the inhabitants of Scotland) and Gallic tribes. Regarding Maximus's preparations for the attack on Italy in 387, the Roman historian Sozomen wrote that he 'raised a large army of Britons, neighbouring Gauls, Celts, and other nations'.[9] Thus, when he set out to attack Italy, Andragathius was actually marching with this vast army of various different nations, just like Arthur in the story.

Arthur is then said to have reached Autun, which is in eastern central France, quite near Italy. He then sent out some men ahead of him and they encountered the Romans. According to the story, they initially aimed to give the Romans an ultimatum, but this quickly descended into a battle. Eventually, a Roman senator named Petreius arrived with several thousand men and briefly forced the Britons to retreat. However, the Britons quickly regained their position and forced the Romans back, capturing Petreius and many other Romans, letting the rest flee.

This corresponds to Andragathius's army reaching Italy, causing Valentinian to flee to Theodosius in the east. The praetorian prefect of Italy at that time was a man called Sextus Claudius Petronius Probus, and it is significant that he was a major opponent of Magnus Maximus. One reference work refers to the formation of 'Valentinian II's loyalist support base against Magnus Maximus, now headed by Petronius Probus and the general Bauto'.[10] Like the Britons' enemy Petreius in the legend, Petronius was a senator. The one major difference is that Petronius was not captured by Andragathius, but fled with Valentinian to the east; however, this still falls comfortably within Geoffrey's boundaries of accuracy. Notably, Petreius was not said to have been killed in this encounter, unlike many other Roman characters in the story. This, again, agrees with his identification as Petronius.

After this, another fight takes place between the Romans and the Britons, involving the Romans trying to get their prisoners back. This is undoubtedly just another battle fought between Andragathius's army and Valentinian's forces in Italy, as the fighting apparently continued, at least against the city of Rome, until the next year.[11]

The Battle of Siesia

This is the final battle between Arthur, king of the Britons, and Lucius Tiberius, leader of the Romans. The two opposing armies travel towards each other and finally clash swords in a valley called Siesia, where Arthur had set up his army in waiting along the route Lucius inevitably had to pass through. This clearly matches the historical reality of Andragathius and Theodosius travelling towards each other and meeting at a place called Siscia. The only major difference between the two events is the geography. In *HRB*, Siesia is located between Langres and Autun, France, whereas Siscia is located in Croatia, to the east of Italy. In line with this, Arthur is not said to have reached Rome or even Italy by this point. In fact, the account says that he never reached Rome, but turned back to Britain after the battle at Siesia to address the uprising of Mordred.

However, just as the Welsh Triads contained significant information regarding Arthur coming to Gaul with Elen, we can also find valuable information regarding the battle at Siesia. In one Triad called 'The Three Dishonoured Men of the Island of Britain', from the collection in the *Red Book of Hergest*, it is said that Arthur and Lucius (or Lles, as he is called in the Triad) met and fought 'beyond the mountain of Mynneu'. The 'mountain of Mynneu' refers to the Alps.[12] This being the case, Siesia cannot be between Autun and Langres; in fact, it cannot be in France at all. But Siscia, in modern-day Croatia, is indeed beyond the Alps. Perhaps Geoffrey of Monmouth, or his source, placed the battle where he did because there is a village called Saussy between Langres and Autun, which he assumed was the location in the story.

A demonstration of the confused geography of the story is the fact that Geoffrey describes Arthur as subduing the Allobroges – a tribe centred a little way outside Italy – after the battle at Siesia as he is heading towards Rome. Yet earlier, in Lucius's letter to Arthur during the interregnum, he mentions that Arthur had subdued the province of the Allobroges. Clearly, Geoffrey's account is confused as to what part of Europe Arthur's campaign took place in, and the Welsh Triads definitely place the final battle *beyond* the Alps.

Whatever the case, the greater part of the account corresponds to the reality of 388. Before the actual battle takes place, *HRB* describes Arthur splitting his army into many different bodies, which seems to relate to this contemporary description of Andragathius's activities: 'Andragathius ... greatly strengthened all the approaches through the Alps and along the rivers, placing there large bodies of soldiers and employing skilful strategy that counted for even more than the strength of numbers.'[13]

Admittedly, the story says that Arthur split up his army *at* Siesia, whereas Andragathius distributed his army among the Julian Alps. But these mountains are very near Siscia, so this is only a minor mistake. It is similar to Geoffrey's earlier mistake in describing Caesar's forces as arriving *at* the Thames, when in reality, their landing place was only *near* the Thames. One body of Andragathius's soldiers went ahead of the rest of the army and started preparing at Siscia, which body did not include Andragathius himself. This matches the specific detail that Arthur stayed behind the rest of the army; he only arrives on the battlefield near the end of the battle to assist his struggling forces. Likewise, Andragathius 'left his army leaderless at Siscia'.[14] Additionally, the fight took place at a location at which Andragathius's army had already placed themselves, with Theodosius being the one to come to them. This specific detail is matched by the story in *HRB*, in which Arthur's army is lying in wait at Siesia for Lucius.

Another interesting similarity is the statement that Arthur set up a golden dragon for a standard. We have already seen how the sixth-century Arthur was a 'pendragon'. Additionally, upon Uthyr assuming the throne in *HRB*, he constructed two golden dragons. Arthur himself is said to have had a golden dragon on his helmet earlier on in Geoffrey's book. However, a dragon as a *standard* is not mentioned anywhere in the context of the sixth-century Arthur. It is only mentioned here, in the context of the war with the Romans. Therefore, it is probably significant to note that Magnus Maximus is known to have carried a battle standard of a dragon when he invaded Gaul.[15] In all likelihood, this is the very standard referred to by Geoffrey of Monmouth.

The one major difference between the Arthurian legend and Andragathius's invasion is the outcome of the final battle. In the former, Arthur won, while in the latter, Andragathius lost. This is the one and only major deviance between the two events that could pose any significant difficulty to equating them. However, as with the siege of Paris, there are precedents for this kind of substantial error in the *Historia Regum Britanniae*. For example, the book claims that the Britons won against the Romans at the battle on the Thames, yet according to Caesar's contemporary account, it was the Romans who won. However, despite their claimed victory, the great loss dealt to the British was still present in Geoffrey's account by virtue of the statement that the Romans 'made no small slaughter'. Similarly, even though the Britons are claimed to have been the victors at the battle at Siesia, they are still said to have received substantial – even devastating – losses.

As well as being informed in plain words that the Britons sustained terrible losses, the account provides many names of significant British leaders who were killed in the battle, including the famous Bedivere and Kay – two of Arthur's most important companions. In fact, out of the sixteen divisions Arthur establishes prior to the battle, the leaders of six of these are killed in this one battle.[16] The death of Gallus, a nobleman previously mentioned in the account of Arthur's feast at Caerleon during the interregnum, is also reported here. Additionally, one more consul and three noblemen die during the battle.[17] This gives a total of eleven of Arthur's companions being killed at the battle of Siesia, which is unprecedented in Geoffrey's book. Even at the Battle of Camlann, which is portrayed as Arthur's eventual loss, fewer than half these numbers are named as among those who were slain.

The *Brut Tysilio* version of the battle even says that 'the number of men killed on both sides could not be counted'. This agrees with another statement from a Welsh source regarding the fight. This source is the same Triad that provided the detail showing that Siesia was 'beyond the mountain of Mynneu' – that is, the Alps. Here, it is said that 'an untold number was slain on each side that day,' and that 'Arthur's best men were slain there'. Further, the Triad says: 'When Medrawd heard that Arthur's host was dispersed...'

This definitely sounds like a defeat for Arthur, even if Lucius was supposedly killed as well. All things considered, the information provided from the various sources regarding the battle at Siesia shows that it was a devastating event for Arthur's side. This conforms to the defeat of Andragathius's army at Siscia. Even though Arthur is portrayed as the victor, this still falls within Geoffrey's boundaries of accuracy, as shown by the example from the account of Caesar's invasion.

The Kings of the East

In the legend, Lucius Tiberius collaborates with the leaders of many nations when preparing for his fight against Arthur. Some of these leaders may possibly be identified as historical figures in the time of 387, when Maximus attacked Italy and Theodosius first began making preparations to return the assault, and in 388, when the final battle took place.

However, in all likelihood, many of the names and specific designations of these kings probably do not come from the original source, whatever that was. It is worth noting that the *Brut Tysilio* simply refers to 'the kings of the east', rather than actually naming any of them or describing which areas they ruled over.

This idea of the Roman leader requesting support from the kings of the east in his war against Arthur directly parallels the fact that Theodosius called on the aid of many foreign nations as he went to attack Maximus, or Andragathius, in 388. His army was notably composed of Huns, Goths and Alans, all of whom are from the east. Even though the exact nations and rulers named by Geoffrey do not reflect the reality of 388, once again, this has a precedent in his account of Caesar's invasion of Britain. He accurately describes a conference held by the British chiefs, yet he calls Tasciovanus, the historical king of the Catuvellauni, the ruler of Cornwall. He also includes otherwise unknown kings from Gwynedd, Dyfed, and even Scotland. While these details are most likely incorrect, he is accurate in the fact that there was a conference held by various British chiefs. Similarly, in the Arthurian legend, though the details of which rulers exactly were involved in the Roman emperor's alliance, Geoffrey is correct in writing that the emperor made an alliance with rulers from the east.

Emperor Leo and Lucius Tiberius

These are two of the most significant characters in the Arthurian legend. Leo is the Roman emperor who is referred to several times but never actually makes an appearance. Lucius Tiberius, meanwhile, is the main enemy of the story – the Roman leader who faces off against Arthur and his army on the battlefield. As discussed in a previous chapter, Geoffrey Ashe considers the Leo of the story to refer to Leo I, the eastern emperor from 457 to 474. Leo does seem to be located in the east, as Arthur never encounters him during all his battles in France, so Leo I would be a good fit. However, this identification must be rejected for the reasons already considered.

In reality, Leo seems to be a shortening and slight corruption of Theodosius. With the exclusion of the characteristic Latin suffix in the British accounts, this would become Theodos as standard. Another common change from Latin is 'Th' to 'T', which would produce Teodos, or perhaps Teudus.[18] From this expected modification of the Latin name into a British form, the only real corruption and shortening would be the scribal error of a 'T' to an 'L' and the drop of the 'dos' or 'dus' from the end. This can be compared to the historical Togodumnus and his *HRB*-counterpart Guiderius; in this instance, it is the beginning rather than the end of the name that has been clipped, along with general corruptions of the name. Another example is the name of Salomon, a king of Brittany in some records. In the Welsh accounts, this name is shortened to Selyf, the ending having been clipped.[19]

This identification is logical, as Theodosius was the reigning eastern Roman emperor at the time of Andragathius's invasion, yet Theodosius was not involved in the defeat of Gratian nor the invasion of Italy, involving Petronius. Of course, he was involved in the attack on Maximus's dominion in 388 and the resultant battle at Siscia, but it cannot be said with certainty that he was present at the battle. Theodosius split his army into two groups as they went west out of the Balkans. It was the southern army that fought at Siscia, while the northern army fought a stronger force led by Maximus's brother Marcellinus at Poetovio. Theodosius may have been with the northern group.

If this is the case, then who is the main enemy of the legend, Lucius Tiberius? The likely solution is that he was one of Theodosius's generals. He would have had to have been very high-ranking to be given such prominence and importance in the legend. It is known that there were four leading generals of Theodosius's army in 388. Two of them – Richomer and Arbogast – were barbarians, so it is unlikely that they would have come to represent Rome in later tellings of this event. The two Roman generals were Promotus and Timasius, respectively the Master of the Cavalry and the Master of the Infantry.

On the face of it, neither of these names seem very similar to 'Lucius' or 'Tiberius'. However, a point that has already been noted is that the letter 'b' would be a 'v' sound to the native Britons. An example of this is seen in the word 'brenhin' – meaning 'king' – which is sometimes spelt 'frenhin'. Another example is Bishop Ufelwy, whose name is spelt with a 'b' instead of an 'f' in some records. Likewise, the exact same applies to the letter 'm'. This is why Salomon, as noted previously, is spelt Selyf in the Welsh chronicles.[20] Perhaps an even more appropriate example would be the fact that Gregory of Tours spells Conomor's name as Chonoober, whereas most other sources spell this name with an 'm' in place of the 'b'. Therefore, to the Welsh writers, Tibasius would likely have been an acceptable alternate spelling of Timasius. It may even have been written down as 'Tivasius', 'Tifasius' or something similar, hiding whether it was originally a 'b' or an 'm'. This would be similar to how the Latin 'Demetia' was written as 'Dyfed' in the Welsh records.

From this alternative spelling, the only real corruption necessary would be the conversion of the first 's' into an 'r'. These two letters were easily confused, so the change from Tibasius to Tibarius is well within reason.[21] It is also worth noting that 'Tiberius' would have been a much more familiar name to the Britons than 'Timasius'. For example, it was during the reign of a Tiberius that Jesus was executed, and this fact – which would have been very prominent to the Christian Britons – is recorded in *Historia Brittonum*. There were many other prominent men in the Roman Empire with that name, such as several Byzantine emperors. All things considered, it is fairly easy to see how 'Timasius' could have developed into 'Tiberius'. The Roman general's full name was 'Flavius Timasius', so 'Lucius' is likely a scribal corruption of 'Flavius'.

This identification makes sense, as Timasius had a very prominent role in the war against Maximus, and is therefore very likely to have gone up against Andragathius's army. Granted, Timasius did not die in the encounter, as did Lucius Tiberius in the story. However, this would be a similar error to one that Geoffrey demonstrably made before. In the account of Claudius's invasion of Gaul, the Roman leader named Lelius Hamo, who clearly represents the historical Aulus Plautius, is killed by Arviragus at the beginning of the invasion, despite Aulus Plautius actually living far beyond this invasion. Therefore, identifying the Tiberius of the story with the historical Timasius does fall within Geoffrey's boundaries of accuracy.

The Battles of Iceland and Norway

Let us now consider the events immediately preceding the first invasion of Gaul. Arthur is said to have made war in Scandinavia, whose rightful ruler was Lot. As we saw in a previous chapter, the Welsh often used the same word for Scotland and Norway, meaning that there could easily have been confusion between the two locations. Considering Lot was a prince of the northern dynasty of Rheged, which encompassed the border of England and Scotland, it seems a virtual certainty that the 'Norway' in which Arthur campaigned for the sake of Lot was actually an area of Scotland. This is supported by the fact that the previous king of the area to which Arthur travels – supposedly an uncle of Lot – is called the king of 'Prydarn', while Scotland is known to have been called 'Prydyn' in Welsh texts.[22] This former word is very likely a corruption of the latter.

The 'Iceland' of the story is spelt 'Isslont' in *Brut Tysilio*, which is not the Welsh name for Iceland.[23] Arthur travels here just after fighting in Ireland. It seems much more likely that this enigmatic 'Isslont' is the name of some region, probably an island, between Ireland and Scotland. It has been convincingly argued that Islay was the intended place, though this cannot be stated with absolute certainty.[24]

It seems logical that this would have been a campaign of the sixth-century Arthur, and that this is what Arthur had been engaged with immediately prior to Hoel asking for his assistance in defeating Conomor. The fact that it is a battle concerning the sovereignty of Lot, who was definitely a sixth-century individual, seems to confirm this. However, the names of the sixth-century Arthur's companions are also used in the story of the war against the Romans, evidently being drafted onto the account for consistency of the story. It is possible that the same thing has taken place with this account of the war in Scotland, meaning it was actually part of Andragathius's activities. However, the line that we considered in a previous chapter occurs at this point: 'Walgan, the son of Lot, was then a youth twelve years old, and was recommended by his uncle to the service of pope Supplicius, from whom he received arms.'

This is chronologically correct, for Walgan (that is, Gawain) would have been around twelve years old in 560, as discussed earlier. This may simply be because, as has already been explained, the story of the Gallic conquest was placed into a specific period of time during the sixth-century Arthur's reign, and this particular event was tied to the events just before Arthur travelled to Gaul in 560 – hence, the writer inserted the fact that Gawain was twelve when this occurred. However, this seems rather unlikely. It is very specific and quite random for a later syncretisation. It seems more likely that this detail was included simply because it is a truthful detail. Therefore, though it cannot be said with certainty, the evidence does appear to support the idea that this event, which evidently took place in Scotland, not Norway, concerned the sixth-century Arthur. Hence, though it at first *seems* to commence Arthur's European conquest, there is not actually any reason to look beyond the historical sixth-century Arthur for the reality behind this particular part of the legend.

Nonetheless, there is a remarkable correspondence with the life of Andragathius. There is nothing known specifically about Andragathius's career in Britain, but there is no evidence or any reason to suppose that Maximus acquired a new leading commander upon invading Gaul. Therefore, we can reasonably assume that what is known of Maximus's activities in Britain would also apply to Andragathius. With this in mind, it is significant to note that Maximus successfully fought against the Picts in 381 or 382, just one or two years before leaving for Gaul. The extent of his engagement up north is indicated by the fact that the genealogical list in the *Harleian MS 3859* for the rulers of the Isle of Man goes back to Maximus through one of his sons.[25]

This would mean that Andragathius also travelled to Scotland shortly before going across the sea to Gaul, just as Arthur does in the legend. It is possible that this is a coincidence, since, as we have just discussed, the attack on Scotland, or 'Norway', is more likely to be correctly attributed to the sixth-century Arthur. Nonetheless, the very least it does is provide an additional point of connection between the activities of Andragathius and Arthur. Just as they both travelled to Gaul – and hence the activities of Andragathius were inserted into the life of Arthur between 560 and 570 – they were also both in Scotland just prior to travelling there. This would encourage the chroniclers to confuse the two figures and combine their activities.

Conclusions

In this chapter, we have seen how the events of 383–388 can account for the legend of King Arthur's campaign into Europe. Frollo was

Gratian, and just as Frollo fled from Arthur, so Gratian fled from Andragathius. His death at the hands of Arthur was Gratian's death at the hands of Andragathius. The nine years in Gaul was from the sixth-century Arthur's time in Gaul, having nothing to do with Andragathius or Magnus Maximus. The interregnum in Britain for four years took place when Andragathius returned to Britain after the defeat of Gratian in 383 and only came back to the Continent when summoned by Maximus in 387. The battle between Arthur's men and the Romans on their way to Rome, involving the senator Petreius, actually took place when Andragathius's army attacked Italy while the senator Petronius was the praetorian prefect. The final battle between Arthur's army of many western nations and Tiberius's army of many eastern nations at Siesia, which, according to the Welsh Triads, took place beyond the Alps, was the final battle between Andragathius's army of many western nations and Timasius's army of many eastern nations at Siscia, beyond the Alps.

This consideration of the activities of Andragathius, from what little we can surmise about him in Britain right up until his well-recorded defeat in 388, shows quite clearly that he is by far the best candidate for the Arthurian figure whose European conquest was grafted onto the life of King Arthur ap Meurig. The general pattern of events in both the reality of 383–388 and the Arthurian legend must be admitted to be remarkably similar. Many of the specific details, likewise, can be seen to connect. Examples include the Gallic army switching sides upon the initial encounter with the British army, the use of a dragon standard, Arthur splitting his army into many bodies and staying behind the rest of the army when they fought at Siesia, and the involvement of an Elen who was known for having never returned to Britain.

The general picture that emerges is one that is very similar to how Geoffrey of Monmouth wrote the other events in his *Historia Regum Britanniae*. With the majority of the events of the Roman era, the overall sequence of events corresponds to what we know from authentic sources and archaeology. There are also often many specific details that are accurate, though there are also occasionally some significant errors in geography, the fates of certain people, or the timing of events. Of course, the European conquest of King Arthur is somewhat more confused and error-ridden than most, simply by virtue of the fact that it has been attributed to the sixth-century King Arthur. Therefore, many of the names of the characters are taken from real individuals of the sixth century. But when this is accounted for, the account reads very much like most of Geoffrey's accounts of known events in the Roman era when viewing it as a description of Maximus's usurpation.

However, what this explanation does not immediately make obvious is why Andragathius's activities would have been combined with Arthur's. The two names are not very similar – they certainly do not seem similar enough to have become confused, leading to their lives being combined. The reason for this confusion – and the final, but vitally important, element of the theory – is inextricably linked to the true identity of Andragathius and his relation to Maximus.

7

The Identity of the First Arthur

The preceding chapter outlined how the activities of Andragathius match up extremely well with the Continental activities of King Arthur in the *Historia Regum Britanniae*. However, what now needs to be explained is how Andragathius could have been confused for Arthur. Their names are not very similar, though it is perhaps possible to see how the first element may have developed into 'Arthur'. The 'd' may have been written as a 't' in the British documents, producing 'Antragathius'. Removing the Latin ending, as expected, would make 'Antragath'. The first actual corruption necessary, then, would be a scribal error that changed the 'n' into an 'r', which would make 'Artragath'. From this stage, perhaps someone could have misread this as 'Artur agath', or assumed that that was what was intended. 'Artur' is simply a variant of 'Arthur', so this may be the explanation for how Andragathius became confused for Arthur.

Perhaps this explanation of how the name may have changed is not convincing enough for some. But the close and consistent similarities of Andragathius's Gallic activities with those of Arthur demonstrate clearly that Andragathius *was* the figure who became combined with Arthur ap Meurig. So, however the process happened, it must have happened somehow. Evidence that Andragathius did become known in British records by a name very similar to 'Arthur' will now be considered.

Andragathius of the Genealogies

By far the most famous of Magnus Maximus's children is Victor, the Augustus of Gaul during his father's reign. He is often described as an infant, so he cannot have been born very long before Maximus came to Gaul in 383. In 388, after the defeat of Maximus's forces, Theodosius sent Arbogast to execute Victor. As such, he left no descendants and does not seem to be mentioned in any ancient Welsh genealogies. We also know that Maximus had several daughters, though we do not know their names from contemporary sources. One ninth-century inscription, in its generally understood interpretation, gives Magnus Maximus a daughter named Sevira, who is, in turn, said to have been the wife of Vortigern. However, no sons other than Victor are referred to in the contemporary Roman accounts. He is the only recorded son who can definitely be said to have existed.

However, other sons are recorded in the earliest surviving Welsh genealogies. These are commonly Constantine, Owain and Dunod. The most common wife given to Maximus is Elen ferch Eudaf, but he is also recorded as producing children by a certain Ceindrech ferch Reiden. Elen is recorded as the mother of Constantine, and the Welsh sources state that this Elen was the one who went to Gaul with Maximus. Therefore, it would seem to be the case that Elen was the wife spoken of in the contemporary Roman accounts, making Ceindrech an earlier wife. The sources are not in total agreement as to which wife was the mother of Owain – the earliest source (*Jesus College MS 20*) claims that it was Ceindrech – but in any case, Dunod would seem to be the eldest son.

The reason for drawing this conclusion is that the descendants of both Dunod and Owain are recorded as ruling in south-east Wales, but Owain's descendants ruled only the area of Glywysing, while Dunod's descendants ruled Glywysing and Gwent.[1] Thus, Dunod's descendants were the overkings, with Owain's descendants as the subordinates. The most logical reason for this would be that Dunod was the older brother. Supporting this conclusion, Dunod's descendants through a different line are recorded as ruling over Dyfed – south-west Wales – and the Isle of Man. The fact that his lineage had control over much more territory than Owain's lineage likewise indicates that he was the older, more powerful, brother.

Additional evidence for Dunod being the eldest is found in Geoffrey's *Historia* itself. As was noted previously, it is likely that the Dionotus of Geoffrey's account was actually the Dunod ap Maxim of the genealogies. Dionotus, of course, was the person to whom Maximus had entrusted the government of Britain. Surely this position would not have been given to any of his sons but the eldest?

There is an extremely significant fact concerning Dunod. This fact is found by comparing two different versions of the same ancestral record. Specifically, let us compare this sequence in the *Jesus College MS 20* with the same sequence in the *Harleian MS 3859*:

Senilth ap Dingat ap Tutwawl ap Edneuet ap Dunawt ap Maxen wledic

Senill ap Dinacat ap Tutagual ap Eidinet ap Anthun ap Maxim guletic

From this comparison, we find that Dunod was known by another name. That name, very significantly, was 'Anthun'. The reason this name is so significant should be obvious. Visually, it is extremely similar to 'Arthur'. Each 'n' in Anthun's name is distinct from each 'r' in Arthur's name merely by one small stroke. The fact that Maximus, a person who is known to have invaded Gaul in a way that strikingly resembles King Arthur's legendary invasion of Gaul, is recorded as having a son – probably the eldest – with a name so very close to 'Arthur' seems more than just a coincidence.

As well as the name, we must also bear in mind the area in which he ruled. If, as the records indicate, he was a ruler of all of South Wales, then his domain would have included the area ruled by the sixth-century King Arthur. And if he was the same as *HRB*'s Dionotus, then as well as being the king of 'Cornwall' (or Cerniw) in particular, he was also the ruler of all of Britain for a time. If a scribe could confuse 'Anthun' for 'Arthur' simply due to their visual similarity, then how much more so if the record described Anthun as ruling all of Britain, but especially being active in territory that the scribe knew was Arthur's. Furthermore, regarding the records placing Anthun at the head of the kings of the Isle of Man, Peter Bartrum wrote: 'H. M. Chadwick believed that the persons in the earlier part of the pedigree belonged to Galloway.'[2] This has been accepted by many others. Anthun, therefore, had particular control of Galloway as well as South Wales, meaning his similarity with the sixth-century Arthur increases, for the latter figure had strong connections to northern England and southern Scotland.

The similarities extend beyond their names and areas of activity. Just as Arthur ap Meurig had Owain ap Urien in his service, records about Anthun may well have included mention of his brother Owain. Anthun's other brother, Victor, shares the name of Arthur's father-in-law, Gwythyr ap Greidawl; 'Gwythyr' is merely the Welsh form of 'Victor'. In fact, it is a remarkable coincidence that, just as Gwythyr ap Greidawl was a ruler in France, Victor the son of Maximus was the Augustus, and therefore nominal ruler, of Gaul, or France.[3] So as well as the same name, they also had a very similar position. It is difficult to see how a chronicler would *not* have been confused, at the least, to read about a ruler of Britain named 'Anthun' active in South Wales and the North, alongside references to such characters as Owain and Gwythyr, the ruler of France. Assuming that 'Anthun' was just a spelling mistake for 'Arthur', or simply misreading it as such, would be quite logical.

The suggestion, of course, is that Anthun was Andragathius. The former's birth date is estimated to have been 355 by Peter Bartrum.[4] This being the case, he would have been around twenty-eight when his father invaded Gaul. That this is a reasonable age for a cavalry commander is evidenced by the fact that the famous Mark Antony was twenty-six when appointed the cavalry commander of Aulus Gabinius. As to how 'Andragathius' could have become 'Anthun', it would presumably have been very similar to the suggestion for how it could have become 'Arthur'. From 'Antragathius', a scribal error could have caused the 'r' to become an 'n', leaving 'Antnagathius', or 'Antnagath'. A scribe may have misinterpreted this as meaning 'Antun agath', the 'Antun' then naturally evolving into 'Anthun'. Alternatively, it might be that Andragathius simply had another name, that other name being 'Antonius'. Perhaps his full name was 'Antonius Andragathius Maximus'. Based on the available information, it is impossible to say which option is more probable.[5]

Bearing in mind the possibility that Andragathius and Anthun were the same, both men would have been recorded as being in Britain but then leaving for Gaul and fighting there – Anthun against Gratian, and Arthur against Conomor. In fact, as was explained near the end of the previous chapter, both men would have been recorded as fighting in the area of Scotland and then, very soon afterwards, leaving for Gaul and fighting there. This would certainly have added to the reasons for the chroniclers to assume that both men were the same.

Another possible cause of confusion may have been in records of their successors. In the *Historia Regum Britanniae*, as well as in many subsequent sources, Arthur is recorded as being succeeded by Constantine. The Constantine in question was Constantine ap Cador of Cornwall. However, after Magnus Maximus, the next officer in Britain to rise up and invade Gaul was a man called Constantine, known as Constantine III to historians. For the accounts that focused more on Andragathius – or 'Anthun', as we are now theorising – the power of Britain may well have been described as being passed on to Constantine after Anthun, rather than after Maximus. This would be a rather specific detail that would make it appear as if the 'Anthun' of the records was the Arthur of the sixth century.

So we can see that, by sheer coincidence, there are numerous points of similarity between Andragathius/Anthun and Arthur ap Meurig, several of which are remarkably specific. Assuming that Andragathius really was the person later recorded as Maximus's son Anthun, then their areas of influence, the names and roles of their associates, their successors, and even their very names could all have contributed to their being confused for a single king, leading to the story of the European conquest being added onto the accounts of King Arthur ap Meurig.

The Brychan Confusion

There is an obscure but very significant detail in the Arthurian mythos that strongly indicates Anthun was, in fact, incorporated into the character of King Arthur. But first, we have to establish the facts regarding a certain figure in Welsh history. This figure is the famous Brychan of Brycheiniog, the son of Anlach.

Brychan is generally believed to have lived in the early to mid-400s, with some evidence even suggesting his life began some way back into the fourth century. For example, a daughter of Brychan named Eleri is recorded as marrying Ceredig ap Cunedda.[6] Ceredig was probably born *c.* 415–420, so the father of his wife would likely have been born *c.* 400 or earlier. Indeed, much of the information about many of Brychan's children indicates a late fourth-century date of birth for him, and this is why most current sources favour this early date. His genealogies link him back to a sixth-generation ancestor recorded as Annhun Rex Gregorium. Annhun is simply an alternative spelling of the name Anthun, the 'nt' being replaced by 'nn'.[7] So the sixth-generation ancestor of Brychan was this 'Anthun king of Greece'. Unfortunately for the modern historian, his father is not recorded. The issue with identifying him as Anthun ap Maxim is the chronology. If Anthun ap Maxim was born in 355, then for Brychan to have been born in *c.* 400, each generation would have had to have been seven and a half years long. Needless to say, this is an impossibility. If we allow a minimum of twenty years for each generation, then for 'Anthun king of Greece' to be the same as Anthun ap Maxim, Brychan could not have been born any earlier than 475.

However, there is good reason to believe that there was more than one Brychan. This is a conclusion that is supported by 'fringe' authors and respected historians alike.[8]

The first piece of evidence comes from the fact that more than one location is recorded as being his grave. This can by no means be taken as proof that there was more than one Brychan, since many historical figures have more than one supposed resting place. However, taken in conjunction with a second piece of evidence – the fact that he is recorded as having more than one wife (which, likewise, would not be unusual on its own) – it is indicative that the records *might* not be referring to a single individual. When the information is looked at more closely, this becomes a virtual certainty.

For example, the Vespasian version of the *Cognatio Brychan* records his grave as being in 'Ynys Brychan, near Mannia', while the Domitian version says he was buried in 'Mynau'. The two most likely locations for Mannia or Mynau are the Isle of Man (called Manau in Old Welsh) or Manaw Gododdin, which is the area of Britain that is roughly adjacent to the Isle of Man. Perhaps Ynys (meaning 'isle') Brychan is the Calf of Man, an island near the Isle of Man. In either case, it is very likely that one of these two locations is the grave of that particular Brychan. As such, it is quite unusual to suppose that a king of Brycheiniog in South Wales would be buried in either of these two northern locations. In light of the fact that there are at least two other supposed locations for Brychan's burial, is it not at least suggestive that this is a different individual altogether?[9]

The existence of a distinct northern Brychan is made more apparent by, peculiarly, Breton tradition. According to the *Life of St Ninnocha*, written in 1130, Brychan married Menedoc, the daughter of Constantine, king of the Scots. This Constantine can only be the son of King Rhydderch of Alt Clut, Scotland. It is presumably this king who is recorded as being converted to Christianity in 588 in the *Annals of Ulster*. The *Great Synaxaristes* records his birth as 570 and his death as 640. If these dates are even roughly correct (and they do agree with information about the dating of his father Rhydderch; for example, the fact that he fought alongside Urien against the Anglian king Hussa in *c.* 590), then Constantine's daughter would have married someone living at the end of the sixth century and the first half of the seventh. It is impossible for her to have married a Brychan of the fifth century. Therefore, Brychan the husband of Menedoc the daughter of Constantine of the Scots must have been a different individual, presumably of the northern kingdoms.

Wilson and Blackett propose the existence of a grandson of Llywarch Hen, of the northern kingdom of Rheged, called Brychan. They do not appear to provide any evidence for this particular relationship, but the probable dating of such a grandson – that is, *c.* 564 or later, using the date of 520 for Llywarch as estimated by Peter Bartrum – would agree with the aforementioned marriage, and as mentioned by those authors, the connections between the

Isle of Man and the family of Llywarch makes such a location likely to be the grave of his grandson Brychan; the alternative possibility of Manaw Gododdin would fit just as well.

We can thus see that there is good evidence for the existence of a late sixth-, early seventh-century Brychan, whether he was specifically the grandson of Llywarch Hen or not. So we are dealing with at least two Brychans – one who lived in the late fourth and early fifth centuries, and one who lived in the late sixth and early seventh centuries. Another piece of evidence for multiple Brychans is the dating of his descendants. Just as some of them can be used to reveal the existence of the first Brychan, others reveal the existence of an additional Brychan.

Consider the relatives of Mordred. As was established in Chapter One, the evidence shows that Urien and Llew were both most likely born in *c.* 523. The reader is encouraged to review the evidence presented in that section if there is any doubt. With this being the case, Cynfarch, the father of those two brothers, was likely born somewhere around the year 501. That this is an accurate estimate is shown by the fact that Cynfarch's brother, Elidyr, had a son who is generally believed to have been born either in the 520s or 530s, this son being Llywarch Hen. Therefore, we can see that both Cynfarch and his brother Elidyr were born at the very beginning of the sixth century.

The reason this is significant is because both of them are recorded as marrying daughters of Brychan. The wife of Cynfarch and mother of Urien and Llew was Nyfain ferch Brychan, while the wife of Elidyr and mother of Llywarch was Gwawr ferch Brychan. Given the unlikelihood of these women being older than their husbands, we can conclude that they were born at least a few years into the 500s.

Then there is Lluan, another daughter of Brychan. She was the mother of Aedan the son of Gabrain. As explained in the first chapter, the sources indicate that Aedan was born in 531, around the same time as Llywarch or perhaps a little later. So his mother, like the mother of Llywarch, would have been born in the early part of the sixth century.

For the Brychan of the late fourth, early fifth century to have been the father of these daughters, he would have had to have been over 100 years old when he fathered them. Such a conclusion can be safely discounted. Logically, the father of these women would have been born an average generation earlier, or *c.* 480. This is a comfortable fit with the lower estimate of 475 for a sixth-generation descendant of Anthun ap Maxim. However, as the records are evidently a confusion of at least three Brychans, the ancestry given to him could be that of the Brychan from *c.* 400, the Brychan from *c.* 480, or the Brychan from *c.* 564. The maternal grandfather in the pedigree is a certain Tewdrig ap Teithfallt – the same names as Meurig's father and grandfather. They are also placed in the same part of the country as the father and grandfather of Meurig. There is no independently recorded Tewdrig ap Teithfallt available to be the subject of the Brychan documents if the pedigree is that of the earlier or the later Brychan. Thus, by far the most logical assumption is that the pedigree is, indeed, that of the Brychan from *c.* 480.

In fact, this conclusion is explicitly supported by a genealogical record contained in the *Life of St Cadoc*. It is recorded that 'Teitfall begat Teudiric. Teudiric, who was made a martyr in Gwent, to wit, Merthir Teudiric, who begat Marchell, mother of Gladusa.' The rest of the document shows that the Marchell of this record is the mother of Brychan, making the Tewdrig of this record the grandfather of Brychan. But, as outlined in the second chapter, it was Tewdrig the father of Meurig who died at Merthyr Tewdrig. Therefore, we have here a clear statement that the Tewdrig ap Teithfallt who was the father of Marchell, and therefore the grandfather of Brychan, is the same as the Tewdrig ap Teithfallt who was the father of Meurig.

With the pedigree now in its correct temporal position, we can see that the 'Anthun king of Greece' at the head of the line does, indeed, fit into position as Anthun ap Maxim. They would have been contemporaries and both would be ancestors of the kings of South Wales. There are very few people in ancient British history recorded as having that name, so given the fact that Anthun king of Greece and Anthun ap Maxim were contemporaries in the same area, there does not seem to be any reason to doubt they were one and the same person.

An issue does seem to arise, however, when more material is considered. The ancestry of Teithfallt the grandfather of Meurig is usually given as the following: Teithfallt ap Ninniaw ap Erb ap Erbic ap Meurig ap Enenni. That is how it is given in the *Jesus College MS 20*, the earliest record, though Teithfallt is exchanged for Llywarch. Similarly, in the list in the *Life of St Cadoc* just mentioned, the ancestry is given: Teithfallt ap Idnerth ap Erb ap Erbic ap Meurig ap Enenni. This is identical, apart from Idnerth being in the place of Ninniaw.

In contrast, the ancestry given for Teithfallt the grandfather of Marchell is given in all the Brychan documents as: Teithfallt ap Teithrin ap Tathal ap Anthun. This is completely different to the pedigrees just mentioned. The reason for this is quite simple. As noted in an earlier chapter, the use of 'ap' in the Welsh genealogies is not strictly limited to the meaning of 'son'. It can also be used in the sense of 'successor'. Notably, the 'genealogical' lists that give 'Ninniaw…' before Teithfallt are usually records of the kings of Glamorgan, as in the *Jesus College MS 20*. In contrast, the records that give 'Teithrin…' before Teithfallt are usually just the ancestral lists of religious figures (specifically, the children of Brychan). The majority of the records follow this pattern; however the *Life of St Cadoc* is an exception, as it makes Teithfallt 'ap Idnerth ap Erb' in a list of the ancestors of Cadoc. But the *Jesus College MS 20* illustrates the point well, for it contains both versions. As already noted, it gives the list of the kings of south-east Wales, recording Tewdrig's father as 'ap Ninniaw…' The first part of this manuscript focuses on the children of Brychan, and the very first list is for the eldest son of Brychan, commonly known as 'saint Cynog'. This list, which logically would not be a king list but merely one of ancestry, as Cynog was not a king, gives the 'ap Teithrin…' version. Therefore, the evidence indicates that Teithfallt was the son of Teithrin, son of Tathal, son of Anthun, son of Maximus, and was simply the successor of Ninniaw.

King Arthur – The King of Greece

This being the case, we can now see that Athrwys, or Arthur, was a sixth-generation descendant of Anthun ap Maxim, being the first cousin of Brychan. But more importantly, it establishes that Anthun, the son of Magnus Maximus, was known as 'King of Greece'. Why is this so important? It is important because of a few obscure, peculiar, but very significant statements in some of the Welsh Arthurian tales.

Near the end of *The Dream of Rhonabwy*, many different individuals assemble at a council of Arthur's. After a long list of individuals, it is said that men from Norway, Denmark and Greece arrived there as well. Shortly thereafter, the story says that men brought Arthur tribute from Greece. The reference to Norway and Denmark can be explained both by the *Historia Regum Britanniae* and the fact that Arthur had long previously been recorded as fighting in Scotland, 'Llychlyn' being a word used for both Scotland and Scandinavia. However, the reference to Greece is quite inexplicable.

As was mentioned in a previous chapter, the earlier Welsh tale *Culhwch ac Olwen* provides the clear, unambiguous statement that Arthur conquered Greece. Needless to say, Athrwys never did that, nor did any other Arthurian candidate, such as Riothamus or Lucius Artorius Castus. At first sight, there does not seem to be any reasonable explanation for this statement.

Of course, Magnus Maximus did not really conquer Greece either. Andragathius got as far as the Balkans, though he did not reach Greece itself. But Greece is certainly the most prominent area in the Balkans, so it is not beyond reason that a statement that Andragathius, or Anthun, fought in the Balkans evolved into a statement that he fought in Greece, which then gradually developed into the belief that he conquered it. In any case, the fact remains that the son of Maximus *was* recorded as the king of Greece. From a consideration of Peter Bartrum's *A Welsh Classical Dictionary*, Anthun seems to be the only character in all of ancient British history or legend recorded as having that position, other than King Arthur himself. It beggars belief that the only two people in British legend who were believed to have ruled Greece just so happened to have had almost identical names. And given that there is no reason whatsoever for the sixth-century Arthur to have been thought of as conquering Greece, the logical conclusion is that such a belief came from Anthun, not the other way around.

If we accept that this is the case, then it demonstrates that Anthun and Arthur *were* combined. Details of the former *were* drawn into tales of the latter. This does not necessarily mean that the Continental wars of Anthun (assuming for the moment that he was the same as Andragathius) were also drawn into tales of Arthur, thus accounting for the otherwise inexplicable European wars attributed to him, but it would be remarkable if that is not what happened.

However, this theory relies heavily on Anthun being the same person as Andragathius. Is this plausible, and, what is more, is there any direct evidence for this?

The whole context of the situation must be examined to get an idea of how likely such a conclusion is. What, then, do we know of Maximus's other family members? Where were they at the time, and did they participate in the war? From the Roman historians, we know that Maximus's wife had come over to Gaul from Britain along with Maximus, and they also had daughters who seem to have been within Continental Europe as well. So we know that at least some of his family came with him. What we also know is that Maximus had a brother named Marcellinus. He did not just participate in the war, but he seems to have been one of the main generals. He led the army that fought against Theodosius at Poetovio, which was the second major defeat of Maximus's forces, after the battle at Siscia. Furthermore, by legend, Maximus also had the military aid of Conan Meriadoc, either his brother-in-law or his wife's cousin.

So we can see that Maximus was joined by at least some of his family members in the fighting, and others, at the very least, came over to Gaul with him. And, as mentioned previously, he made his youngest son – who would not have already possessed any government in Britain, as would have Anthun and perhaps Owain – the Augustus of Gaul. Is it not reasonable to suppose that his eldest son may have been the one to whom 'the general direction of the war' was given?

However, reasonable as it may be, this is not proof. Is there any actual evidence that Maximus's son, the sixth-generation ancestor of Arthur, or Athrwys, was the person who led the invasion of Europe and killed Emperor Gratian?

The Pillar of Eliseg
Before we consider this first piece of evidence, we must first establish what really became of Andragathius. The Roman histories claim

that, after he heard reports of Maximus's execution, Andragathius committed suicide by hurling himself into the Adriatic Sea, through which he was sailing at the time. However, the fact that this is what the surviving reports say does not necessarily mean that this is what actually happened. We know that Andragathius, as well as being an excellent commander and strategist, was also very deceptive. During the initial invasion of 383, he had his men spread reports that Gratian's wife was coming to meet him, when in reality it was Andragathius hiding in a cart. Evidently, he was perfectly capable of deception and spreading false reports, and there is no issue with him having done the same when his life was in danger in 388. In fact, such a claim would easily have been faked, for the only people who would have been on the ship to confirm or deny the story would have been Andragathius's own men. He could easily have sneaked off the ship, just as he had hidden in a cart five years previously. The fact that the reports of his death are inconsistent, some saying it occurred in the Adriatic with others saying it occurred in a river, gives genuine reason to doubt the story. It is within reason to believe that he may have secretly retreated to Britain and, perhaps, lived in Galloway, which would have been beyond the reaches of the Roman Empire. Or it may be that Wales was sufficiently secluded, given that the Roman army apparently ceased to be active there after 383.

When Constantine III became the usurping British emperor in 407, Andragathius could well have returned to the limelight. We do not know how Constantine chose to organise the government of Britain, and he may have allowed Andragathius to control much of it, being the son of the previous usurping emperor from Britain (as we are theorising). Alternatively, if he did go to Wales, where the Romans had already left, then he could easily have made himself high ruler of that area immediately. He would have been outside the confines of the Roman Empire. And just as Teithfallt, later, is recorded as 'Little Emperor', Andragathius likewise may have been considered a kind of emperor.

Evidence that something like this did happen is found in the ninth-century *Historia Brittonum*. In this, Nennius records the Roman emperors who spent time in Britain. After Magnus Maximus, there are two more. The first is Severus Æquantius and the second is Constantius. The issue is that there never was a Roman emperor called Severus Æquantius. So, perhaps this was really Anthun, the son of the previous emperor. 'Severus', while being a name, is also just a Latin word, cognate with the English 'severe'. 'Æquantius', meanwhile, could be a corruption of 'Anthun', or rather, 'Anthunius' or 'Antonius'. The fact that 'Æquantius' was a name in its own right would have made such a corruption easier than it might at first be thought. So to reiterate, perhaps Maximus's son became accepted by the inhabitants of Wales as their new ruler, or even emperor, after the death of Maximus. Thus, he came to find himself recorded by Nennius as the next Roman emperor who spent time in Britain.

Interestingly, Constantine III is identified in *HRB* as Constantine the son of Maximus.[10] This being the case, it is possible that Anthun was not only the ruler of much of the non-Roman part of Britain after his father's death in 388, but he may even have been given control of the rest of Britain by Constantine III, as they would have been brothers, when the latter left for Gaul on his own campaign there.

It is impossible to say for certain what the facts are. But concluding that Anthun had some kind of significant level of control over Britain after the death of Maximus – either by being accepted as the ruler of what was then non-Roman Wales, or by being given control of Roman Britain by his brother Constantine III, or both – makes sense of Nennius's otherwise inexplicable 'Æquantius'. But, how does this relate to the issue of whether or not Anthun was the same as Andragathius?

In Denbighshire, North Wales, there is a stone pillar known as the Pillar of Eliseg. It was erected in the ninth century and bears an inscription regarding a king called Eliseg (known in Welsh history as Elisedd). In the second half of the inscription, it records an otherwise unknown marriage between Sevira, an otherwise unknown daughter of Maximus, and Vortigern. The 'Maximus' in question is universally understood to be Magnus Maximus, partially due to the fact that the inscription refers to Maximus as the 'king of Britain', and Magnus Maximus is the only Maximus 'king of Britain' known from the pertinent time period, and also due to the fact that the inscription mentions that the Maximus in question had killed Gratian the king of the Romans.

However, there are definitely issues with such a conclusion. Ambrosius began his defeat of the Saxons, in addition to slaying Vortigern, no earlier than in the 470s, as we know from Bede. However, Vortigern began his reign in 425, after some time spent as Constans' adviser. With these two key pieces of information in mind, we can hardly imagine that he was born far off CE 400.

In contrast, any daughter of Magnus Maximus must obviously have been fathered before Maximus's death in 388. In reality, though, considering the likelihood that a newborn child of Maximus's would have been mentioned in the Roman accounts, the daughter would almost certainly have had to have been born before the usurper came to power in 383.

It is common for a man to marry a younger woman; the reverse is historically very rare. While it would not be impossible for Vortigern to have married a daughter of Magnus Maximus, it is extremely unlikely that he did so. The Pillar of Eliseg is almost certainly mistaken – or, alternatively, Magnus Maximus is not the subject of the statement. According to Roman naming customs, Magnus's children would likely have borne the name 'Maximus' as well, including Anthun. Without any preconceived notion that the 'Maximus' of the inscription was Magnus Maximus, the logical conclusion would be that it was one of his sons. The only objection to such a conclusion is the fact that the individual is called the 'king of Britain'. However, as we have established, there is no reason why Anthun could not have set himself up as the ruler of the non-Roman parts of Britain after 388. In fact, if he was the Dionotus of the *HRB*, the one to whom Magnus had entrusted the government of Britain, then it would have been more a case of simply keeping the position he had already held for several years, though presumably he would have relinquished control of the Roman parts of Britain after his father's demise, to hide himself away from the Roman Empire. These parts of Britain may have been returned to him when his brother, Constantine III, was declared emperor by his troops. The fact that Nennius records the next emperor in Britain after Magnus Maximus as having a name that could plausibly be related to

'Anthun' or 'Antonius' indicates that one of these things, if not both, really did take place.

With this in mind, we see that it is indeed plausible for Anthun to be the Maximus of the Eliseg inscription. In fact, all this speculation about what Anthun might have done after 388 and what position he might have had during Constantine III's reign and how he might relate to Nennius's 'Æquantius' need not be necessary. Simply having control of Britain *during* his father's reign, as the *HRB*'s Dionotus indicates was the case, would be sufficient reason for him to later be recorded as the king of Britain.

Given this genuine likelihood that Anthun would have been referred to as the king of Britain in later records, there is no reason to favour Magnus over his son as the 'Maximus' of the Eliseg inscription. The chronological considerations involving Vortigern certainly favours the idea that it was his son.

Of course, we are now faced with the fact that the inscription tells us that this Maximus killed Gratian the king of the Romans. The killing could indeed have been attributed to Magnus, as he was the chief of the man who actually held the blade, but the same cannot be said for Anthun; he would have had to have been directly involved in the killing. This fact strongly supports the conclusion that he was Andragathius, the actual killer of Gratian.

To summarise so far, the fact that Anthun was recorded as the king of Greece could conceivably be explained if he was Andragathius. This latter individual is known to have fought in the Balkans, with Greece as the most prominent part of that area. Thus, as mentioned before, it is conceivable that records of Andragathius fighting in the Balkans developed into records of him fighting in Greece, which, in turn, developed into the propaganda that he had conquered that area (this would link into the idea that his final defeat at Siscia was transformed into a victory). On the other hand, if Anthun was not Andragathius, then how would he have acquired the title of 'king of Greece'? There does not appear to be any alternative explanation. We have also seen that it is far more likely for the 'Maximus' of the Eliseg inscription to have been a son of Magnus rather than Magnus himself, due to chronological reasons. The particular son would almost certainly have been

Anthun, due to the fact that the inscription calls the 'Maximus' the 'king of Britain', a title that Anthun would have been entitled to on the basis of his rulership of Britain during his father's reign and, possibly, afterwards too. If this is correct, then this inscription attributes the killing of Gratian to Anthun, indicating that he was Andragathius, the historical killer of Gratian.

The Prophecies of Merlin

More direct evidence is found in Geoffrey of Monmouth's work itself, though not in the main narrative. In the section of the book in which Vortigern is attempting in vain to construct a tower, his men bring him a boy whose sacrifice should, supposedly, be sufficient to ensure the construction can be completed. However, this boy turns out to be Merlin, and he saves himself by revealing the true cause of the problems. Furthermore, he makes an extended prophecy regarding Britain, which contains repeated reference to the 'Red Dragon', signifying the native Britons, and the 'White Dragon', signifying the Anglo-Saxon invaders. Consider, very carefully, the beginning of this 'prophecy':

> Woe to the red dragon, for his banishment hasteneth on. His lurking holes shall be seized by the white dragon, which signifies the Saxons whom you invited over; but the red denotes the British nation, which shall be oppressed by the white. Therefore shall its mountains be leveled as the valleys, and the rivers of the valleys shall run with blood. The exercise of religion shall be destroyed, and churches be laid open to ruin. At last the oppressed shall prevail, and oppose the cruelty of foreigners. For a boar of Cornwall shall give his assistance, and trample their necks under his feet. The islands of the ocean shall be subject to his power, and he shall possess the forests of Gaul. The house of Romulus shall dread his courage, and his end shall be doubtful. He shall be celebrated in the mouths of the people; and his exploits shall be food to those that relate them. Six of his posterity shall sway the scepter, but after them shall arise a German worm. He shall be advanced by a seawolf, whom the woods of Africa shall accompany.[11]

The first lines are self-explanatory. They refer to the first few years after the Saxons turned on the Britons, driving them out of their land – their 'lurking holes'. Next comes apocalyptic imagery to describe the war, referring to mountains being levelled and rivers flowing with blood. We are already familiar with the fact that the churches were destroyed in the Saxon invasion (causing the cessation of the exercise of the Britons' religion), leading to Ambrosius, or Teithfallt, restoring them. This restoration, along with the recovery against the Saxons in general, is evidently what is referred to by the line 'At last the oppressed shall prevail...', meaning the Britons will start winning against the Saxons – the 'foreigners'.

It is the second half of this passage that is the revealing part. It attributes the recovery to 'a boar of Cornwall', that is, Cerniw. Teithfallt did indeed rule Cerniw. In fact, the *Bonedd y Gwyr Gogledd* calls Teithfallt the 'prince of Kerniw'. This same designation would apply equally well to Teithfallt's descendants, who continued to rule the same area. Teithfallt did 'give his assistance' to the native Britons and figuratively (and perhaps even literally) trample the necks of the foreigners. However, the next few lines cannot be attributed to Ambrosius. We have already established that he was in Brittany from 425 until the 470s. He was married to a daughter of the king of Brittany, so he would probably have been considered a prince of that kingdom. But there is no evidence that he ever actually ruled any part of Gaul. There is certainly no evidence that he ever clashed with the Romans, as is implied by the line 'the house of Romulus shall dread his courage'. Nor was Ambrosius's end 'doubtful'. These lines would fit very well with the legendary Arthur, but not with Ambrosius. *HRB*'s Arthur did 'possess the forests of Gaul' and cause the Romans to dread his mightiness. So, just as the two dragons do not represent any specific Briton or Saxon, but simply represent the two different nations in general, it is evident that the boar represents a dynasty, and not any specific king. Teithfallt was the first to lead a major, effective counter-offence against the Saxons, and then the role of the boar in this 'prophecy' is assumed by Arthur.

The confusion between Arthur and the secondary Arthurian figure has been repeated here, as Athrwys did not actually conquer Gaul and attack the Romans. But nonetheless, the prophecy is now describing the legendary Arthur of the *HRB*. However, the line immediately after the reference to the European invasion is what is most relevant to this investigation. Note the following: 'Six of his posterity shall sway the scepter, but after them shall arise a German worm.'

So after six descendants had ruled, the German worm – that is, the Saxons – would rise. The question is, when *did* the Saxons 'rise', or become especially prominent (more so than they had been during the previous part of the invasion)? Surely it was after the death of Arthur, who acted as the main restraint against the Saxon uprising. This is supported by the archaeological record, and the *Anglo-Saxon Chronicle* likewise attests to a period of cessation regarding their advancement through the country, with their first major advancement into the west being in 577, immediately after Arthur had abdicated. This understanding is reinforced by the description found in the *Life of St Goeznovius*, thought by some to have been written before Geoffrey of Monmouth's time. It tells us the following: 'When this same Arthur, after many victories which he won gloriously in Britain and in Gaul, was summoned at last from human activity, the way was open for the Saxons to go again into the island, and there was great oppression of the Britons.'

This reveals that Arthur was indeed believed to have been the main restraint against the Saxons. As this passage shows, the Saxons then 'arose' after his death. Further evidence of the general time period being described in Merlin's prophecy is seen by the following line: 'He shall be advanced by a seawolf, whom the woods of Africa shall accompany.'

'He' is the 'German worm' mentioned in the previous line. This means that the Saxons would be 'advanced', or 'exalted', as other translations render it, by 'a seawolf, whom the woods of Africa shall accompany'. According to Geoffrey of Monmouth's history, a certain 'Gormund king of Africa' invaded Ireland relatively soon after Arthur's death, in the reign of the British king Ceredic. The Saxons then invited Gormund over to Britain, resulting in Gormund causing extensive devastation to the island. With the British king, Ceredic, defeated, Gormund handed over 'the greater part' of the island to Saxon control.[12] Gormund, with his African hordes, is evidently the seawolf who exalted the German worm. After this, he left for Gaul to assist a Frank named Isembard, who had been expelled from his kingdom by his uncle.

At least some of this story shares an origin with an eleventh- or twelfth-century epic poem (from a genre known as the *chansons de geste*) called *Gormont et Isembart*, the events of which may have been based on an incident in the ninth century involving Norsemen. But there must be a reason as to why it was mistakenly placed in the sixth century in the *HRB*. Perhaps there was a separate Germanic tribe that did invade Ireland and then ally itself with the Anglo-Saxons. If the leader of this tribe was named Gormund, then the story of Gormund and Isembard could easily have found itself falsely attached to this earlier ruler.

In any case, the point being made is that this is what is referred to in Merlin's prophecy. This, in turn, demonstrates that the aforementioned rise of the German worm, or the Saxons, as mentioned by Merlin, occurred soon after Arthur's demise. Arthur was, as everything indicates, the one holding back the tide of the Saxons.

With this fact in mind, let us consider that part of the 'prophecy' once more. Give special attention to the final sentence: 'The islands of the ocean shall be subject to his power, and he shall possess the forests of Gaul. The house of Romulus shall dread his courage, and his end shall be doubtful. He shall be celebrated in the mouths of the people; and his exploits shall be food to those that relate them. Six of his posterity shall sway the scepter, but after them shall arise a German worm.'

So if the German worm rose after six of 'his' posterity, or descendants, ruled, yet they rose upon Arthur's death, then logically Arthur would have to be the last of these six descendants. Therefore, counting back six generations will reveal to us who 'he', the conqueror of Gaul, really is:

Arthur – Generation 6
Meurig – Generation 5
Tewdrig – Generation 4
Teithfallt – Generation 3

Teithrin – Generation 2
Tathal – Generation 1
Anthun – Conqueror of Gaul

This demonstrates two things. Firstly, it demonstrates that Anthun ap Maxim was believed to have conquered Gaul and fought against the Romans, which can only have been when accompanying his father in 383–388. For the conquest to have actually been attributed to him, he would have needed to have had an extremely prominent position in the war. Hence, identifying him as Andragathius, the cavalry commander and the one who actually led the war, is the most logical conclusion.

Secondly, it demonstrates that Anthun was confused with the later, sixth-century King Arthur. This is proved by the fact that the prophecy places the conqueror of Gaul *after* the Britons start winning against the Saxons. It is clear from the description that it is meant to be the King Arthur of legend, with him succeeding Uthyr and in turn Ambrosius, continuing the fight against the Saxons as the 'boar of Cerniw'. Yet it is presented as being a full six generations later before the German worm rises, followed by its exaltation by the seawolf, identifiable as Gormund, still in the sixth century – an obvious impossibility. These lines *require* an earlier individual to have been confused with a much later one, thereby causing the chronology of the prophecy to take a massive leap back.

In all likelihood, whatever ancient Welsh sources this 'prophecy' was constructed from contained the lines, or essence thereof, 'the islands of the ocean shall be subject to his power, and he shall possess the forests of Gaul ... Six of his posterity shall sway the scepter, but after them shall arise a German worm' separately from the preceding lines, but due to the conqueror of Gaul being assumed to be King Arthur, these poetic lines were placed immediately after some other, unrelated poetic lines describing the Saxons being conquered by the boar of Cerniw.

Conclusions

In summary, we have seen that the activities of Andragathius in 383–388 correspond very closely to the activities of Arthur as recorded by Geoffrey of Monmouth. We have seen that there are certain characteristics of King Arthur that cannot be attributed to the sixth-century Athrwys, but could very easily be explained by Anthun. We have seen that there are multiple good reasons for Anthun to have been confused with the sixth-century Arthur, causing the stories about them to be unwittingly combined. We have seen that there are several pieces of evidence that indicate that Anthun was the military leader who fought in the Balkans and killed Gratian, thus identifying him with Andragathius. Finally, we have now seen that Geoffrey of Monmouth's work contains direct evidence that Anthun played a major leading role in his father's invasion of Europe, and was therefore almost certainly Andragathius.

In an earlier chapter, it was highlighted that other theories regarding the origin of Arthur's European campaign as recorded by Geoffrey of Monmouth cannot even begin to explain the brief description of Arthur's Continental campaign in *Culhwch ac Olwen*. It says that Arthur fought in Europe, as in the *Historia Regum Britanniae*, but it goes on to say that Arthur had been in Africa, the islands of Corsica, Greece, and India. All but one of these can easily be explained by Andragathius. By defeating and killing Gratian, he conquered the Western Roman Empire, including North Africa and Corsica. While there is no evidence that he was personally present in these places, the fact that he can be said to have conquered them naturally lends itself to such a conclusion, and thus could easily have led to the lines in *Culhwch ac Olwen*.

Regardless of quite how and why Andragathius, or Anthun, became known as the king of Greece, the evident fact that he did explains the line that Arthur conquered Greece. It is interesting to note that this reference to Greece is the very last place outside of Britain mentioned in the passage. This ties in with the fact that Greece – or the Balkans, more correctly – was the furthest place to which Andragathius went. While it is true that Andragathius never went to or conquered India, the reference to India is, peculiarly, at the very beginning of the list of places outside of Britain. It is *after* India that Llychlyn ('Scandinavia', or Scotland), Europe, Africa, Corsica, and Greece are mentioned. If India really is meant, then this is hardly logical. It is quite possible that this is merely a misrendering of some location within the British Isles.

So even though this theory does not perfectly match what is provided in the Welsh sources, it is remarkable for being extremely close. Considering this Welsh material is generally very different from and far grander than Geoffrey of Monmouth's account, yet Andragathius's career ties up remarkably well with both – in addition to the evidence that he was known by a name very similar to Arthur – it seems hardly possible to dismiss the foregoing as coincidence.

This appears to be the answer to that part of the Arthurian mystery. Just as Geoffrey of Monmouth did not invent the story of Gormund being summoned over to France by Isembard and fighting there, but seems to have combined two unrelated Gormunds who were separated by several hundred years of history, it is virtually certain that he also confused two 'Arthurs'; hence, the tale of King Arthur of Caerleon, son of Uther Pendragon, fighting the Saxons in Britain in the sixth century and the Romans on the Continent also in the sixth century was born. It was a case of real history being combined, not imaginary history being invented.

APPENDIX 1

The Dating of Gildas

We saw in Chapter One how the majority of sources indicate that the Battle of Badon took place around CE 548. However, the one potential significant stumbling block to such a conclusion is the dating of Gildas himself, the earliest surviving source to mention the battle. As he describes it as having taken place forty-three years prior to the time of his writing, determining the period in which he wrote is of vital importance. The most secure way to do this is to establish the dates of the reigns of the five kings to whom he directs some of his comments.

The five kings condemned by Gildas were Maelgwn, Vortiporius, Aurelius Caninus, Constantine and Cuneglasus. A consideration of each one shall follow.

Maelgwn
The next earliest source for Maelgwn after Gildas is the *Historia Brittonum*, and this states that Maelgwn began ruling 146 years after the arrival of Cunedda in North Wales. Based on the familial information about Cunedda provided by Nennius and later genealogical records, Peter Bartrum concluded that the migration could not feasibly have taken place before around 430.[1] If Maelgwn began ruling 146 years after this, then his accession must have taken place in 576 or later.

The *Historia Brittonum* provides even more information about the general time frame of Maelgwn's rule, and it is not the first half of the sixth century. Section 61 concludes with the statement that Ida, son of Eoppa, became king and ruled for twelve years. According to the *Anglo-Saxon Chronicle*, this is the Ida whose reign began in 547. The next section then begins with the statement that a certain Outigern fought bravely against the Angles 'at that time'. Several poets are then listed as having been famous for their poetry 'at that time'. Two of these poets are well known from other sources: Taliesin and Aneirin. The former poet was the bard of Urien and his son Owain, while Aneirin is famous for having composed *Y Gododdin*, which concerns the Battle of Catraeth in *c*. 600. Thus, these two figures lived from the mid- to late sixth century. This is significant, for the very next line is the one mentioning Maelgwn ruling among the Britons, with the detail that his rule began 146 years after Cunedda came down from the North. Hence, we can see that not only does the actual figure given by Nennius indicate he was ruling in the late sixth century, but so too does the information about his contemporaries.

This chronology continues to be supported by Geoffrey of Monmouth's *Historia Regum Britanniae*. During the section concerning the rule of Constantine, the immediate successor of Arthur, the death of David is mentioned. The account then says that David was buried at a particular location 'at the command of Malgo, king of the Venedotians', the Venedotians being the inhabitants of Gwynedd. This is immensely significant, for all the records of David's death place it in the late sixth century – the year 589 is particularly favoured today. Yet here we have an account that explicitly makes Maelgwn outlive David. This supports the conclusion derived from the *Historia Brittonum* that Maelgwn became king sometime after 576 and was a contemporary of late sixth-century poets.

Maelgwn still being alive this late into the sixth century is supported by the fact that *The Dialogue of Myrddin and Taliesin*, from the eleventh century, states that Maelgwn was present at the Battle of Arthuret. This battle is placed in the second half of the sixth century by virtually all authorities. The *Welsh Annals*, for instance, places it in the year 573.

Further support is given by the fact that Maelgwn Gwynedd appears in Jocelyn's *Life of St Kentigern*. This Kentigern was the grandson of Llew ap Cynfarch, whose daughter was raped by her cousin Owain ap Urien. Since Owain was born in *c.* 545 (see Chapter One), the year of his son Kentigern's birth is unlikely to have been any earlier than *c.* 565. Therefore, any interaction between Kentigern and Maelgwn could only have occurred in the 580s at the earliest.

However, this still does not address one of the two main pieces of evidence used to support Maelgwn's early date. We have already dealt with the first, which is the 547 record of Maelgwn's death (see Chapter Six). The second piece of evidence used is the genealogical record of Maelgwn. In the *Harleian MS 3859*, his ancestry is given as the following: Maelgwn ap Cadwallon Lawhir ap Einion Yrth ap Cunedda.

The ancestry given by the *Jesus College MS 20* is identical. Does this tie in with the information provided by Nennius? Well, if we suppose that Maelgwn was as old as sixty when he became king, and that Einion was not born before Cunedda arrived in Wales, but perhaps was born in that year, then each generation would have had to have been forty-three years long. Bear in mind that Geoffrey includes Cadwallon as one of the kings present for Arthur's special coronation. Using this scenario of forty-three years starting from the mid-430s, Cadwallon would have been born *c.* 478, which would make him around eighty-two at the time of the coronation. While such a scenario is unlikely, it is by no means impossible.

However, there is a specific detail provided by Nennius that categorically denies this pedigree. Cunedda is described as Maelgwn's *atavus*, which is a word meaning 'great-great-great-grandfather'. Contrast this with the genealogies, which make him Maelgwn's great-grandfather. However, *atavus* was apparently a technical term used in Roman law to denote the meaning just considered.[2] In more generic terms, it was simply used to denote an ancestor of any kind, which is what one scholar argues was its intended meaning in this passage of the *Historia Brittonum*.[3] On the other hand, when we consider the use of this specific word, as opposed to one of several other Latin words which mean 'ancestor', in conjunction with the explicit time frame given between the two men, it seems more likely that 'great-great-great-grandfather' really was meant. We are confronted with the distinct possibility, then, that there are two missing generations in the pedigrees of the kings of Gwynedd.

Alternatively, it may be the case that this record of 'Maelgwn ap Cadwallon ap Einion ap Cunedda' is actually a succession list. We simply do not know. But whatever the case, there is plenty more information about Maelgwn himself that can help us to determine when he lived, regardless of his actual ancestry.

One particularly telling piece of information is the fact that the mother of his illegitimate son Rhun was a certain Gwallwen ferch Afallach. The reason this is significant is because another daughter of Afallach, named Modron, was the wife of Urien Rheged. As was established in the first chapter, Urien was very probably born in the first few years of the 520s, perhaps 523. Assuming the two sisters were not particularly dissimilar in age, and we have no reason to believe they were, it would be logical to conclude that Urien and Maelgwn were roughly the same age as well, meaning that Maelgwn's birth would have been in *c.* 523.

One of Maelgwn's actual wives was part of a well-known and easily positioned family. According to Elis Gruffudd of the early sixteenth century, she was the sister of Asaph, the son of Sawyl Penuchel. In the *Life of St Kentigern*, Asaph was said to have been a disciple of Kentigern, who, as concluded earlier, was probably born around the year 565. Kentigern was probably not younger than twenty when he came to have disciples, meaning that Asaph must have still been alive in *c.* 585. Similarly, Asaph's brother Dunod is said, in a Triad, to have been present at the Battle of Arthuret, which took place in *c.* 573. Furthermore, the Welsh poem *The Death of Urien* seems to portray Dunod as fighting against Owain after his father Urien died. Since Urien fought against the Anglian king Hussa, who ruled from 586 to 592, Urien can only have died in 586 at the earliest. Therefore, if Dunod fought against Owain after Urien's death, he must have still been alive and active in this year. So Dunod and Asaph are both recorded as still being active in the 580s, if not later. In fact, the *Welsh Annals* reports that Dunod died in 595. With no preconceived notion, it would be logical to assume that Maelgwn was roughly the same age as his brothers-in-law. Just as Urien being active in battle as late as *c.* 590 indicates that he was most likely born after 520, Dunod was likewise probably born around the year 520 or later. All this information agrees fully with the estimated date of *c.* 523 for Maelgwn's birth.

Another of his wives was Sanan ferch Cyngen. She was the sister of a man called Brochwel Ysgithrog, and this Brochwel married Arddun the sister of Dunod and Asaph. From this information, we can immediately see that Sanan was of the same generation as Maelgwn's other wife, as she was also a sister of Dunod and Asaph, as we have just considered. However, there is additional information to support this. Sanan's mother, the wife of Cyngen, was Tudglid, one of the daughters of Brychan. As we have established and reiterated through the course of this book, Brychan must have been born in *c.* 480. Tudglid may have been born somewhere between 500 and 520. Her daughter Sanan must, in turn, have been born around eighteen to thirty years later, or any time from 518 at the very earliest to 550 at the very latest. This estimate conforms well to the information that she was of the same generation as Asaph and Dunod, neither of whom died until the close of the sixth century. It also agrees with a birth date of roughly 523 for her husband Maelgwn.

Let us see how well this estimated birth year of *c.* 523 ties in with information about Maelgwn's own mother. She was, so the records tell us, named Meddyf ferch Maeldaf. In turn, her mother was the daughter of Tallwch, the father of Tristan.[4] And who was this Tallwch? It is most likely that he was Talorc mac Mordeleg, a Pictish ruler from this era. He is not recorded as having a son called Tristan (or 'Drest', which is considered to be the Pictish equivalent), but he was succeeded by a man of that name. Tristan (specifically 'ap Tallwch') is mentioned in the Welsh tale *The Dream of Rhonabwy* as one of Arthur's men, and it would thus seem that this was, in fact, the Drest ap Talorc of Arthur's time ('ap' being used, in this case, in the sense of 'successor'). The start of his reign is generally held to have been 552.[5] His predecessor Talorc ruled for eleven years, most likely from 541 to 552. If this Talorc is the 'Tallwch' of the Welsh records, which he does appear to be, then we have a clear chronological fix. He would have been the great-grandfather of Maelgwn, yet he was still alive by *c.* 552.

If we assume that Maelgwn's mother was as young as eighteen when she gave birth to him, then using the estimated birth year of 523 for Maelgwn, she would have been born in 505. If we then assume that her mother, the daughter of Tallwch, was likewise eighteen years old when she gave birth, we arrive at 487 for her birth. If we then assume that Tallwch was as young as twenty when he fathered this daughter, his birth would have taken place in *c.* 467. This would mean that he was seventy-four when he became king and eighty-five when his reign ended. The chronology is tight, but it is just about possible. The idea that Maelgwn's birth was much earlier than 523 is simply not viable with the information concerning his mother, unless Tallwch is not the Talorc of the Pictish records.

This chronology is supported by the record in the twelfth-century *Black Book of Chirk* which states that, after the death of Maelgwn, a certain Elidir Mwynfawr rejected the sovereignty of Rhun ap Maelgwn on the grounds that he was illegitimate and then proceeded to march into Gwynedd. Rhun killed Elidir, but then Clydno Eidyn, Nudd Hael, Mordaf Hael and Rhydderch Hael came down from the North to avenge him. If Gildas was writing in around 591, then Maelgwn must have died after that year. Let us suppose he died in 592, at the age of approximately sixty-nine. Do these four men conform to such a chronology?

Rhydderch Hael is very well known. He is recorded in the *Historia Brittonum* as fighting alongside Urien against Hussa (586–593). He is also recorded as fighting against Aedan mac Gabrain, who ruled from *c.* 574 to *c.* 609. The *Life of St Kentigern* records him as a contemporary of the titular individual. Thus, this was a king who ruled in the late sixth century. In fact, the aforesaid *Life* claims that he died in the same year as Kentigern, which the *Welsh Annals* puts in 612.

Clydno Eidyn was the son of Cynfelyn ap Dyfnwal Hen. For reference, the above-mentioned Rhydderch Hael was the great-grandson of Dyfnwal Hen. Clydno had a son named Cynon, and he is recorded in *Y Gododdin* as being present at the Battle of Catraeth. This battle took place around the turn of the seventh century, so we can see roughly when Clydno must have lived.

Nudd Hael was also descended from Dyfnwal Hen; he was a first cousin of Rhydderch Hael. To reaffirm the chronology, his father Senyllt is mentioned in *Y Gododdin*, apparently indicating that he was still alive in *c.* 600 when the Battle of Catraeth took place.

Hence, it is clear that his son Nudd Hael was definitely a late sixth-, early seventh-century king.

Mordaf Hael was likewise a first cousin of Rhydderch, and that is all that is known about him beyond the record in the *Black Book of Chirk*.

It is clear from all this information that the four kings who fought against Rhun apparently very soon after Maelgwn's death were late sixth-century kings. This agrees completely with Maelgwn dying in the early 590s, but it does not agree at all with Maelgwn dying in 547 or any time around then. It likewise agrees with Rhun being roughly the same age as Owain (born *c.* 545), as we would expect from the claim that their mothers were sisters.

And what about the other children of Maelgwn? Well, the wife of the above-mentioned Elidir Mwynfawr is recorded as being Eurgain ferch Maelgwn. So this king who was, as we have just seen, a contemporary of late sixth-century individuals married one of Maelgwn's daughters. This agrees with her being born in the 540s or later, as would be expected if Maelgwn was born in the 520s. The sons Alser and Doeg are also recorded, but nothing of chronological note seems to be known about them.

However, one apparent obstacle to this chronology is the record of the descendants of Rhun. They are recorded in the genealogies (such as the *Harleian MS 3859* and the *Jesus College MS 20*) as the following: Cadwaladr ap Cadwallon ap Cadfan ap Iago ap Beli ap Rhun ap Maelgwn.

If Rhun was born around 545, then we can conclude that Beli was born *c.* 567, Iago was born *c.* 589, Cadfan was born *c.* 611, Cadwallon was born *c.* 633, and Cadwaladr was born *c.* 655. This does not fit with the available information concerning some of these individuals. For example, Cadfan's wife was said to have been a daughter of Cynan Garwyn. This man was the son of Brochwel, whose wife was Arddun the sister of Dunod and Asaph. From this information, considering the fact that Dunod and Asaph, as concluded earlier, should have been born no earlier than *c.* 520, it is likely that Cynan, their nephew, was born *c.* 540 (this conclusion is additionally supported by the fact that his son Selyf is recorded in the *Welsh Annals* as dying at the Battle of Chester, which was in 616), which would mean his daughter would presumably have been born at some point between 560 and 580. It is extremely improbable that he fathered a daughter who married a man born *c*. 611. So Cadfan must have been born much earlier.

In all probability, it is almost certainly a simple case of this 'ancestral' list actually including several successors rather than sons. It is most interesting to note that Geoffrey of Monmouth makes Beli the son of Einion ap Maelgwn rather than Rhun ap Maelgwn. But this is not simply an alternative name for Rhun, for both individuals are present in Geoffrey's account. This is significant. There does not appear to be anything gained whatsoever by having Einion be the father of Beli rather than Rhun. Would Geoffrey really have just chosen to randomly change this individual's father? It seems reasonable to conclude that there must have been a genuine source for this otherwise inexplicable claim. However, there are a number of later references in Welsh poetry that refer to the later princes of Gwynedd as being the descendants of Rhun. Bearing this in mind, and if we assume that Geoffrey was not wrong in making Einion the father of Beli, then it is immediately clear that the rulership of Gwynedd must have passed over from the children of Beli to the children of Rhun at some point.

Perhaps what happened is this: Maelgwn died in the early 590s. Rhun succeeded as king. After he died, his *nephew* Beli, perhaps born *c*. 567, succeeded, and he was, in turn, succeeded by his son Iago, perhaps born *c*. 587. Then Iago died in 616, the year of the Battle of Chester. After his death, Cadfan, the son of Rhun, born *c*. 567, succeeded as king and then came to be succeeded by his son Cadwallon, followed by his grandson Cadwaladr. Hence, the descendants of Rhun ruled Gwynedd after a brief intermission of rule by the son and grandson of Rhun's brother. This ties in with the detail that Cadfan's wife was a daughter of Cynan Garwyn. As Cynan must have been born *c*. 540, his daughter would have been born around the year 560 or later. This matches Cadfan being born in the 560s, as the son of Rhun. There is an inherent unlikelihood in the concept of Maelgwn marrying a sister of Dunod and Asaph, as he is recorded as doing, while his great-great-grandson married a granddaughter of another of their sisters. There is a two-generation disunity in such a conclusion. On the other hand, making Cadfan the son of Rhun makes the generations exactly equal.

We have seen through this section that the information as a whole strongly supports Maelgwn still being alive in the 590s, allowing for Gildas to have written that late. All the information provided about him in the *Historia Brittonum* supports a late sixth-century *floruit*, as too does the information provided in the *Historia Regum Britanniae*. The information concerning his wives and mistresses consistently makes him a contemporary of late sixth-century figures. There are records that explicitly place him in the late sixth century, such as the *Dialogue of Myrddin and Taliesin* and the *Life of St Kentigern*. Then there is the information about events that happened apparently very soon after his death, involving late sixth-century kings raiding Gwynedd. The information about his mother, likewise, supports the conclusion that he was not born until the 520s, indicating that he was still alive in the late sixth century. The only information that contradicts this conclusion is the genealogical record of Maelgwn's descent from Cunedda and the record of Cadfan's descent from Maelgwn. But the overwhelming weight of evidence requires *this* information to be what needs explaining – which explanation has been provided – not the other way around.

Cuneglasus

On the basis of there being no other king of this general time period with a name equivalent to Gildas's 'Cuneglasus', it is generally held that this must have been Cynlas Goch of Rhos. He was a relative of Maelgwn, with his lineage being recorded as Cynlas ap Owain ap Einion ap Cunedda.

From this, it can be seen that Cynlas and Maelgwn were supposedly first cousins. Of course, we have already established that most of the evidence overwhelmingly points to Maelgwn being a mid- to late sixth-century king, probably being born *c.* 523. There are almost certainly missing generations in the record for Gwynedd, so it may likewise be the case that there are missing generations after Einion in this list as well. Alternatively, it may be that the Gwynedd record serves more as a succession list. This would explain both the excessive cluster of kings after Maelgwn (which kings actually had a 'son, nephew, son, first-cousin once removed, son' relationship, if the conclusions concerning Rhun and his successors in the previous section are correct) as well as the paucity of kings between Cunedda and Maelgwn. If this is the case, then we may conclude that Einion was a long-serving king. Perhaps he ruled for sixty-five years, starting from some time in the 430s, when Cunedda came down from the North. This would place the end of his rule around 500. Maelgwn's father Cadwallon, as well as Cynlas's father Owain, would then have ruled after that.

A sufficient amount of information is known about Maelgwn to be able to determine that his 'genealogy' is deficient. Unfortunately, almost no other information is known about Cynlas, but given the close relationship between the dynasties of Gwynedd and the dynasties of Rhos, it is reasonable to conclude that the same could apply to him.

Vortiporius

Vortipor was the son of Aircol Lawhir of Dyfed. Cynan Garwyn, the king of Powys, is recorded in the *Book of Taliesin* as having caused Aircol to flee, presumably by raiding his country. As we have established, Cynan was probably born *c.* 540, and therefore could not have fought against Aircol until the late 550s at the very earliest; more realistically *c.* 560. Therefore, Aircol was apparently still alive by this point in the sixth century. Even if we allow him to have been as old as seventy when this raid took place, his birth would have been no earlier than *c.* 490. Vortipor would then have been born between *c.* 510 and *c.* 530. Gildas describes the king as growing grey and nearing the end of his life, which would indicate that he was at least sixty, though probably quite a bit older. If we conclude that he was between sixty and seventy years old, the time of Gildas's writing would be somewhere between *c.* 570 and *c.* 600.

How does this tie in with other information? Well, it accommodates Aircol being a contemporary of Teilo, as recorded in his *Life*. It also ties in with Budic, born *c.* 500, fleeing to Dyfed in the time of Aircol. Apart from these few references, the only real information to be used to date this dynasty is to be found in the genealogies. And what do these indicate?

The genealogies for the kings of Dyfed are notoriously contradictory, but we may make an attempt to use them. Firstly, it must be noted that there are primarily two fundamentally distinct versions: the Irish version and the British version. The Irish are recorded as having invaded and settled in Dyfed at the beginning of the fifth century or a little earlier. In the Irish record of the kings of Dyfed, found in the eighth-century *Expulsion of the Déisi*, Aircol is the son of Triphun, son of Aed, son of Corath, son of Eochaid, the one who is said to have migrated from Ireland to Dyfed in the first place. In the British *Harleian* version, Triphun is the son of Clotri, son of Gloitguin, son of Nimet, son of Dimet, son of Maxim (that is, Magnus Maximus – the Dimet here is Dunod, or Anthun). These two pedigrees are distinctly different. One goes back to an Irish settler, while the other goes back to a Roman emperor. The logical conclusion would be that one of them is a succession list, while the other is an actual genealogical list. But which one is which? Needless to say, the list that includes a series of individuals who were never in control of the country cannot be a succession list. Since the Irish were in control of that part of Wales after the time of Maximus, it is evident that the *Harleian* record, which traces Triphun back to Maximus through non-Irish individuals, is not simply recording the rulers of Dyfed but is truly meant to be an ancestral record. As is noted in the second chapter of this book, there is a sudden change in the Irish version of this list from Irish names to Roman names around the year 500. 'Triphun' is generally held to be derived from the Latin *tribunus*, while his son Aircol bears the Latin name 'Agricola'. The most logical conclusion, then, is that the Irish document simply records Triphun as 'mac Aed' because he succeeded the Irish king; he was the descendent of Maximus who gained control of the region after a period of Irish rule.

This being the case, how well does our estimated date of *c.* 490 for Aircol's birth conform to this pedigree? If Dimet – that is, Anthun – was born in 355, which estimated date is taken from Peter Bartrum and is used throughout this book, then each subsequent generation until Aircol would have had to have been twenty-seven years long. This seems somewhat too long, though perhaps there was just one unusually long generation at some point down the line of descent. In any case, twenty-seven years per generation is within reason and conforms to the other evidence available – that concerning Aircol and Cynan Garwyn.

Therefore, we certainly cannot be far wrong with the estimate of *c.* 490 for the birth of Aircol. Then his son Vortipor, as established previously, would have been born somewhere between *c.* 510 and *c.* 530. If Gildas was writing in *c.* 591, Vortipor would have been between sixty-one and eighty-one years of age, which agrees very well with Gildas's comments on the king's age.

Aurelius Caninus

This king is not especially useful for establishing the chronology, for it is not clear which king in the genealogies this is meant to be. It is generally felt that 'Caninus' was a pun on the man's real name, which would have been Conan, or Cynan. This is certainly what the Welsh versions of *HRB* indicate, for they name him 'Cynan Wledig'. However, there were a number of men by that name in this general period. The most famous Cynan of the era, though, was the Cynan Garwyn to whom we have already referred several times. Gildas describes Caninus as enjoying war and plunder; this certainly fits with Cynan Garwyn, a warlord who is recorded in a poem in the *Book of Taliesin* as leading many campaigns throughout Wales and even into Cornwall.[6] If this identification is correct, then it is obvious that Gildas must have been writing well into the 560s, given Cynan's birth of *c.* 540. If this Cynan is the king in question, Gildas could easily have been writing in 591.

Evidence that actively supports such a conclusion is found in Geoffrey's *Life of Merlin*. There, the narrative largely takes place in the aftermath of the Battle of Arthuret, which the *Welsh Annals* places in 573. In this account, the reigning king is specifically identified as Aurelius Conan. This information clearly places Aurelius's rule in the latter half of the sixth century. The identification with Cynan Garwyn, therefore, does seem to be correct, but in any case, the chronology of the matter is clear.

Constantine

This king was a ruler of Dumnonia, as per the testimony of Gildas. According to Geoffrey of Monmouth, this king was the son of Cador, a ruler of Cornwall during Arthur's time. Constantine's father Cador, more usually spelt Cado or Cadwy in other records, has a fairly stable lineage, which is usually given as the following:

Cadwy ap Geraint ap Erbin ap Constantine ap Cynfawr ap Tudwal ap Gwrfawr ap Gadeon ap Cynan Meriadoc.

The final figure here is the Conan who, according to the *HRB*, went with Maximus to the Continent and became the ruler of Brittany. Given his engagement in battle in this war of 383, though also bearing in mind his relation to Octavius, it would be reasonable to assume he was born some time around 330–340. If we assume twenty-two years per generation, then Constantine ap Cador should have been born around 528–538.

However, it is perhaps likely that he was born a little later than that. His grandfather, Geraint, was killed at the Battle of Llongborth. In Chapter Six of this book, evidence was provided that this battle was the initial fight against Mordred upon Arthur's return from Brittany in *c.* 570. If Geraint was born in 484–494, in line with our rough guide of twenty-two years per generation from a start of 330–340, he would have been between seventy-six and eighty-six years old when this battle was fought. This is not impossible, but a younger age would be preferable. If he was around sixty at the time of the battle, then he would have been born in *c.* 510. This would give an average generation gap of just over twenty-four years, if starting from *c.* 335. Such a conclusion is reasonable and would indicate a birth of *c.* 554 for Constantine, the grandson of Geraint. If Gildas was writing in 591, Constantine would have been about thirty-seven; an age that is perfectly compatible with Gildas's description, as he says the king has been sinning 'many years'.

Additional support for this chronology is, again, found in the *HRB* itself. In the section describing Constantine's rule, the account says that David died at this time. His death is most commonly accepted as having occurred in 589 – all versions, in any case, place it near the end of the sixth century or even at the beginning of the seventh. A religious individual named Daniel (also known by the Welsh form 'Deiniol'), is also said in the *HRB* to have died in the time of Constantine. The *Welsh Annals* record that man's death as being in 584.

It really is impossible to find any information from the sources we have that actually supports an early sixth-century *floruit* for this king. To the contrary, all the information that is there in the various sources supports Constantine being a king who flourished in the late sixth century. This fully agrees with Gildas writing in *c.* 591.

Gildas Albanius and Gildas Badonicus

If the sources regarding the Battle of Badon itself indicate that it took place in the mid-500s, and the sources regarding the kings about whom Gildas wrote show that they ruled in the latter half of the sixth century, then one final avenue to consider is the evidence regarding Gildas himself. Is there any evidence that he was born in *c.* 548, as would be required by the other information?

In the first *Life of St Gildas*, written in the eleventh century, we are told that Gildas went to Ireland in the reign of Ainmericus. This is generally accepted as referring to Ainmuire mac Sétnai, the high king of Ireland from 566 to 569. After preaching there for an unspecified amount of time, he travelled all the way to Italy and spent some time in Rome and then Ravenna. After this, he travelled back towards Britain and ended up in Armorica, or Brittany. At this point, Gildas is said to be in the thirtieth year of his life – that is, he was twenty-nine years old. We cannot say for sure how much time passed between the beginning of his visit to Ireland, in the reign of Ainmuire, and his arrival in Armorica after returning from Italy, but clearly we must allow a fair amount of time for the events to have happened. Consider the description of his stay in Ireland:

> Then St Gildas, protected with the shield of courage and the helmet of salvation, went round all the territories of the Hibernians and restored the churches, instructed the whole body of the clergy in the catholic faith, that they might worship the holy Trinity, healed the people who were severely wounded by the bites of the heretics, and drove far away from them the heretical conceits along with their authors.

After describing the spiritual blessings that resulted from his preaching, the account continues by describing how Gildas built many monasteries in the island, 'rearing in them not a few sons of noble men, and fashioning them by the rule of a regular discipline. And, that he might be able to present more disciples to the Lord, being a monk, he now gathered monks to himself'.

Clearly, we must conclude that Gildas spent at least several years in the country. It is also likely that several years separated his leaving Ireland for Italy and his arriving back in Armorica.

Thus, if the beginning of this whole period was somewhere between 566 and 569 (Ainmuire's reign), then by the end of this whole period, when Gildas arrived back in Armorica, we can reasonably conclude that this was some time in the 570s. If he was twenty-nine years old by this point, as the account explicitly says, then his birth would have been somewhere in the 540s. Seeing as the other evidence points to *c.* 548 as being the year of the Battle of Badon, and hence the year of Gildas's birth, this is a comfortable fit.[7]

At the same time, however, there is plenty of evidence that Gildas lived much earlier. For example, Gildas was one of the prominent individuals who helped arrange the downfall of Count Conomor, which happened in 560. We can hardly attribute this to a twelve-year-old. Similarly, he was said to have preached in Dyfed during the reign of Triphun, the father of Aircol Lawhir. As we have already seen, the birth of Aircol seems to have occurred somewhere around the year 490, with his father, of course, being born around twenty to twenty-five years prior to that. For a man born in *c.* 548 to have preached during his reign, Triphun would have had to have continued ruling as king until he was in his nineties. This is not impossible, though it is very unlikely. More significantly, Gildas was said to have spoken to David's mother, Non, while she was pregnant with David. The exact year of David's birth is debated, but it was certainly long before the 540s. It is generally placed somewhere in the two decades either side of the year 500. This would indicate that Gildas, allowing for him to have been as young as a teenager at the time of David's birth, was born a little before the turn of the sixth century. This is a much better fit for someone who was preaching in the time of Triphun, and it would mean that he was an elderly and respected figure at the time of Conomor's downfall in 560. This information matches with the claim in the *Chronicon Britannicum*, written in 1356, that Gildas was born in 490.[8]

Nonetheless, different evidence points, again, to a mid-sixth-century birth for Gildas. In his second *Life*, written in the twelfth century, Arthur was said to have killed Gildas's brother Hueil. When this happens, Hueil is repeatedly referred to as a youth. Perhaps he was in his early twenties. Yet, he is described as Gildas's older brother. If Gildas was born in *c*. 490, yet Hueil was older than him, then Hueil would have had to have been born a little before that. If he was still considered a 'youth' when Arthur killed him, then we can hardly imagine the year of this event to have been much beyond *c*. 512. However, Arthur would have been around ten years old at that time. This becomes even more unbelievable when a later version of the legend is considered, which includes the detail that Hueil took a mistress of Arthur.[9] On the other hand, if Gildas was born in *c*. 548 and his brother was born a few years earlier, then we are looking at a date toward the end of the 560s for Hueil's death. Needless to say, Arthur would have been old enough to have engaged in the alleged activities if this is when the event really took place.

Similarly, there is a record of Mordred marrying a daughter of 'Gawolane, great prince of the Britons'. As revealed by Geoffrey of Monmouth, Mordred's brother Gawain was twelve years old in, or very shortly before, 560. Mordred would presumably have been born at roughly the same time – that is, in the late 540s. Considering the improbability of a man marrying a woman much older than him, it is most probable than Mordred's wife was born around 550 or later. It has been suggested that 'Gawolane' was Cadwallon, the father of Maelgwn, but it is improbable that Cadwallon was still fathering children by the mid-sixth century. The more traditional interpretation, that Gawolane was Caw, the father of Gildas, is preferable. This would, again, mean that the children of Caw belong to the mid-sixth century, not the late fifth and early sixth.

So we are faced with a mass of contradictory evidence. One set of evidence indicates that Gildas was born in the late 540s, while another set of evidence requires him to have been born towards the end of the 400s. As a result of this, we are forced to come to the same conclusion that was reached by historians hundreds of years ago: there were two men called Gildas. Traditionally, these are divided into 'Gildas Albanius', the native of Scotland (Albania), and the younger 'Gildas

Badonicus', the writer of *De Excidio*. Though the idea that the younger Gildas was not from Scotland seems to be without foundation, the evidence does agree with the tradition inasmuch as it was clearly the younger Gildas, born in the middle of the sixth century, who wrote about Badon.

Thus, this is the answer to the enigma of the dating of the Battle of Badon. All the sources regarding the battle itself indicate that it took place somewhere around 548, and the evidence regarding the kings about whom Gildas wrote, forty-three years after the battle, shows that they ruled their territories well into the second half of the sixth century, even into the 590s. The reason that there is evidence regarding the dating of Gildas himself that does not accommodate this late chronology is simply the fact that there were two men of that name in this general period. One of these men was probably born in the late 540s, and would therefore have been the man who wrote about Badon.

The State of Britain

However, in spite of all this evidence for a late sixth-century date for Gildas's writing, there is one apparent obstacle that cannot just be dismissed as a later mistake. It is found in the words of Gildas himself. He describes how the Saxons caused havoc in Britain and caused the Britons to flee. Then, at last, under the command of Ambrosius, they began pushing back and won many battles against the Saxons. From that time onwards, the Britons and the Saxons continued warring against each other, until eventually the Battle of Badon took place, which was 'almost the last but certainly not the least' slaughter against the enemy. He then describes the peace that ensued thereafter, and how those who had grown up after Badon did not appreciate the value of the 'present security'. They descended into civil wars. This was, apparently, the state of Britain at the time Gildas was writing.

How could this be, if he was writing as late as 591? There are many battles between the Britons and the Saxons recorded in the *Anglo-Saxon Chronicle* for the years between 548 and 591, including the capture of Bath and Gloucester in 577. Furthermore, the evidence is clear that Urien, along with others, fought against Anglo-Saxon kings in the 570s and 580s. Surely this completely precludes the possibility that Gildas's comments were written so late in the sixth century?

One possible way to reconcile the information would be to conclude that his comments were not meant to be taken to be referring to the entirety of Britain. It could be that he was confining his comments, by this point in his narrative, at least, to the non-Romanised Britons. This may seem arbitrary, but there are numerous records that refer to distinct regions of Britain. The boundaries given to one of these regions – Lloegyr – corresponds very well with the Romanised part of Britain. Of course, all of Britain up to the border of Scotland was controlled by the Roman Empire. But certain parts of the island were distinctly more Romanised than others. That is, they were more thoroughly incorporated into the Roman culture, becoming part of the Roman society, contributing in return to the economy and functioning of the empire, and just generally living with a thoroughly Roman way of life. The distribution of Roman villas illustrates this point very well. The other parts of Britain, while being in subjection to Rome, largely maintained their cultural identities and kept to themselves. Dumnonia was one such non-Romanised area. The main part, though, was known as the land of the Cymry (known today simply as Wales – the modern Welsh word for this is 'Cymru', which will therefore be used in this discussion to refer to the full extent of the original 'land of the Cymry'). The border of the land originally designated by this term extended diagonally from the border of Wales, somewhere along the Severn, to the Humber in the north-east of England.

In fact, these parts of the island were culturally distinct long before the time of the Romans. More or less exactly the same part of Britain that came to be Romanised had also been inhabited by the tribes that minted coins, traded extensively with the Continent, and were generally more industrial. This division appears to have existed from as early as the emergence of the Brythonic Celts in *c.* 500 BCE. At this time, the La Tène culture was brought over from the Continent and likewise covered much of the later 'Lloegyr' area. The Arras culture in York, for example, is La Tène, employing the extensive use of chariot burials and burials in square barrows. While originally thought to have been confined to Yorkshire, these La Tène square barrows have been recognised down through the Midlands and into Essex, near London. The majority of La Tène artefacts have been found in this general area, such as the famous Battersea Shield, discovered in the Thames. It was thus these La Tène inhabitants of Britain who continued to have a greater material culture than the rest of the inhabitants. It was these inhabitants who continued to have the greatest contact with the Continent. And it was these Britons who were exposed to almost 400 years of Roman rule, living in Roman villas with Roman customs and a Roman society.

Due to all this, it is likely that the Cymry considered themselves, certainly by the end of the Roman era if not before, to be a distinct people to the inhabitants of Lloegyr. Dumnonia was equal in all regards to Cymru. All five kings to whom Gildas directs his comments reigned within the confines of this non-Romanised British territory. Maelgwn was the king of Gwynedd, in north-west Wales. Cynlas was the king of the neighbouring kingdom of Rhos. Vortipor was the king of Dyfed, in south-west Wales. Constantine was the king of Dumnonia. Finally, Aurelius Caninus, if we accept his identification as Cynan Garwyn, was the king of Powys, along the eastern side of Wales. It is also interesting to note that Gildas refers to Magnus Maximus as having removed all the Roman forces from Britain, while the archaeological evidence shows that Roman military presence seems to have entirely ceased only in Wales at this time. This supports the idea that Gildas was particularly concerned with events that affected the non-Romanised Britons – the Cymry – and was primarily aiming his words at them, not the Romanised Britons of Lloegyr. Thus, when he referred to the freedom from foreign wars that his people were now experiencing, it may well be that he simply meant that the *Cymry* were no longer experiencing foreign wars.

According to the *Genealogy of Iestyn the Son of Gwrgan*, which records the triumphs of Teithfallt against the Saxons, they came to Wales in his time, slew many of the natives, and destroyed churches and choirs. Teithfallt lived in the fifth century. In the *Book of Llandaff*, Tewdrig is recorded as dying after fighting the Saxons on the River Wye, in the south-east of Wales. This took place in the early sixth century. Gildas himself refers to several shrines of martyrs as having been destroyed by the Saxons, and he seems to give the burial place of Julian and Aaron as an example. Their place of burial is most widely accepted as being at Caerleon, which is in south-east Wales.

Thus, it seems clear that the Saxons had been warring in Wales right through from the fifth century to at least the early sixth. It may be that Julian and Aaron's burial site was destroyed during Arthur's ninth battle, which was said to have been at 'Cair Lion'. Similarly, many of Arthur's other battles took place in the north of Britain, such as Edinburgh, Celidon, and other places around southern Scotland and northern England, outside the territory of the Romanised Britons. Nennius and Geoffrey are both explicit in that the Saxons were warring in this general area. Yet there does not appear to be any evidence of Saxon wars being fought in this area after Arthur's last battle. In short, the theory being presented here is that the Battle of Badon marked the end of the foreign wars in the land of the non-Romanised Britons, or the Cymry.

Granted, Urien and others were said to have fought against the kings of Bernicia, which was north of the Humber and therefore within the territory that would normally be considered 'Cymru'. However, it is self-evident that the actual area ruled by the Anglo-Saxons would obviously not have been considered part of the land of the Cymry. It could easily be the case that Urien and his allied kings invaded Bernicia and fought their wars there, rather than the Anglo-Saxon kings invading the British territory. As such, it could still be said that the foreign wars had ceased, for this would simply be an act of aggression on the part of certain British kings and would not have had an impact on the peace being experienced by the inhabitants of Cymru, which was the point Gildas was making. There does not appear to be any definite record of a Saxon war taking place in Cymru itself between the years 548 and 591. Therefore, this seems to be a satisfactory interpretation of Gildas's words.

Conclusions

It was outlined in the first chapter how all the available information regarding Arthur shows that he lived from the very beginning of the sixth century to some way into the latter half of that century.

Further, it was explained how the information regarding the Battle of Badon indicates that it took place in the mid-sixth century, probably in *c.* 54. Independently, the information concerning the Battle of Camlann requires it to have taken place some way into the latter half of the sixth century, which reaffirms the conclusion about Badon, as they were supposed to have been separated by about twenty years.

Now, in this appendix, we have seen that by far the greater part of the evidence concerning the five kings agrees with the date of 591 for Gildas's writing. The only evidence to the contrary is that of the record of Maelgwn's ancestors and descendants and the related record of Cynlas's ancestors. However, sufficient evidence exists concerning Maelgwn himself to demonstrate that this record is deficient, which gives us reason to question Cynlas's ancestry. Every other piece of evidence concerning Maelgwn places his reign thoroughly in the second half of the sixth century. We have seen that the same applies to Vortipor and Constantine. Similarly, the scant information we have about Aurelius Caninus, provided by Geoffrey of Monmouth, completely agrees with a late sixth-century date and indicates that he should be identified with the famous Cynan Garwyn, a king who lived from *c.* 540 to *c.* 610.

Additionally, we have seen that there is evidence for two distinct individuals named Gildas, both of whom lived in the sixth century. There is evidence that one of these men was substantially younger than the other, being the younger brother of someone active in battle but described as a 'youth' during or just after the 566–569 reign of Ainmuire of Ireland. This is a perfect correspondence to the estimated birth year of *c.* 548 for one of the two men named Gildas.

Finally, an explanation has been provided for how Gildas was able to refer to the foreign wars as having ended after Badon and not begun again until his time even though the Saxons continued to advance and make war with the Britons between 548 and 591. Though this interpretation of Gildas's words may not seem obvious, it is surely permissible. It is improbable in the extreme to suppose that later chroniclers over various parts of the country and across hundreds of years would, apparently by pure coincidence, make false claims covering almost all avenues that consistently placed

Arthur, the battle, the five kings, and Gildas himself much later in the sixth century than they actually were. Surely an allowable interpretation of Gildas's words that does not require such a conclusion is the preferable one.

In conclusion, it is clear that the corpus of evidence points definitively towards a particular conclusion: the Battle of Badon took place in *c.* 548.

The Thirty-three-year Error

In *The Chronicles of England* we find the statement that King Arthur died 546 years after the Incarnation of Our Lord. As we have seen throughout this book, an abundance of information about Arthur proves unequivocally that he lived beyond CE 546. The Battle of Camlann seems to have occurred in *c.* 570, though the evidence indicates that he did not die then. After an indeterminate period of time, he was taken away to 'Avalon' to be healed of his wounds.[1] A date of 579 for Arthur's death, in accord with the idea that the 'Incarnation' (the birth of Jesus) has been confused with the 'Passion' (the death of Jesus, thirty-three years later), matches this information well.

Another example of this thirty-three-year error comes from the *Historia Regum Britanniae*. In this book, Geoffrey wrote that King Lucius died 155 years after the Incarnation. Yet he was supposed to have written a letter to Pope Eleutherius asking for a Christian to be sent to the country. Eleutherius did not become pope until *c.* 174, showing that Lucius cannot have died as early as CE 155. Certainly for him to have caused Christianity to make any progress during his life, there must have been a good number of years between the letter being sent to Pope Eleutherius and his death. A date of 188 (thirty-three years later than 155) for his death accords much better with this information. This is backed up by the fact that he is credited with having founded St Peter-upon-Cornhill Church in 179. Again, this would not be possible if he died in 155, but would be quite possible if he died in 188.

Yet another example of an apparent thirty-three-year error is found in the words of Nennius. Towards the end of his work, he refers to the fact that the Saxons came to Britain in the fourth year of Vortigern, and he says that this was when Felix and Taurus were Roman consuls. Historically, it is known that Felix and Taurus were consuls in 428. However, Nennius then says that this was in 'the 400th year from the Incarnation of our Lord Jesus Christ'. Though not exactly corresponding to the thirty-three-year principle, this is within five years of what it would be expected to be. Considering Nennius's imperfect accuracy with other dates he provides, and the fact that the figure of 400 may have been rounded up, this can be taken as evidence that 'Incarnation' dates sometimes were originally dated from the 'Passion' but became mistakenly copied.

That dates were sometimes based from the Passion rather than the Incarnation is shown by the fact that Nennius explicitly does this sometimes in *Historia Brittonum*. It may be that when subsequent copyists or chroniclers came across such a statement, they simply, but incorrectly, understood it to refer to the number of years from the birth of Jesus. Reading the line without much thought, they may have experienced a case of mental blindness and substituted the word 'Incarnation' for 'Passion'. Alternatively, it may be the case that the phrase 'In the xth year of the Passion of our Lord' was sometimes shortened to just 'In the xth year of our Lord'. This could then, by a later reader, have been assumed to mean from his incarnation, or birth.

It is known that a standardised dating system based on Jesus's death was commonly used on the Continent. It is known as the Victorius system. It is generally held that it was actually this system that Nennius was using, and that he or a later copyist mistakenly inserted 'Incarnation' instead of 'Passion'. It may, in fact, be the Victorius system that is responsible for all the errors mentioned in this appendix. The only issue with this explanation is that it is five years short of reflecting the actual year of Jesus's death (that is, CE 33). In other words, it is only twenty-eight years ahead of the CE (or AD) calendar, rather than being thirty-three years ahead. This fits Nennius's error perfectly, and it is adequate for Lucius's death, but it is not ideal for explaining the errors involving Arthur.

For example, if the dates in the *Welsh Annals* were mistakenly placed where they were due to being taken from a record that used the Passion dating system, as seems to be the most logical explanation, then, if this was specifically the Victorius system, the 516 entry for Badon should actually signify CE 544. Alternatively, if it was based on a Passion dating system which used the correct date of CE 33 for Jesus' death, then the entry would signify CE 549. Of the two, the later one is closer to the post-547 date indicated by Nennius's statement that the twelve battles continued until the time of Ida, and it is also closer to the 553 date found in the *Red Book of Hergest*. Similarly, the information regarding Cheldric, or Cerdic, would place the battle in 553. So regarding the *Welsh Annals*, the option that is closest to these other pieces of evidence is clearly preferable. Thus, based simply on this, it is more logical to conclude that the Passion dating system used was one based on CE 33, as opposed to the Victorius system, based on CE 28. Similarly, the correspondence between the events and chronology presented in the *Historia Regum Britanniae*, the other records regarding the great plague, and the contemporary history presented by Gregory of Tours (see Chapter Six) works much better when the Battle of Badon is placed in 548 and the Battle of Camlann is placed in 570 than it does when the former is placed in 544 and the latter is placed in 565.

It cannot be stated with absolute certainty whether the Passion dating system used for the Arthurian dates was specifically the one produced by Victorius, or whether the Britons developed and used their own version that counted from the correct starting year (that is, 33 CE). The information regarding Arthur supports this latter option. Evidence against it includes the fact that such a system is not unequivocally known to have existed, in contrast to the Victorius system. It is simply impossible to provide exact dates for the reign of Arthur with total confidence, but what we can be sure of is that the Battle of Badon was fought roughly in the mid-sixth century, while the Battle of Camlann was fought just over twenty years later. Arthur, then, must have died somewhere in the 570s.

Constans and the Family of Brittany

According to the *Historia Regum Britanniae*, Ambrosius and Uthyr were younger brothers of Constans, and they were all sons of Constantine the king of Britain. This Constantine was said to have been the brother of Aldroen the king of Brittany. This does not conform to the idea that Teithfallt was Ambrosius, inasmuch as the father of Teithfallt was Teithrin ap Tathal ap Anthun. There is no real evidence that Teithrin was known by the name 'Constantine', nor that this family had any power over Brittany before Teithfallt married Amlawdd's (Aldroen's) daughter. Additionally, the chronology does not allow Teithfallt to have had an older brother who was old enough to have become king while Teithfallt was still a child, as in the relationship between Ambrosius and Constans. So, what can explain this apparent issue?

Firstly, the true identity of Constantine and Constans must be established. It is usually taken for granted that these men were meant to be Constantine III, the British usurper of 407, and his historical son Constans. In the *HRB*, Constans is a monk, which would certainly fit Constantine III's son, who was indeed a monk for a time. Given that this story is set at the very end of the Roman era, the common identification does, on the face of it, seem very likely.

In reality, though, there are serious issues with such a conclusion. For instance, later in the book, when Arthur is speaking, he refers to the fact that 'Constantine the son of Helena and Maximian' acquired the Roman Empire. Given that 'Maximian' is the name used for Magnus Maximus in Geoffrey's work, it is evident that the

HRB identified Constantine ap Maximus as Constantine III, the man who usurped the empire, controlled much of Britain and Gaul, and marched into Italy. On the other hand, Constantine the brother of Aldroen is never called a son of Maximus, or Maximian. Nor is he described as crossing over into Gaul and warring with the Romans, or having any Continental expeditions. He is simply portrayed as a king of Britain, and his parentage is not given. Another difference is the fact that Constantine the brother of Aldroen is said to have reigned for over ten years, while Constantine III only ruled for four years, and he only had control over Britain for two years. Their deaths are also different. The Constantine of the *HRB* (the brother of Aldroen) is said to have been treacherously killed by a Pict who had come into his service, while Constantine III was defeated by the Romans by means of a siege and then executed.

Furthermore, the Constans of the *HRB* is described as outliving his father, whereas Constans the son of Constantine III was actually killed before his father. His manner of death is completely different too. The Constans of the *HRB* is treacherously killed in his sleep by Picts, who had been manipulated into doing so by Vortigern, Constans' advisor. In contrast, Constans the son of Constantine III was captured by the Romans and executed. The timing involved is also incorrect, for Vortigern, according to Nennius, became king in 425. Geoffrey portrays him as immediately succeeding Constans, yet how could this be the case if Constans actually died in 411, as did the son of Constantine III?

It is clear that Geoffrey was not describing Constantine III and his son. These figures are wildly different. The truth behind Geoffrey's account seems to be found in Nennius's 'Constantius'. He is the last in his list of 'Roman Emperors', after Magnus Maximus and the seemingly non-existent Æquantius. His reign is said to have lasted sixteen full years, being 'treacherously murdered' in the seventeenth year of his reign. Interestingly, if we count back sixteen years from 425, Vortigern's first year and therefore the last year of Geoffrey's Constans, we come to 409. This is the very year that the native Britons are recorded by Zosimus as expelling the Roman administration from Britain.

It is also interesting to note that both Constantine and Constans, in the *HRB*, are recorded as being treacherously murdered by

Picts, and in both cases the Picts are specifically shown to have been in the service of the king, rather than simply being Picts who sneaked down from Scotland and attacked the king. And Nennius's Constantius, too, is said to have been treacherously murdered, though no detail is given.

What seems to have happened is this. By the end of the first decade of the 400s, the Britons on the outer parts of Roman Britain – such as Wales and northern England – had been neglected by the Roman forces for a number of years and were facing trouble with raids from the Picts and the Scots. They first appeal to a Roman later recorded as Agitius, but he does not offer any assistance.[1] They then appeal to Aldroen of Brittany, as the *HRB* tells us, and he chooses to send his brother, named Constantius, to become their king rather than going himself. Under the command of this Constantius, the Britons expel the Roman administration of Constantine III, thus ending the Roman era of Britain. Constantius then rules Britain for sixteen years, until 425, and is then treacherously murdered by Picts. Due to some confusion with the contemporary and similarly named Constantine III and his son Constans, the writer of Geoffrey's source mistakenly divided Constantius into two men – one named Constantine and one named Constans. This explains why their death stories are so similar. Making Constans a monk is most probably a detail drawn from Constans the son of Constantine III.

A similar conclusion was reached by Peter Bartrum, who said:

> The fact that the story told by Geoffrey about Constans son of Constantine is clearly based on that of Constans son of the usurping emperor of AD 407, has led some writers to assume that Geoffrey's Constantine is to be identified with the usurping emperor ... Nothing, however, that Geoffrey says about Constantine himself is drawn from the history of the emperor.[2]

So how does this relate to the lineage of Arthur? Well, we can now see that there was no Constans. There was simply Constantius, and this is the man whom Vortigern succeeded. And when this took place, in 425, Ambrosius and Uthyr were 'only children in their cradles' according to *HRB*. In Chapter Two, it was shown how, in accord with the words of Gildas regarding Ambrosius, Uthyr was far more probably the son, rather than the brother, of Ambrosius. Thus, the reality of 425 would have been that Ambrosius, alone, was a child when this happened. This ties in with the estimated date of *c.* 420 for Teithfallt's birth. However, what does not tie in is Teithfallt's father, Teithrin. He should have been born around the turn of the fifth century, which would mean that he was only about ten years old in 409. Obviously, he could not have been Constantius. So what is the explanation for this?

Firstly, let us see who Constantius really was. The scribes of the British genealogies identified him as Constantine ap Cynfawr ap Tudwal ap Gwrfawr ap Gadeon ap Cynan Meriadoc. This is shown by the fact that Aldroen, or Aldwr (specifically called 'king of Brittany'), is given the same ancestors in the British genealogies, thus making him the brother of this particular Constantine. However, given that Cynan Meriadoc must have been born somewhere in the region of 335, this Constantine would have been born around 435 if we assume twenty years to a generation. This would increase to *c.* 445 if we assume twenty-two years to a generation. Clearly, the Constantine of this genealogical record cannot be the Constantius who ruled before Vortigern, who began his reign in 425. Perhaps the suggestion might be made that it is actually a king list, thus allowing for many of the men preceding Constantine and Aldroen to have actually been of the same generation. However, this conclusion does not conform to Geoffrey of Monmouth's statement that Aldroen was the *fourth* king from Cynan.

Another reason for supposing that this list truly is one of ancestry, not succession, is the fact that Geraint, the king who was killed at Llongborth in *c.* 570 at the end of the great plague, is listed as 'ap Erbin ap Constantine ap Cynfawr'. As was said in the first appendix, it is unlikely that Geraint was more than sixty years old when he fought in this battle. This would put his birth *c.* 510, and his appointment as king no earlier than *c.* 524. More realistically, he would not have become king until *c.* 530 or later. If the Constantine of this list was the one who was killed in 425, then, if it is a succession list, that leaves a space of around 100 years occupied by a single person – Erbin. On the other hand, if we suppose that the list is simply one of ancestry, we comfortably arrive at the year of *c*. 510 for Geraint's birth with an average generation gap of just over twenty-four years.

It is clear that the scribes were simply mistaken in thinking that Constantine the king of Britain before Vortigern was the Constantine of this list. This then caused them to mistakenly give this ancestry to Aldroen (and, by extension, Amlawdd). The actual ancestry of these men seems to be entirely unknown. However, they were presumably from the family of Cynan, given Aldroen's position as the king of Brittany.

But finally, how did Teithfallt come to be thought of as the child of Constantius? It is possible that this is simply a random mistake, in line with Geoffrey mistakenly making Helena the daughter of a British king, making Leolin, Trahern and Marius the uncles of Helena and also mistakenly making Sulgenius the brother of Caracalla's mother. On the other hand, it may be that the explanation is that it came from a list showing the succession from Constantius. As Vortigern acquired power illegally and was considered to have been a wicked king, bringing about the downfall of Britain by inviting over the Anglo-Saxons, it is entirely plausible that some king lists would have omitted him. This would then make Teithfallt, or Ambrosius, 'ap Constantius'.

To expand on this point, consider the fact that Teithfallt is recorded as having married Dywanwedd the daughter of Amlawdd, Amlawdd actually being Aldroen (see Chapter Two). This would mean that Teithfallt may well have actually been the rightful heir of Constantius, if neither Constantius nor Aldroen had any sons. This would support the idea that some king lists may have simply listed 'Teithfallt ap Constantius', skipping the reign of Vortigern. This would also explain why Vortigern is said, in the *Historia Brittonum*, to have been in fear of Ambrosius throughout his reign – because he had a greater right to the throne of Britain than Vortigern did.

However, while this explains why Vortigern would have been fearful of Teithfallt *during* his reign, this does not explain why Teithfallt would have needed to have been taken away to Brittany as a child upon Vortigern's rise to power. If Teithfallt only became the heir to the throne after marrying Dywanwedd, surely he would have posed no threat at all to Vortigern's kingship before that point?

The answer to this seems to lie in Teithfallt's descent from Maximus. It seems that Vortigern's only claim to the rulership of the whole of Britain was the fact that he married into the family of Maximus (see Chapter Seven). Teithfallt, on the other hand, was a direct descendant of the emperor through the senior male line. While it seems that these descendants had lost control of much of their territory (explaining why the Britons had to request for help from the Romans and then from Aldroen of Brittany), they were still the ones to whom Britain belonged by right. Thus, when Constantius became king and managed to re-establish order in the country, it was understood that Teithfallt, the senior descendant of Maximus, would succeed him when the time came. This would certainly have been good reason for Vortigern to have wanted Teithfallt dead after he caused the death of Constantius.

Alternatively, perhaps the agreement was that the kingship would permanently be passed over to Constantius and his family. But of course, when Constantius died and Vortigern succeeded, Vortigern's only claim to the throne was through the family of Maximus. His problem, though, was that if a connection to the family of Maximus was to be used as a basis for declaring oneself a legitimate overking, Teithfallt was the one who had the better claim.

So, whether Constantius was brought over simply to re-establish control over the whole country and then pass the throne back over to the descendants of Maximus, or whether it was intended to be a permanent change in dynasties, the basis for Vortigern's claim meant that his kingship would have been under constant threat as long as Teithfallt was still alive. This is why he would have wanted him dead, and this is why Teithfallt's guardians would have carried him away to the safety of Brittany.

Thus, it is likely that Teithfallt (Ambrosius) came to be considered the son of Constantius (Constantine) for several reasons. Firstly, he was the rightful heir of Constantius, while Vortigern was considered a usurper. Thus, some king lists likely omitted Vortigern, recording Teithfallt as 'ap Constantius'. Additionally, simply by seeing him described as the heir of

Britain after Constantius's death, a later scribe could easily have assumed that the reason he was the heir was because he was the son of Constantius. This conclusion would have been reinforced by seeing a reference to Teithfallt being a kinsman of Aldroen. Whether it was a combination of reasons or just one, we can now see that there are good reasons for why the legends speak of Ambrosius as the son of Constantine.

Notes

1 Establishing the Identity of King Arthur

1. This attribution is no longer widely accepted, but it will be used throughout this book for the sake of simplicity.
2. *Historia Brittonum*, 50, translation by J. A. Giles.
3. Kirby, D. P., *The Earliest English Kings: Second Edition* (London: Routledge, 2000), p. 40.
4. Cunliffe, Barry, *Wessex to A.D. 1000* (Abingdon: Routledge, 2014), p. 298.
5. Bartrum, Peter, *A Welsh Classical Dictionary* (Aberystwyth: National Library of Wales, 1993), p. 697.
6. For a more extensive discussion of why the family of Mordred precludes the possibility that the Battle of Camlann took place as early as 537, see Wilson, Alan & Blackett, Baram, *Artorius Rex Discovered*, pp. 127–129, 150–157.
7. Ashley, Mike, *The Mammoth Book of King Arthur* (London: Constable and Robinson Ltd, 2005), p. 273.
8. *Historia Regum Britanniae*, 9: 15, translation by Thompson and Giles.
9. Darch, John H. & Burns, Stuart K., *Saints on Earth: A Biographical Companion to Common Worship* (London: Church House Publishing, 2004), p. 34; Cross, F. L., & Livingstone, E. A., *The Oxford Dictionary of the Christian Church: Third Edition Revised* (Oxford: Oxford University Press, 1997), p. 456; Lloyd, T., Orbach, J. & Scourfield, R., *The Buildings of Wales: Carmarthenshire and Ceredigion* (London: Yale University Press, 2006), p. 501.
10. *Historia Regum Britanniae*, 9: 15, translation by Thompson and Giles.

11. Bartrum, Peter, *A Welsh Classical Dictionary* (Aberystwyth: National Library of Wales, 1993), p. 693.

12. Charles-Edwards, T. M., *Early Christianity Ireland* (Cambridge: Cambright University Press, 2000), p. 487; *The Annals of the Four Masters; The Annals of Ulster*.

13. In the *Life of St Illtud*, he is said to have outlived Samson, who was still alive in 560 when he had a hand in the overthrow of Count Conomor. This takes place with a considerable portion of the *Life* still ahead of it, indicating that Illtud did not die, according to this source, until quite a while after 560 (at the earliest, for we do not know how much longer after 560 Samson lived).

14. Bartrum, Peter, *A Welsh Classical Dictionary* (Aberystwyth: National Library of Wales, 1993), p. 604.

15. Ibid.

16. It has been claimed that Artuir had a sister called Morgan, or Muirgein, which would match with Arthur's legendary half-sister Morgan le Fay. This relies on the record of 'Muirgein, daughter of Aedan' in the ninth-century *Martyrology of Óengus*. In Whitely Stokes's 1905 edition, he lists her birth place as Belach Gabrain. Since Gabrain was the name of Aedan's father, and the area of Gowrie in Scotland was possibly named after him, it is not an unreasonable viewpoint that this Muirgein was Artuir's sister. However, it seems that Belach Gabrain is much more widely accepted to have been in Ireland (see Kostick, Connor, *Strongbow: The Norman Invasion of Ireland*). Stokes himself thought it was the modern Gowran Pass in Ireland. In fact, the *Tripart Life of St Patrick* mentions Bealach-Gabhran, placing it in the area of Ossory, Ireland. Therefore, it is highly unlikely that the Aedan who fathered Muirgein was Aedan mac Gabrain. The abovementioned *Life* records an Aedan son of Colman in Ireland, and it is much more probable that Muirgein was his daughter. Therefore, there is no evidence that Artuir had a sister named Muirgein.

17. *The Annals of Tigernach; The Annals of Ulster*.

18. Gidlow, Christopher, *The Reign of Arthur: From History to Legend* (Stroud: Sutton Publishing Limited, 2004); Lacy, N. J., Ashe, G., Mancoff, D. N., *The Arthurian Handbook: Second Edition* (Abingdon: Routledge, 2013); Moffat, Alistair, *The British: A Genetic Journey* (Edinburgh: Birlinn Limited, 2013).

19. Bartrum, Peter, *A Welsh Classical Dictionary* (Aberystwyth: National Library of Wales, 1993), pp. 693, 695.

20. Farmer, David, *The Oxford Dictionary of Saints: Fifth Edition Revised* (Oxford: Oxford University Press, 2011), p. 166; Cross, F. L., & Livingstone, E. A., *The Oxford Dictionary of the Christian Church: Third Edition Revised* (Oxford: Oxford University Press, 1997), p. 616; *The Annals of Ulster.*

21. Rees, W. J., *Lives of the Cambro British Saints: of the fifth and immediate succeeding centuries, from ancient Welsh & Latin mss. in the British Museum and elsewhere* (Llandovery: William Rees, 1853), p. 354.

22. Bartrum, Peter, *A Welsh Classical Dictionary* (Aberystwyth: National Library of Wales, 1993), p. 77.

23. If this seems to conflict with the concept of Dubricius stepping down as bishop in *c.* 560 in favour of David at the Synod of Brefi, let it be noted that there is a record of a 'Dubricius son of Brychan' whose life would comfortably overlap this synod if the Brychan in question is Brychan II. See Chapter Seven for a discussion of the Brychans.

24. Bartrum, Peter, *A Welsh Classical Dictionary* (Aberystwyth: National Library of Wales, 1993), p. 244.

25. Baring-Gould, S. & Fisher, J., *The Lives of the British Saints: The Saints of Wales and Cornwall and Such Irish Saints as have Dedications in Britain: Vol. IV* (London: The Honourable Society of Cymmrodorion, 1913), p. 140; Rees, Rice, *An Essay on the Welsh Saints or the Primitive Christians, Usually Considered to Have Been the Founders of Churches in Wales* (London: Longman, Rees, Orme, Brown, Green, and Longman, 1836), pp. 218, 253.

26. Cross, F. L., & Livingstone, E. A., *The Oxford Dictionary of the Christian Church: Third Edition Revised* (Oxford: Oxford University Press, 1997), p. 1460.

27. Rees, Rice, *An Essay on the Welsh Saints or the Primitive Christians, Usually Considered to Have Been the Founders of Churches in Wales* (London: Longman, Rees, Orme, Brown, Green, and Longman, 1836), p. 219.

28. Ibid.

29. Bartrum, Peter, *A Welsh Classical Dictionary* (Aberystwyth: National Library of Wales, 1993), p. 34.

30. Sweeney, R. D., *Prolegomena to an Edition of the Scholia to Status* (Leiden: E. J. Brill, 1969), p. 88.

31. Bartrum, Peter, *A Welsh Classical Dictionary* (Aberystwyth: National Library of Wales, 1993), p. 32 (see references).

32. Barber, Chris & Pykitt, David, *The Legacy of King Arthur* (Abergavenny: Blorenge Books, 2005), p. 22.

33. It has been claimed by some that Athrwys appears as 'Andrus' in one of the Llancarfan charters, showing that the name was originally spelt 'Antres' in Old Welsh. This is incorrect. There is a certain Andres ap Morcant mentioned in the narrative that introduces the charter in which 'Andrus' is a witness. The 'Andrus' who appears is listed immediately after 'Meurig and his sons', but a full reading of the line makes it clear that Andrus is not to be included as one of these sons. In reality, the sons are left unnamed. In all probability, the 'Andrus' who appears in this list is the same as 'Andres ap Morcant', who appears in the narrative just a few lines previously. That 'Athrwys' does not come from 'Antres' is evident from the rule that 'nt' is reduced to a single 'n' sound, as in 'Morgan' from 'Morcant'. Thus, 'Antres' would have become something like 'Anrys', not 'Atroys'.

2 The Family of King Arthur

1. Wilson, Alan & Blackett, Baram, *Artorius Rex Discovered* (Cardiff: King Arthur Research, 1986), p. 194; Barber, Chris & Pykitt, David, *Journey to Avalon: The Final Discovery of King Arthur* (Samuel Weiser, Inc., 1997), p. 54.

2. Koch, J. T., *Celtic Culture: A Historical Encyclopedia: Volume 1* (Santa Barbara: ABC-CLIO, 2006), p. 1722.

3. Williams, Taliesin, *Iolo Manuscripts: A Selection of Ancient Welsh Manuscripts, in Prose and Verse, from the Collection Made by the Late Edward Williams, Iolo Morganwg, for the Purpose of Forming a Continuation of the Myfyrian Archaiology; and Subsequently Proposed as Materials for a New History of Wales* (Llandovery: William Rees, 1848), p. 127.

4. Bartrum, Peter, *A Welsh Classical Dictionary* (Aberystwyth: National Library of Wales, 1993), p. 172.

5. Ibid.

6. Bartrum, Peter, *A Welsh Classical Dictionary* (Aberystwyth: National Library of Wales, 1993), p. 544.

7. *Historia Regum Britanniae*, 8: 19, translation by Thompson & Giles.

8. Historically, it seems that Lot of Lodonesia was the son-in-law of Meurig, thus showing how the legend has conflated Meurig and his father Tewdrig into one 'Uthyr Pendragon'.

9. Similar to how Tewdrig's son Meurig was turned into Meurig's son-in-law Lot in the previously discussed event.

10. Morris, John, *Arthurian Period Sources: Arthurian Sources, Vol. 3: Persons* (Chichester: Phillimore & Co. Ltd, 1995), p. 59.

11. Ibid.

12. To compare this and other names, see *Brut Tysilio*, the Welsh version of *Historia Regum Britanniae*.

13. Baring-Gould, S. & Fisher, J., *The Lives of the British Saints: The Saints of Wales and Cornwall and such Irish Saints as have Dedications in Britain: Vol. I.* (London: The Honourable Society of Cymmrodorion, 1907), pp. 229–231.

14. Morris, John, *Arthurian Period Sources: Arthurian Sources, Vol. 3: Persons* (Chichester: Phillimore & Co. Ltd, 1995), p. 169.

15. Barber, Chris & Pykitt, David, *The Legacy of King Arthur* (Abergavenny: Blorenge Books, 2005), p. 35.

16. Bartrum, Peter, *A Welsh Classical Dictionary* (Aberystwyth: National Library of Wales, 1993), p. 15.

17. Baring-Gould, S. & Fisher, J., *The Lives of the British Saints: The Saints of Wales and Cornwall and Such Irish Saints as have Dedications in Britain: Vol. III* (London: The Honourable Society of Cymmrodorion, 1911), p. 305.

18. Bartrum, Peter, *A Welsh Classical Dictionary* (Aberystwyth: National Library of Wales, 1993), p. 14.

19. Additionally, a certain Marchell is said to have been the daughter of Tywanwedd and Hawystl Gloff, which brings to mind Tewdrig's daughter Marchell – though obviously not the same person, it is consistent with the idea that Marchell was a name used by that family.

20. The spelling of 'Winchester' in *Brut Tysilio* is 'kaer Wynt'. Given everything else that is known about Arthur and his family, Caerwent in south-east Wales is much more likely to be the intended location than Winchester in England.

21. That Arthur survived the Battle of Camlann, in contrast to the claim found in the *Welsh Annals*, is a fact that is supported by, in addition to the aforementioned legend, which explicitly speaks of his survival, the fact that Geoffrey gives 541 – actually 574 – as the year of Arthur's abdication. Yet, the Battle of Camlann certainly took place in 570 (as well as the evidence found in the previous chapter for such a date, it is reaffirmed by the information provided in Chapter Six of this book). In like manner, the date of Arthur's death is given as

546 – actually 579 – in another record, which is substantially beyond the year in which the Battle of Camlann occurred. Furthermore, Meurig was still alive after the end of the great plague, in the same year as Camlann, as he was there for Oudoceus's appointment as bishop after returning to Britain. Athrwys is recorded in the *Book of Llandaff* as king after the death of Meurig, so if Meurig lived beyond the Battle of Camlann, then Athrwys certainly must have done. Thus, the evidence from both Arthur and Athrwys supports the fact that the man continued living until at least several years after Camlann.

22. Bartrum, Peter, *A Welsh Classical Dictionary* (Aberystwyth: National Library of Wales, 1993), p. 428.
23. In yet other charters, Ufelwy is shown to be a contemporary of Dubricius, providing even more evidence that Meurig belongs to the sixth century, not the seventh.
24. Morris, John, *Arthurian Period Sources: Arthurian Sources, Vol. 3: Persons* (Chichester: Phillimore & Co. Ltd, 1995), p. 170.
25. The Llandaff charters reveal that there was a student of Dubricius named Cynfarch in Glamorgan in the early sixth century, and it is possible that this was Cynfarch the father of Urien.

3 The History of the Kings of Britain: Book Four

1. *De Bello Gallico*, 4: 24, 26, 32, translation by McDevitte and Bohn.
2. *Historia Regum Britanniae*, 4: 3, translation by Thompson and Giles.
3. *Ecclesiastical History of the English People*, 1: 2, translation by L. C. Jane.
4. The oldest known examples of written Old Welsh date from the ninth century, which was the century after Bede and the same century as Nennius. This is not to say that Welsh was not written down before that century, but there is simply no surviving evidence of it of which we are currently aware. However, what this means is that Geoffrey's 'very old Welsh book' could have been at least as old as the *Historia Brittonum*, which would have been just over 300 years old at the time of Geoffrey's writing. If we assume it was exactly contemporary with the *HB*, then it would have been written about 250 years after the death of Arthur. This dramatically reduces the temporal difference of 550 years between the death of Arthur and Geoffrey's writing.
5. *Historia Regum Britanniae*, 4: 1, translation by Thompson and Giles.
6. *De Bello Gallico*, 4: 20, translation by McDevitte and Bohn.

7. The Durolevum location for Dorobellum is supported by the fact that the name is written as 'Doral' in the *Brut Tysilio*, as well as the fact that 'Dorobernia', which is a known spelling for the Latin name for Canterbury, is mentioned soon after in *HRB*. Hence, the fact that 'Dorobernia' is not used in this part of the text is indicative that Canterbury is not the place intended.

8. *De Bello Gallico*, 5: 9, translation by McDevitte and Bohn.

9. The fact that Caesar's account tells us that the result of a later attack on the Romans, arranged by Cassivellaunus, was *reported* to the British leader seems to favour the conclusion that Cassivellaunus himself was trapped in his stronghold.

10. *De Bello Gallico*, 5: 21, translation by McDevitte and Bohn.

11. Attar, Rob, *BBC History Magazine* (London: Immediate Media Company, December 2014), p. 26.

12. *Geographica*, 4: 5, translation by Jones.

13. *Roman History*, 60: 19, 20, translation by Cary.

14. The 'cester' suffix comes from a later Anglo-Saxon word meaning 'fort', and thus has nothing to do with the original name.

15. *The Lives of the Caesars – The Life of Vespasian*, Vol. 4, translation by Rolfe.

16. Southern, Patricia, *Roman Britain: A New History 55 BC – AD 450* (Stroud: Amberley Publishing, 2011).

17. Bartrum, Peter, *A Welsh Classical Dictionary* (Aberystwyth: National Library of Wales, 1993), p. 32.

18. *Historia Regum Britanniae*, 4: 17, translation by Thompson and Giles.

19. The clipped beginning would be similar to the clipped beginning of 'Togodumnus' in the name 'Guiderius'.

20. And, if Miles Russell is correct, the glorious Fishbourne Roman Palace was built for Lucullus.

4 The History of the Kings of Britain: Book Five

1. *Historia Regum Britanniae*, 5: 2, translation by Thompson and Giles.

2. Severus's entire military force on this campaign is generally thought to have been around 40,000.

3. *Roman History*, 77: 15, translation by Cary.

4. Such a claim is found at least as early as the *Historia Augusta*, written towards the conclusion of the Western Roman Empire.

5. *Historia Regum Britanniae*, 5: 3, translation by Thompson and Giles.

6. *Historia Regum Britanniae*, 5: 4, translation by Thompson and Giles.

7. *Nant* is the Welsh word for 'stream', or 'brook'.

8. *Panegyrici Latini 8.*

9. In the early 2010s, a team of archaeologists concluded that these skulls had been deposited downstream from a Roman cemetery, their heads having been torn off the bodies by the force of the flowing water. This conclusion was reached largely due to the evidence of flowing-water action present on the skulls, showing that they were not placed *in situ*. However, such logic is flawed, for one could hardly expect that the skulls would *not* have been moved by the flowing water, producing exactly the same physical evidence, if they had been deposited directly into the stream as in the story.

10. *Historia Regum Britanniae*, 5: 5, translation by Thompson and Giles.

11. Bede's *Ecclesiastical History*, 1: 6, translation by Giles.

12. *Historia Regum Britanniae*, 5: 7, translation by Thompson and Giles.

13. Birley, Anthony, *The Roman Government of Britain* (New York: Oxford University Press, 2005), p. 411.

14. *Historia Regum Britanniae*, 5: 8, translation by Thompson and Giles.

15. Also spelt Gewissi, Gewisse and Gewissae in various modern sources.

16. Snyder, Christopher, *Age of Tyrants: Britain and the Britons, A.D 400–600* (University Park: The Pennsylvania State University Press, 1998), p. 8; Birley, Anthony, *The Roman Government of Britain* (New York: Oxford University Press, 2005), p. 412.

17. Southern, Patricia, *Roman Britain: A New History 55 BC – AD 450* (Stroud: Amberley Publishing, 2011).

18. Merrifield, Ralph, *London: City of the Romans* (Berkeley and Los Angeles: University of California Press, 1983), p. 210.

19. Birley, Anthony, *The Roman Government of Britain* (New York: Oxford University Press, 2005), p. 412.

20. M'Dermot, Martin, *A New and Impartial History of Ireland, from the Earliest Accounts to the Present Time* (London: J. M'Gowan, 1820), p. 399.

21. Bromwich, Rachel, *Trioedd Ynys Prydein: Fourth Edition* (Cardiff: University of Wales Press, 2014), p. 88.

22. Bartrum, Peter, *A Welsh Classical Dictionary* (Aberystwyth: National Library of Wales, 1993), p. 291.

23. Southern, Patricia, *Roman Britain: A New History 55 BC – AD 450* (Stroud: Amberley Publishing, 2011).

24. Ibid.

25. The statement that Eudaf possessed the kingdom until Gratian and Valentinian's reign does not necessarily mean that Eudaf's rule ended at the very beginning of their reign.

26. *Historia Regum Britanniae*, 5: 9, translation by Thompson and Giles.

27. It is unclear whether this should indeed be Cornwall, or rather Cerniw in south-east Wales; the place is referred to as 'Kerniw' in the *Brut Tysilio*, which could refer to either the location in Dumnonia or to the location in Wales.

28. *New History*, Book 5, 35: 4.

29. That is not to say that 'Caernarvon' was misunderstood by Geoffrey to be London, but that his source may have used some other term for Caernarvon, or a nearby area, which was similar enough to 'Londinium' for Geoffrey to be confused.

30. Bartrum, Peter, *A Welsh Classical Dictionary* (Aberystwyth: National Library of Wales, 1993), p. 265.

31. This is a strong indication that Geoffrey did not take the story from the earlier sources that are still available to us, as the earlier sources claim that these virgins were martyred in Cologne, which is in Germany but far from the coast.

32. Jones, Michael E., *The End of Roman Britain* (Ithaca: Cornell University Press, 1996), p. 245.

33. For such a discussion, however, see Appendix 3, 'Constans and the Family of Brittany'.

5 Proposed Theories

1. *The Origin and Deeds of the Goths* XLV, 237, 238, translation by Mierow.

2. In this case, it would be changing Euric into Glycerius.

3. *Historia Regum Britanniae*, 9: 11, translation by Thompson and Giles.

4. For example, the Roman place name 'Moridunum' was reduced to 'Myrddin', which can now be found in 'Caerfyrddin', or Carmarthen.

5. Philadelphus, Theodulus, *The True Portraiture of the Church of Jesus-Christ* (Pater Battut, 1670), p. 115.

6. Arthur subdues Gaul over a period of nine years. He returns to his kingdom in peace, and then just as his men are about to engage in battle against Lucius, Arthur comments that it has been five years since they last fought.

7. Leo II's rule did not last anywhere near long enough to be the Leo of the story.

8. Sims-Williams, Patrick, *Irish Influence on Medieval Welsh Literature* (Oxford: Oxford University Press, 2011), p. 161, 163.

9. The logic of this is that 'Llawwynnyawc' seems to be similar to one of Lugh's epithets, either 'Lamfhota' or 'Loinnbeimnech', but Patrick Sims-Williams describes this as 'not very plausible'. See Patrick Sims-Williams, *Irish Influence on Medieval Welsh Literature*, p. 162.

10. According to Peter Bartrum, nothing is known of Lleenog other than his place in the genealogies. See Peter Bartrum, *A Welsh Classical Dictionary*, p. 462.

11. Even if it were, there are alternative possibilities for the origin of Lancelot that do not involve Lugh, and therefore have nothing even arguably to do with Llwch Llawwynnyawc.

12. *Culhwch ac Olwen* does seem to be describing the same European conquest, as it mentions Llychlyn (Scandinavia) immediately before mentioning Europe, in line with the pattern of events in *HRB*. It should be noted, however, that Geoffrey certainly did not take his account of the Gallic conquest from this particular source, as *Culhwch ac Olwen* explicitly says that Arthur conquered Greece, while Geoffrey has the king of Greece fight against Arthur. Additionally, he does not include any mention of Africa or India.

6 The Man Who Conquered Europe

1. *Historia Regum Britanniae*, 9: 11, translation by Thompson and Giles.

2. Baring-Gould, S. & Fisher, J., *The Lives of the British Saints: The Saints of Wales and Cornwall and Such Irish Saints as have Dedications in Britain: Vol. II* (London: The Honourable Society of Cymmrodorion, 1908), p. 193; Cartwright, Jane, *Mary Magdalene and Her Sister Martha: An Edition and Translation of the Medieval Welsh Lives* (Washington, DC: Catholic University of America Press, 2013), p. 7.

3. Compare the 777 men who came with Gwinear to Cornwall, discussed in an earlier chapter.

4. This would tie in with his estimated age of birth. If Arthur was born *c.* 503, then Meurig is unlikely to have been born later than 483. That would make him ninety years old at his death if he died in 573. Yet if he died no earlier than 588, as would be required if the great plague began in 580, then he would have been 105 years old at the time of death. Of the two, the former option is clearly more likely.

5. It is possibly significant that in the earliest version of the presumably related story 'Jack and the Beanstalk', the giant is said to have murdered Jack's father, just as how Conomor murdered Judwal's father.

6. Charles-Edwards, T. M., *Wales and the Britons, 350–1064* (Oxford: Oxford University Press, 2013), pp. 65, 67, 68.

7. As to how a comet could cause a plague, it should be noted that the physical devastation caused by cometary debris would naturally lead to a great loss of life and destruction of food and water sources, as well as housing and other areas of infrastructure. All these things would contribute to a plague developing and spreading rapidly.

8. The reason for Andragathius returning to Britain as soon as he could, or even at all, will become apparent in the following chapter.

9. Sozomen's *Ecclesiastical History*, 7: 13.

10. McEvoy, Meaghan, *Child Emperor Rule in the Late Roman West, AD 367–455* (Oxford: Oxford University Press, 2013), p. 101.

11. See *The Dream of Macsen Wledig*.

12. Owen, Robert, *The Kymry: Their Origin, History, and International Relations* (Carmarthen: W. Spurrell and Son, 1891), p. 237; Bromwich, Rachel, *Trioedd Ynys Prydein: Fourth Edition* (Cardiff: University of Wales Press, 2014), p. 144.

13. Orosius's *History Against the Pagans*, 7: 35.

14. Liebeschuetz, J. H. W. G., *Ambrose of Milan: Political Letters and Speeches* (Liverpool: Liverpool University Press, 2010), p. 106.

15. Davies, Norman, *The Isles: A History* (London: Pan Macmillan Ltd, 2000), p. 121.

16. These leaders are Bedivere, Kay, Holdin, Leodegarius, Cursalem, and Urtgennius.

17. These individuals are Kimarcoc, consul of Trigeria, and Richomarcus, Bloccovius and Jagivius.

18. Such as in the name 'Teudubric' from 'Theodoric'.

19. In Welsh, the letter 'm' is pronounced as a 'v', which is what the letter 'f' in Selyf signifies.

20. Another example of this is seen in the place name Carmarthen, which is spelt Caerfyrddin in Welsh.

21. Sweeney, R. D., *Prolegomena to an Edition of the Scholia to Status* (Leiden: E. J. Brill, 1969), p. 88.

22. Hubert, Henri, *The Rise of the Celts* (New York: Dover Publications, Inc., 2002), p. 208; Broun, Dauvit, *Scottish Independence and*

the Idea of Britain: From the Picts to Alexander III (Edinburgh: Edinburgh University Press, 2007), p. 95.

23. Griscom, Acton, *The Historia Regum Britanniae of Geoffrey of Monmouth* (Genève: Slatkine Reprints, 1977), p. 545.

24. Ibid.

25. In fact, there is a Triad that mentions Maxen Wledig leading a host to Llychlyn. This might mean Scotland, though others consider this to be a corruption of Llydaw; that is, Armorica, on the Continent. See *Rachel Bromwich – Trioedd Ynys Prydein – Fourth Edition*, p. 88.

7 The Identity of the First Arthur

1. The evidence for this will be considered shortly.

2. Bartrum, Peter, *A Welsh Classical Dictionary* (Aberystwyth: National Library of Wales, 1993), p. 20.

3. That Welsh accounts could consider a ruler in Brittany to be a ruler of France is demonstrated by the fact that Ionas, the king of Brittany murdered by Conomor, is called 'king of France' in *Culhwch ac Olwen.*

4. Bartrum, Peter, *A Welsh Classical Dictionary* (Aberystwyth: National Library of Wales, 1993), pp. 20, 645, 714.

5. An objection might be raised to the idea that Andragathius was the son of Magnus Maximus on the grounds that 'Andragathius' is not a Roman name. However, mixing Roman and barbarian names was not that uncommon in this era. For example, Theodosius's barbarian general Arbogast was actually named 'Flavius Arbogastes'. His other barbarian general, Richomer, was actually 'Flavius Richomeres'. In both these instances, a barbarian personal name is preceded with the Roman 'Flavius'. If Maximus's first wife, the mother of Anthun, was Celtic – and the record of 'Ceindrech ferch Reiden' suggests that she was – then this would explain how a son of Maximus was able to possess a Celtic name. And he may, quite easily, have had a Roman name as well, as did many barbarian individuals of the fourth century.

6. *The Cambro-Briton: Vol III* (London: J. Limbird, 1821), p. 202.

7. As in 'Morgan' from 'Morcant'.

8. Berkley, Grant, *The King Arthur Conspiracy* (Trafford Publishing, 2006), p. 243; Bartrum, Peter, *A Welsh Classical Dictionary* (Aberystwyth: National Library of Wales, 1993), p. 71.

9. Berkley, Grant, *The King Arthur Conspiracy* (Trafford Publishing, 2006), p. 243.

10. This is gleaned from the words of Arthur when talking to his men about the letter from the Romans. He refers to the fact that Belinus (a figure from the BCE part of Geoffrey's book) and Constantine, the son of Helena (Elen) and Maximian (the name used for Magnus Maximus in *HRB*) both possessed the Roman Empire for a time. It is clearly Constantine III, the person who took over Roman Britain and Gaul and even marched into Italy for a time, who is being referred to by Arthur.
11. *Historia Regum Britanniae*, 7: 3, translation by Thompson and Giles.
12. *Historia Regum Britanniae*, 11: 10, translation by Thompson and Giles.

Appendix 1: The Dating of Gildas

1. Bartrum, Peter, *A Welsh Classical Dictionary* (Aberystwyth: National Library of Wales, 1993), p. 173.
2. O'Sullivan, T. D., *The De Excidio of Gildas: Its Authenticity and Date* (Leiden: E. J. Brill, 1978), p. 117.
3. Ibid.
4. This is almost certainly not the Tristan of the romance tales, whose uncle was Mark of Cornwall. That Tristan was probably the son of Meliavus, a prince of Brittany. But evidently there has been some confusion in the Welsh records regarding the Tristans.
5. Ashley, Mike, *The Mammoth Book of King Arthur* (London: Constable and Robinson Ltd, 2005), pp. 54, 368; Venning, Timothy, *The Kings and Queens of Scotland* (Stroud: Amberley Publishing, 2013).
6. The poem is known as *Trawsganu Kynan Garwyn mab Broch*.
7. The account in his *Life* goes on to say that the king of Armorica at this time was 'Childeric son of Meroveus'. This must be a mistake, for this king was actually alive in the previous century, and there was not another king of the Franks called Childeric until 662. However, the king of a certain part of Gaul – Austrasia – from 575 to 585 was Childbert, a name that could conceivably have been mistaken for Childeric, especially considering the similarity of the letter 'c' and the letter 't' in medieval texts. Alternatively, the king of the region of Gaul more closely connected with Armorica – that is, Neutrasia – from 561 to 584 was Chilperic, a name that is merely one letter different from Childeric. Either one of these kings could have been the Childeric of Gildas's *Life*.
8. Bartrum, Peter, *A Welsh Classical Dictionary* (Aberystwyth: National Library of Wales, 1993), p. 316.
9. Ibid.

Appendix 2: The Thirty-three-year Error

1. This would appear to derive from an allegorical account in which Arthur represented his kingdom. Britain had been devastated by the plague, so Arthur sailed away in an attempt to find new, healthy land. That this is the correct understanding is indicated by the fact that the later romance tales portray the 'Lame King' as becoming lame due to a strike from a holy spear, which also caused his kingdom to become a wasteland. The 'holy spear' is obviously the comet of 563, just as the comet of 499 was described as a 'rod', and this evidently did cause much of Britain to become a wasteland. So, while the Lame King was not Arthur, this demonstrates the principle of a king being portrayed in a later record as being wounded due to the destruction caused to his kingdom by a comet.

Appendix 3: Constans and the Family of Brittany

1. Almost certainly not Aetius, for numerous chronological reasons.
2. Bartrum, Peter, *A Welsh Classical Dictionary* (Aberystwyth: National Library of Wales, 1993), p. 179.

Bibliography

Ashe, Geoffrey, *The Discovery of King Arthur* (Stroud: The History Press, 2010)

Ashley, Mike, *The Mammoth Book of King Arthur* (London: Constable and Robinson Ltd, 2005)

Attar, Rob, *BBC History Magazine* (London: Immediate Media Company, December 2014)

Barber, Chris & Pykitt, David, *Journey to Avalon: The Final Discovery of King Arthur* (Samuel Weiser, Inc., 1997)

Barber, Chris & Pykitt, David, *The Legacy of King Arthur* (Abergavenny: Blorenge Books, 2005)

Baring-Gould, S. & Fisher, J., *The Lives of the British Saints: The Saints of Wales and Cornwall and such Irish Saints as have Dedications in Britain: Vol. I.* (London: The Honourable Society of Cymmrodorion, 1907)

Baring-Gould, S. & Fisher, J., *The Lives of the British Saints: The Saints of Wales and Cornwall and Such Irish Saints as have Dedications in Britain: Vol. II* (London: The Honourable Society of Cymmrodorion, 1908)

Baring-Gould, S. & Fisher, J., *The Lives of the British Saints: The Saints of Wales and Cornwall and Such Irish Saints as have Dedications in Britain: Vol. III* (London: The Honourable Society of Cymmrodorion, 1911)

Baring-Gould, S. & Fisher, J., *The Lives of the British Saints: The Saints of Wales and Cornwall and Such Irish Saints as have Dedications in Britain: Vol. IV* (London: The Honourable Society of Cymmrodorion, 1913)

Bartrum, Peter, *A Welsh Classical Dictionary* (Aberystwyth: National Library of Wales, 1993)

Berkley, Grant, *The King Arthur Conspiracy* (Trafford Publishing, 2006)

Birley, Anthony, *The Roman Government of Britain* (New York: Oxford University Press, 2005)

Bromwich, Rachel, *Trioedd Ynys Prydein: Fourth Edition* (Cardiff: University of Wales Press, 2014)

Broun, Dauvit, *Scottish Independence and the Idea of Britain: From the Picts to Alexander III* (Edinburgh: Edinburgh University Press, 2007)

Carleton, Don, *Arthur, Warrior and King* (Stroud: Amberley Publishing, 2018)

Cartwright, Jane, *Mary Magdalene and Her Sister Martha: An Edition and Translation of the Medieval Welsh Lives* (Washington, DC: Catholic University of America Press, 2013)

Charles-Edwards, T. M., *Early Christianity Ireland* (Cambridge: Cambright University Press, 2000)

Charles-Edwards, T. M., *Wales and the Britons, 350–1064* (Oxford: Oxford University Press, 2013)

Cross, F. L., & Livingstone, E. A., *The Oxford Dictionary of the Christian Church: Third Edition Revised* (Oxford: Oxford University Press, 1997)

Cunliffe, Barry, *Wessex to A.D. 1000* (Abingdon: Routledge, 2014)

Darch, John H. & Burns, Stuart K., *Saints on Earth: A Biographical Companion to Common Worship* (London: Church House Publishing, 2004)

Davies, Norman, *The Isles: A History* (London: Pan Macmillan Ltd, 2000)

Farmer, David, *The Oxford Dictionary of Saints: Fifth Edition Revised* (Oxford: Oxford University Press, 2011)

Gidlow, Christopher, *The Reign of Arthur: From History to Legend* (Stroud: Sutton Publishing Limited, 2004)

Griscom, Acton, *The Historia Regum Britanniae of Geoffrey of Monmouth* (Genève: Slatkine Reprints, 1977)

Hubert, Henri, *The Rise of the Celts* (New York: Dover Publications, Inc., 2002)

Jones, Michael E., *The End of Roman Britain* (Ithaca: Cornell University Press, 1996)

Kirby, D. P., *The Earliest English Kings: Second Edition* (London: Routledge, 2000)

Koch, J. T., *Celtic Culture: A Historical Encyclopedia: Volume 1* (Santa Barbara: ABC-CLIO, 2006)

Lacy, N. J., Ashe, G., Mancoff, D. N., *The Arthurian Handbook: Second Edition* (Abingdon: Routledge, 2013)

Liebeschuetz, J. H. W. G., *Ambrose of Milan: Political Letters and Speeches* (Liverpool: Liverpool University Press, 2010)

Lloyd, T., Orbach, J. & Scourfeld, R., *The Buildings of Wales: Carmarthenshire and Ceredigion* (London: Yale University Press, 2006)

M'Dermot, Martin, *A New and Impartial History of Ireland, from the Earliest Accounts to the Present Time* (London: J. M'Gowan, 1820)

McEvoy, Meaghan, *Child Emperor Rule in the Late Roman West, AD 367–455* (Oxford: Oxford University Press, 2013)

Merrifeld, Ralph, *London: City of the Romans* (Berkeley and Los Angeles: University of California Press, 1983)

Moffat, Alistair, *The British: A Genetic Journey* (Edinburgh: Birlinn Limited, 2013)

Morris, John, *Arthurian Period Sources: Arthurian Sources, Vol. 3: Persons* (Chichester: Phillimore & Co. Ltd, 1995)

O'Sullivan, T. D., *The De Excidio of Gildas: Its Authenticity and Date* (Leiden: E. J. Brill, 1978)

Owen, Robert, *The Kymry: Their Origin, History, and International Relations* (Carmarthen: W. Spurrell and Son, 1891)

Philadelphus, Theodulus, *The True Portraiture of the Church of Jesus-Christ* (Pater Battut, 1670)

Rees, Rice, *An Essay on the Welsh Saints or the Primitive Christians, Usually Considered to Have Been the Founders of Churches in Wales* (London: Longman, Rees, Orme, Brown, Green, and Longman, 1836)

Rees, W. J., *Lives of the Cambro British Saints: of the fifth and immediate succeeding centuries, from ancient Welsh & Latin mss. in the British Museum and elsewhere* (Llandovery: William Rees, 1853)

Sims-Williams, Patrick, *Irish Influence on Medieval Welsh Literature* (Oxford: Oxford University Press, 2011)

Snyder, Christopher, *Age of Tyrants: Britain and the Britons, AD 400–600* (University Park: The Pennsylvania State University Press, 1998)

Southern, Patricia, *Roman Britain: A New History 55 BC–AD 450* (Stroud: Amberley Publishing, 2011)

Sweeney, R. D., *Prolegomena to an Edition of the Scholia to Status* (Leiden: E. J. Brill, 1969)

The Cambro-Briton: Vol III (London: J. Limbird, 1821)

Venning, Timothy, *The Kings and Queens of Scotland* (Stroud: Amberley Publishing, 2013)

Williams, Taliesin, *Iolo Manuscripts: A Selection of Ancient Welsh Manuscripts, in Prose and Verse, from the Collection Made by the Late Edward Williams, Iolo Morganwg, for the Purpose of Forming a Continuation of the Myfyrian Archaiology; and Subsequently Proposed as Materials for a New History of Wales* (Llandovery: William Rees, 1848)

Wilson, Alan & Blackett, Baram, *Artorius Rex Discovered* (Cardiff: King Arthur Research, 1986)

Index